Praise for
Three Girls from Bronzeville

"Unmissable."

—*Vogue*

"Wholehearted . . . Turner . . . interrupts the monolithic narrative of Black Chicago as ruined and broken, as well as the one-note stereotypes about growing up in public housing. In their place she offers a textured portrait of a moment in time in a particular place . . . Like the poet Gwendolyn Brooks and the playwright Lorraine Hansberry, she is a native daughter of Black Chicago with a bone-deep knowledge of the place and its people."

—*The New York Times Book Review*

"An exceptional work, a memoir told with honesty, grit, and a sly wit that continually takes readers to unexpected places. . . . I'm hooked on these women."

—*The Washington Post*

"Evocative."

—*Chicago Tribune*

"Vivid . . . incisive."

—*Shelf Awareness*

"Dawn Turner is the *perfect* person to tell this heartbreaking yet gorgeous tale of three Black girls from the Bronzeville section of Chicago as they come of age during the 1970s. And not just because it's partially *her* story, but because her lengthy career as a journalist who has reported on stories from all across the globe makes her uniquely capable of weaving an intricate, deeply researched and reported tale, but also one with heavy personal implications, an enormous amount of heart, and a remarkable measure of poise.

Turner's memoir is an achievement on many levels, not the least of which is the fact that it's just downright entertaining as well. Highly recommended."

—Shondaland

"By turns beautiful, tragic, and inspiring, [*Three Girls from Bronzeville*] is a powerful testament to the bonds of sisterhood and the importance of understanding the conditions that shape a person's life choices."

—*Publishers Weekly* (starred review)

"Astounding . . . Turner's candid memoir of entwined yet divergent lives is a probing inquiry into fate, frailty, tenacity, and ultimately, redemption."

—*Booklist* (starred review)

"[Dawn Turner] has a stellar ability to present the personalities of her loved ones, especially the women in her life. This memoir is a compelling testament to the power of women's relationships."

—*Library Journal* (starred review)

"Exceptional . . . This deeply personal and thought-provoking read is the nonfiction pick your book club has been waiting for."

—*Real Simple*

"Turner's writing often feels like reading [Gwendolyn] Brooks for the first time."

—*Chicago Review of Books*

"Heartfelt . . . This book offers hope to anyone who wonders whether, after a terrible crime, attempts at reconciliation are worth it. Turner doesn't sugarcoat the difficulties, but she leaves no doubt that—when the process works—the gains are vast."

—*Kirkus Reviews*

"Poignant and nuanced."

—*Ms.* magazine

"*Three Girls from Bronzeville* is such a beautiful and shattering book, and a rare read in which the delicate craft of the writing itself matches the depth of the themes it explores: coming of age, the invisible burdens of abandonment and poverty and racism, the impossible loyalties of friendship, triumph and regret, and—above all—love. This story is told with grace, humility, and courage. It will remain with me always."

—Jeff Hobbs, author of
The Short and Tragic Life of Robert Peace

"Dawn Turner's *Three Girls from Bronzeville* is a beautiful ode to friendship and family, and an openhearted story of the unique journeys of Black women. Turner's story, told with unwavering candor, is by turns heartbreaking and stirring. This poignant memoir wouldn't let me go."

—Alex Kotlowitz, author of
An American Summer

"Deep love and deep loss thrum throughout Dawn Turner's poignant and stunning memoir, a tale of sisterhood and friendship between three girls across time and place. Heartbreak but also redemption fuel this complex and nuanced story, upending everything we think we know about Black women who lose their way. The seamless blend of personal tale and astute reportage is remarkable, given that the book is also a suspenseful page-turner. I read breathlessly and choked up often, thinking, *There but for the grace of God go I.*"

—Bridgett M. Davis, author of
The World According to Fannie Davis

also by Dawn Turner

■ ■ ■

Only Twice I've
Wished for Heaven

An Eighth of August

Three Girls *from* Bronzeville

A Uniquely American Memoir
of Race, Fate, and Sisterhood

Dawn Turner

Simon & Schuster Paperbacks
New York London Toronto Sydney New Delhi

Simon & Schuster Paperbacks
An Imprint of Simon & Schuster, Inc.
1230 Avenue of the Americas
New York, NY 10020

First Simon & Schuster trade paperback edition June 2022

SIMON & SCHUSTER PAPERBACKS and colophon
are registered trademarks of Simon & Schuster, Inc.

For information about special discounts for bulk purchases,
please contact Simon & Schuster Special Sales at
1-866-506-1949 or business@simonandschuster.com.

The Simon & Schuster Speakers Bureau can bring authors to
your live event. For more information or to book an event,
contact the Simon & Schuster Speakers Bureau at 1-866-248-3049
or visit our website at www.simonspeakers.com.

Interior design by Lewelin Polanco

Manufactured in Italy

1 3 5 7 9 10 8 6 4 2

Library of Congress Cataloging-in-Publication
Data is available on file.

ISBN 978-1-9821-0770-3
ISBN 978-1-9821-0771-0 (pbk)
ISBN 978-1-9821-0773-4 (ebook)

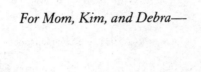

For Mom, Kim, and Debra—

We shape our buildings and afterwards our buildings shape us.

—Winston Churchill

Kick a man when he's down because that's when his head is closest to your foot.

—My mother

contents

Part Three

author's note

During the course of writing this book, I conducted hundreds of hours of interviews and pored over hundreds of pages of court documents. In addition, I have relied on three decades' worth of correspondence in the form of letters and telephone conversations as well as diary and journal entries. The following names are pseudonyms: Henry, Loretta Tyson, Sam, Sadie, Betty, Andrew, Pamela, Carl, Hayes, Keesha, Bunny, Lila, Jack, Greta, Jodie, Tate, Jerry, Ronnie Matthews, Lance Matthews, Ted, Brittany, and Frank. Lastly, some of the stories here were first chronicled in the *Chicago Tribune* and on National Public Radio, and one was included in the anthology *Rise Up Singing: Black Women Writers on Motherhood.*

part one

chapter one

Our Ledge

■ ■ ■

I often think about my sister and my best friend. Not every minute. Not even every day. I mostly think of them when I am experiencing something I would have wanted to share. Some moment that would allow us to tug on a line, thin as a filament, that begins "Remember when . . ." and draws a seemingly ever-present past nearer.

When I imagine us, we come into focus at our beginning—three young girls walking through our neighborhood under a prickly summer sun. I am nine years old, tall and lanky with long, ropy braids. Debra, my best friend, is shorter than me and, at eight and a half, is already prom-queen pretty. And then there's my sister, Kim, three years my junior. She's stealthily trailing us, even though I've bribed her with our mother's secret stash of lemon drops to stay away.

Mom is watching us from our eleventh-floor apartment window. She has told us to go outside and play.

"You two are the nosiest children God ever gave breath to," she always says. "Get out from under grown folks' business."

Later, she will ask me why I didn't hold Kim's hand, why I allowed her to hang so far behind. But right now, Debra and I are walking through our apartment complex on our way to our special place. We are Thing-Finders, two Black girls who have little in common with the popular children's book character Pippi Longstocking, an orphaned white girl with red hair and freckles. But we admire the way she spends her day collecting castoffs for her "Thing-Finders

Club." We live in a neighborhood that has specialized in the broken, the halved—so in the tradition of this little white girl, we traverse our community, sifting through the past, searching for discarded items that we believe can be made new again. We call our hideout our "love spot," and it's a couple of blocks away. It's where we've stashed a rusty metal tin we stole from the janitor's closet. We've seeded it with the artifacts of our lives: my father's fake gold cuff link and a knob from her father's CB radio; a couple of dried pomegranate seeds; the obituary of our third-grade teacher's daughter; a scarred flashcube from an Instamatic; the shoehorn we lifted off the grocery store bagger who has gnarled hands and likes to pat us kids on our heads. We allow him when we're trying to show how brave we are.

To understand Debra, Kim, and me—to understand what will happen to us—you have to know the place that has begun to shape us. We live in Chicago's historic Bronzeville community. At three square miles, it's the cradle of the city's Great Migration, the epicenter of Black business and culture. Over the decades, it's been home to some of the country's most esteemed Black folks: journalist and antilynching activist Ida B. Wells, cardiac surgeon Daniel Hale Williams, jazz trumpeter Louis Armstrong, novelist Richard Wright, Pulitzer Prize–winning poet Gwendolyn Brooks. Kim and I are beginning to understand Bronzeville's storied past because our mother, grandmother, and aunt grew up here in this corner of Bronzeville that hugs the lakefront. Kim and I are the fourth generation of our family to live here. Anything you can imagine, or want, or hope for is here. The good life, made evident by Black politicians, doctors, lawyers, judges, and professors. A good time, as offered by prostitutes, street vendors, and drug dealers. It's all here, not on the other side of the tracks or the other side of a river or even the next "L" stop. It's just across the street. For generations, Bronzeville has been a place where all that was good and bad is simultaneously at your fingertips yet a walled-off world away.

We girls are coming of age at a time when the country is just beyond the civil rights movement and at the threshold of what our parents hope is a new, postracial era for Blacks. A country that finally seems amenable to giving us the opportunities it has denied generations. But that dream will soon be dashed.

Debra's family and mine have just moved into the privately owned Theodore K. Lawless Gardens apartment complex. Like us, it is still young and unblemished, brimming with promise. The twenty-four-story buildings, three of them in a row, are gleaming concrete monuments to upward mobility and are still pristine. A tall chain-link fence encases the property, forming a barrier along Rhodes Avenue from the Ida B. Wells Homes, a once-idyllic public housing project where my mother grew up. But by the 1970s it's crumbling from misbegotten policies and abandonment, the despair of drugs and gangs. Two decades later, an adjacent housing project will draw national attention after two boys, ages ten and eleven, dangle and then drop five-year-old Eric Morse from a fourteenth-floor window for refusing to steal candy. The country will think it knows everything about our neighborhood and us, but it won't. It can't possibly know.

On this summer afternoon, all of that is far in the distance. As we walk—sometimes skipping, sometimes jogging—I am acutely aware that my sister is gaining on us. I can feel Kim without even turning around. That will never change. But Debra is unaware. She's too busy talking, planning today's adventure, gesturing vigorously. We reach the main street and wait for an opening in the traffic. When the coast is clear, Debra grabs my hand and we run as fast as we can across four lanes to the other side.

"No, Don. No!" my sister yells.

Mom says Kim sometimes speaks out of spite. Calls me "Don" instead of "Dawn," says "Duperman" instead of "Superman." She's little and scrappy, scuffed about the knees like a footstool and unafraid of most things—except speeding cars. Ever since she almost got hit by one. "Don't leave me!"

I pretend not to hear her. I pretend not to know that she will cross if I go back and hold her hand. I'm tired of being the big sister. I'm tired of her always sidling so close to me. I'm tired of sharing.

"Let her come, please," Debra says, clasping her hands. I'm not surprised by her insistence. Like Kim, Debra is the younger of two siblings, two sisters. Though Debra and I are best friends, she and Kim are the true soul mates. Both hear but don't hear. Both see the world through their wants. Mom says, "Kind takes to kind."

"No," I say. And now I'm the one walking ahead. "Maybe tomorrow."

Reluctantly, Debra gives in. We leave Kim behind and continue to walk about a block. I'm thinking, *We have the whole summer. We have a lifetime.*

Debra and I are unencumbered when we pass the sign that reads, "Welcome to Lake Meadows." It's a high-rise apartment development neighboring ours, designed for Chicago's Black elite. We play tennis and ice skate in Lake Meadows. There's no fence, but clearly a divide. Even the air feels lighter as we make our way to a small utility building that's built into a hill. We hike the short but steep incline to the roof, about twelve feet above an asphalt driveway, and walk out onto the ledge of the "love spot." We settle amid pigeon droppings as, beneath us, the building's gigantic boilers hum and breathe. We sit astride our world.

Weekend after weekend, summer after summer, we return to this place, later riding our ten-speeds. Kim joins us when she's lost her fear of speeding cars. Conversations graduate from Debra's growing brood of toy dinosaurs to training bras and tampons. We talk about how we plan to be doctors and live next door to each other in houses like the white folks have on the black-and-white television shows.

Although we are easily seen by passersby, we feel invisible to everyone but ourselves.

Every once in a while a security guard demands that we come down, and I get ready to run. But Debra doesn't budge. Neither does Kim when she's with us.

Debra yells, "You can't tell us what to do!"

Kim follows with, "Try to make us!"

I remain quiet, chock-full of enough anxiety for the three of us.

By the time Debra and I are in the eighth grade and Kim is in the fifth, we have begun to go our separate ways. Debra is hanging out with a faster crowd. Kim is ditching school. My teachers are increasingly telling me how smart I am. The three of us growing up scares me, but not nearly as much as us growing apart. As children, we had moved freely around our world of low-slung public housing and gated high-rise developments. But right around adolescence we have to start making a choice. If we choose right, a promising future lies within our grasp. If we choose wrong, the path is unforgiving. The ground has already begun to harden around each of us, and soon it will be impossible to undo who we have become.

The summer before Debra and I start high school, we return to our ledge, not knowing it will be our last time.

"We should jump," she says, out of nowhere. "You double dare me?"

The drop is only about twelve feet, but we've never talked about jumping before. Not when we were younger and used to go sockless in our high-top All Stars. The ones whose shoelaces we soaked in vinegar to make white. So, why now when it is our sandaled feet that hang over the ledge and gravity isn't at all kind to tube tops?

"I'm not jumping," I say and lean away from her.

"I'll hold your hand if you're scared," Debra says. She spits down onto the asphalt to shush her own fear. And before another word is spoken, she scoots forward on the ledge, extending arms straight out in front of her like Frankenstein, and jumps, landing on her feet, then falling backward. We are both shocked by the way she takes flight and then more surprised by the fall. After a few seconds, I see her trying to laugh away the sting that travels up through the soles of her sandals. I realize that I have Frankenstein arms, too. Not because I'm going to jump. I am reaching for her. My instinct is to save her the same way she has saved me. Debra stands and brushes off her shorts. She looks up at me and says it isn't so bad—to jump, then to fall and then hit the ground hard.

"I'll do it again next time," she says.

Only there is no next time. Not long after, she moves away.

Years later, when we are separated by much more than miles, I will think of our ledge and that jump. In my dreams, I will see Kim standing at that intersection, waving goodbye. And I will be haunted by the paths we each took.

chapter two

Bricks and Blood

. . .

My earliest memory of myself is of my sister. My earliest under-standing of my world comes from three women—my mother, grandmother, and aunt.

When I was a toddler and still an only child, my mother said that I began hiding under the dining room table. My parents and extended family had moved into a three-flat apartment building on Chicago's far South Side, ten miles away from Bronzeville. It was my father's idea for everyone to pool their resources in a rent-to-own plan to purchase the building. Mom, Dad, and I lived in the second-floor apartment with its two bedrooms and two baths. Granny and Uncle Al, Granny's younger brother, moved into the first-floor apartment. Aunt Doris, pregnant with fraternal twins, Uncle Henry, and their two older sons moved into the garden apartment. Uncle Anderson, Granny's older brother, and his wife and their two daughters occu-pied the third-floor unit.

Some Sundays, Mom invited everyone to our apartment for dinner. Afterward, my father, on the rare occasion when he was home, and my uncles pushed away from the dining table, eager to watch the last innings of a baseball game or *The Ed Sullivan Show* on the new color television console. Mom, Granny, and Aunt Doris remained seated at the table, nibbling on leftovers and reminiscing about the past. Mom called it "pinching off pieces of time." I have no memory of when or why I joined the women. But I know I felt safe near them. The men existed as clouds of cigarette smoke and spicy cologne and nylon sweaters and booming voices that pitched far away even when they scooped me up after I'd fallen asleep. But the women were flesh and blood, bricks and mortar. They were my fort. I felt cocooned in the cocoa butter and camphor smell of their legs, the sheer raucousness of their laughter. Over the years, I would come to savor their stories while watching the way the hem of the tablecloth draped over their round knees. It was similar to the way their lace handkerchiefs rested on their laps when they worried their white Sunday dresses might ride up too high.

For the longest time, I didn't understand their conversations, especially when they scooted their chairs together, leaned into one another, forgetting the desiccating bones of the fried chicken or roasted turkey; forgetting the men just beyond the pocket doors, and even the little girl who had tucked herself in near their feet.

Granny would sigh: "Umph, umph, umph. When Mr. Right is alright!"

Mom strummed the table: "Make a rabbit hug a hound."

Aunt Doris exclaimed: "Good Lord Almighty!"

Invariably, one of the men would holler from the living room: "Y'all calling me? Somebody call the Lord?" Then the men would laugh, even though they knew better than to expect the women to answer; or to enter that dining room, the women's domain.

Mom lowered her voice: "You know what Lessie would have said . . ." A brief pause always followed my great-grandmother's name. Lessie, Granny's mother, had been gone nearly two years by then, and her loss still felt like a wound that would never scab over. She had sat at the head of the table, and at the head of their lives. "'If the Lord had made anything better, He'd have kept it for Himself!'"

The women stomped their feet and their laughter shook loose heaven and earth.

With my great-grandmother gone, Granny sat at the head of the table. She was a maid at a fine-glass company in Chicago's Merchandise Mart. Although we called her "Granny," the word does not call forth the proper image of a beautiful woman who was statuesque with light-brown skin and fashionably short galloping curls. But she had massive bunions that made her feet wide and boxy. They were the only part of her that she was self-conscious about, and she could spot someone sneaking a peek at her feet the way a buxom woman knows when her cleavage is under inspection.

Granny's stories transported the women back five decades to when her parents fled Mississippi and the Jim Crow South for Chicago, joining tens of thousands of new migrants on their way to the city. It was during the first wave of the Great Migration and Granny was just three years old. If a newcomer to the table asked her where in Mississippi she was born, she flashed the same scowl she reserved for someone who sat in her seat.

"Who cares?" she snapped. "We said good riddance to all of Mississippi. All of it was the same place."

The hard wood of the table muffled the women's words, and for years I thought the Jim Crow South was the *Kim* Crow South; the struggle for civil rights was for *silver* rights; the Great Migration was the Great *Miration*.

"One of the first things my mama did after she arrived was get that long, thick hair of hers chopped off," Granny said. "She wanted to wear the hats that the more sophisticated Black women wore."

Lessie, tall with a beautiful deep mocha coloring, had wide hips and bowlegs. She weighed fifty pounds more than her husband, who was short and slight. Mom and Aunt Doris called him "Granddad." Granny called him "Pops." He died before I was born. When he arrived in Chicago in 1916, he got a job in the stockyards. After his first day, he ran home and told everybody about the traitor sheep— or "house nigga," as he put it—that rounded up the other sheep for slaughter and then looked shocked and bewildered before his own throat was slit. He met a neighbor lady who proclaimed that Chicago indeed was the land of milk and honey. She would get into a car with her pail, driving to the stockyards to steal milk from cows before they met their fate.

"Then, it all quickly went to hell," Granny said.

It was the narrow strip of land—initially called the Black Belt and later dubbed Bronzeville—where the city forced the influx of new Black residents to live. *It* was the place officials abandoned and neglected, allowing burned-out stores to stand, alleys to fill with mud, and mountains of trash to accumulate. Squalid tenements occupied blocks, and some were so run-down that their toilets at times flushed all by themselves from the reverberations of the nearby Illinois Central Railroad trains. The same ones depositing Blacks from the South. When Granny was six, her family lived in a tenement that was in such disrepair that one of its rats bit her on the forehead while she was asleep. She would dab makeup over the scar, two indentations left by the rat's teeth, above her brow for the rest of her life.

"We did what Black people have always done," she said, picking crumbs from the tablecloth, retiring the past. "We took a bunch of scraps and stitched together a world."

M y mother had become quite skilled at salvaging scraps and mending frayed seams. Her marriage had been an exercise in both. Pockets wadded with racetrack winnings, my father had promised her that this building would be a new start, an opportunity to build wealth and well-being. But on a Sunday night when the family did not come down for dinner, Mom sat at the kitchen table watching me eat. From there, she could see the lights from the white Christmas tree in the living room. Dad entered the kitchen wearing his overcoat, Sunday suit, nylon socks, and Old Spice cologne. He said he wore it loud so everybody knew he was coming.

"I'm going out," he said. "Trying to make something happen for the rent."

"Out where?" Mom asked.

"Out, out," he said.

"Okay, then. Just go."

He closed the door and a few minutes later she heard the ignition on his black 1964 DeVille sedan attempting to start, flatlining and misfiring again before turning over. The car had three years on it but looked brand-new. It had been in an accident, which was the only way Dad could afford it on his cabdriver's salary. It still broke down more than it ran. The car, Mom would later say, was like her husband: slick and shiny on the outside but unreliable and filled with deception.

On the kitchen table lay her dream book for divining lottery numbers, her husband's Rules of the Road booklet, and a hostile pile of bills that stared as hard at her as she stared at it. We had been in the building for four months and envelopes held notices demanding two months of rent. How Dad had convinced the owner that he could afford to buy the building in that rent-to-own agreement spoke to his charm and guile. Mom empathized. He had conned her, too, but she was no longer under his spell. She'd been married to Dad for four years. Four years wedded to a man who lacked fidelity to her, to bill collectors, and, most of all, to the truth. For four years, she'd watched his dreams outdistance him because he'd been born in the wrong skin at the wrong time with the wrong ambitions. Still, why did he have to take it out on her? She decided to leave him. She had a part-time job as a receptionist at a dry cleaners a friend owned, and she'd begun bringing home plastic sheaths to wrap clothes in when she packed. No one else knew. Not even Granny and Aunt Doris, in whom she confided everything.

In the beginning—a time hard to fathom now—Granny and Aunt Doris believed my father was the perfect mate for Mom. She and Dad had met in church and sung in the gospel choir. Dad, like Mom, neither smoked nor drank any form of alcohol. Granny, who was also in the choir, loved the way his eyes closed and his jaw trembled when he sang "Precious Memories" in his thundering bass. She took careful note of the way he watched Mom, a soprano, hit her high notes during her signature solo, "The Only Hope We Have." Granny and Aunt Doris stood slack-jawed the first time they heard Mom sing. They had no idea she possessed such a beautiful voice. Granny understood why this man looked at her daughter as though she wore a scarf of incandescent light.

Dad took Mom on a date, dinner at Gladys' on the South Side. He told her that he wanted to own a fleet of cabs. When Mom told Granny, she loved that he aspired to something and had vision. And he was sincere and quiet, reserved about it, unlike her ex-husband, who was nicknamed Rooster for a reason.

"He's a keeper," she'd said to Mom. "He will increase you."

Only he hadn't. At least not in the way she hoped. Now, years later, it wasn't just the bills that were past due, Mom thought as she touched her stomach. So was she.

The next morning, she told our family doctor that she'd had two irregular periods in a row during which she'd only spotted. He recommended a pregnancy test. She insisted she couldn't be pregnant. Her husband hadn't touched her in several weeks, and when he had, she'd used Preceptin-gel birth control religiously.

When the blood test came back positive, Mom demanded that he readminister it using her other arm. She knew it wouldn't make a difference. Sure enough, Mom's other arm betrayed her. She was so upset that she nearly left me in the doctor's office as she grabbed her handbag to leave.

That night, she lay on her bed and asked me to play a game in which I would stand on the bed and jump on her stomach. But after my first landing, it was clear that I was too light to alter her predicament, and with the second jump, she caught me in her arms. Her thick, dark brown hair, straightened into a shoulder-length style, swept like a curtain over one eye, ushering in resolve. Resigned to her pregnancy, Mom decided that if she had a boy, she'd leave my father and make him take "his little bastard" with him. Never mind the irony. And she wasn't going to tell her mother and sister. Aunt Doris would have offered to rear the little boy. Teary-eyed, she would have said, "I've got three hardheaded boys. What's one more? Give him to me."

Mom couldn't have allowed that. She was six months pregnant when the family—minus my father—gathered in our living room, eyes fixed on the television and early reports about the Rev. Martin Luther King Jr. being shot on the balcony of the Lorraine Motel. Mom had spotted off and on during her pregnancy, but when the news confirmed King's assassination, blood gushed from her. It was the one moment she feared she might lose the baby. Then, as quickly as the flow came, it stopped. It was as though the little interloper in her body, determined to get here, had used both hands to turn off a spigot. The following day, the family—again, minus Dad—gathered to watch footage of protesters exacting revenge by burning down their already beleaguered neighborhoods. While everyone wondered how long the protests would last, no one questioned why they were underway. The scars protesters inflicted on their neighborhoods seemed superficial compared to the ones the neighborhoods and the city had inflicted on them.

Dad had been away for several days again, "trying to make something happen at the racetrack." When Mom arrived at the Jiffy Cab Company searching for him, the dispatcher said he *probably* was among the drivers who had gone to the West Side, to communities teeming with protesters, firefighters, police officers, and the National Guard. Cabbies had been dispatched to ferry out residents trying to get to their jobs. Mom stared at the dispatcher. Maybe Dad had convinced the men in the garage that he was the heroic type. But he had left his pregnant wife to smooth things over with a landlord threatening eviction. Every time she looked down at her round midsection, she was propelled forward by the thought of getting this man and his son behind her.

By early June, when Robert Kennedy was assassinated, she was eight months pregnant and we'd been evicted from the three-flat and were living in a motel. In a photograph from the time, I'm wearing a baby-blue dress with a white collar and white ankle socks, standing on a balcony similar to the one at the Lorraine Motel. The bulk of our possessions—the red sectional sofa, a coffee table, new beds, kitchen appliances, and Mom's wedding china—sat in a rat-infested storage facility. The small motel room had paper-thin walls with stock landscape paintings and smelled mostly of bleach and mildew and sometimes ass. The room had two full-size beds, both as swaybacked as old mules and burdened from either newlyweds or prostitutes doing their business. While my aunt Doris and uncle Henry complained that the beds in their room were punishingly uncomfortable, Mom appreciated the sunken space, the way it conformed and acquiesced to her pregnant frame. Nothing else in her life had much give in it. No one, including the baby, had been so accommodating.

Mom and I slept together. The other bed, which would have gone to Dad, remained made and undisturbed. Now he was away for long stretches checking on a chicken farm he said he bought in Michigan. Mom knew that was another lie. Still, she welcomed his absence as long as he paid the motel's weekly fees. In her nation sack, a pouch she kept inside her bra, was about $200 from which she refused to pinch. To pass the time when she wasn't working, she watched *Dark Shadows* and bonded with the maids by helping to scour the motel room. By the way she scrubbed the bathroom and picked the pilling off the nubby bedspreads and held vigilance over the mattresses for bedbugs, she must have appeared to be nesting, preparing for the baby. But, in reality, she was disassembling a life, reconfiguring the nest without my father, and reimagining her world with only me, a child who looked so much like the man she was leaving that to her great dismay he could never be fully gone.

In return for Mom's work, the maids gave her extras from their carts—towels, bars of Ivory soap, hard candies in cellophane sleeves, and books of matches for quieting loud odors. One maid, a Caribbean woman named Dovie, lugged two brown paper bags of hand-me-downs to our motel room. Mom happily accepted them and placed them in the closet next to a mound of my father's belongings. She looked forward to seeing Dovie, and loved the way she pronounced "morning" like "moaning" as she knocked on the motel door, announcing, "Good moaning, how y'all feel?" When Mom craved black cherries and black coffee, Dovie raided the on-site diner. And, after an unpleasant interaction with Dad, the maid turned to Mom and doled out advice: "Baby, I can see you married a mule. But you gotta ride him."

The hell you say, Mom thought as she smiled. She had just a few more weeks of her husband's nonsense and this ordeal would be over. Although Mom had refused to consider baby names, the one thing she couldn't deny the child was conversation: "Little boy, I don't care how much you kick," she would say, rubbing her abdomen. And, "Do you ever sleep?" And, "Child, why are you so darn restless?"

The next day, Mom and I took a bus downtown to the Office of Immigration and Naturalization. She needed a higher-paying job, so she applied to the one she had when she was single, typing the statements of immigrants hoping to become citizens. When she learned she got the job, she began looking for a place to live. Listening to the radio, she heard about an apartment complex opening in Bronzeville. In the summer of 1967, a groundbreaking ceremony was held for Lawless Gardens on the thirteen-acre site directly across the street from the Ida B. Wells housing project. It was a big deal. The principal developers were "Negroes," *Jet* magazine announced. Among them were magazine publisher John H. Johnson and Dr.

Theodore K. Lawless, an internationally known dermatologist who revolutionized skin treatments for leprosy and syphilis. At the ground-breaking, Lawless said he wanted to create a *middle-income* development for people displaced by urban renewal. The community was quickly filling with housing for the very poor and for the well-to-do but had little to nothing for people in the middle. Mom had admired Theodore K. Lawless for years, but that name. How unfortunate for a Black development.

She telephoned the dispatcher where Dad worked to have a taxi sent to the motel. The driver took her four miles north on the street that would soon be named King Drive to the new complex. A third tower and several townhouses were under construction. Fledgling trees lay on their sides awaiting planting. Sidewalks were still being installed. Granny told Mom that she and Uncle Al would move into Lawless Gardens, too, if Mom thought the development was suitable. Uncle Al had to live with Granny because he'd returned from World War II depressed and a bit damaged— her word was "nervous"—and she'd promised their mother she would always care for him. So Mom asked the property manager to show her two two-bedroom apartments. It just so happened that units 306 and 307 were available on the third floor, right around the corner from each other. The rents ranged from $115 to $155 per month. In the apartment that would be ours, the living room windows faced west and looked out onto the rear parking lot, be-hind which was a cluster of nineteenth-century brownstones and graystones. One had been owned by Ida B. Wells herself. In the apartment Mom believed to be perfect for Granny and Uncle Al, the living room windows faced south, framing the building's cir-cular driveway with its manicured berm in the center. Beyond that, a playground was still under construction. And just across the street from Lawless's southernmost border was the Ida B. Wells Homes row houses where she grew up. When it opened in 1941, it was Chicago's first public housing project for African Americans and designed to be an oasis. More than 18,000 people applied for only 1,662 apartments. The housing authority carefully screened the final candidates, checking their backgrounds and visiting their current homes. My grandmother got one. My great-grandparents got another. Ever determined, Granny made sure her daughters partook of every amenity the development offered.

"Low-income people don't have to be low-ceilinged people," Granny said as she signed her girls up for swimming classes in the Madden Park swimming pool. In the field house, she scheduled them for piano, ballet, and etiquette lessons taught by the neighborhood's teachers, who also tutored them in Latin, philosophy, and plane geometry. They learned sewing and knitting from the white nuns from the Holy Angels Catholic Church convent a few blocks away. Aunt Doris had the proper temperament and patience for needlework. Mom did not. But she loved milk, and the nuns allowed their students to line up to get a bottle after each session. That's why Mom attended. She gulped down her milk, wedged the bottle back into the crate, and returned to the line for more. On days when milk was delivered throughout the community, though, she ran from stoop to stoop secretly prying open bottles and slurping the cream off the top. After having her fill, she lay under the cascading clotheslines that reached from building to building. They displayed the community's class diversity. The steel-mill workers' jumpsuits scarred by flames. The bloodstained slaughterhouse workers' aprons. The medical students' monogrammed lab coats. The print blouses and A-line skirts of schoolteachers and social workers. All spirited by the wind, swaying and dancing on the lines.

While standing at the window in Lawless, Mom could see Madden Park. She thought about Mrs. Patterson, an old woman who had been born into slavery. As a young girl, Mom ran to the store for her, and the woman compensated Mom with shiny pennies. Mom, just five years old, sat with Mrs. Patterson in the park and tried to teach her how to read. Mom thought about the day she asked Uncle Al to teach her to fight. He'd been a boxer in the army. He, too, had grown up in Bronzeville, and before he left for the war, he'd been formidable. As a girl, Mom walked through the community believing it was her legend that held bullies at bay. But it was actually his. He also taught her how to catch and hit a baseball. She thought about the boys who didn't want her to play with them no matter how many times she stood in the outfield. And then, one afternoon, a fly ball arced toward her from a blindingly blue sky. She closed her eyes just before it slammed into her chest, laying her flat on her back. She caught it with both hands. When she came to, the boys were standing over her. Mildly impressed, one extended his hand.

"I don't need no help." She lifted herself without losing her prize. "I can do it."

That same determination anchored her that day as she made a decision. She would move us to Lawless—it would be ground zero for her fresh start. And yet, she couldn't help feeling the pangs of a setback. The property manager handed her a folder, and on the cover was an artist's rendering of the complex with a well-dressed mother, father, and child walking down a sidewalk. She placed her thumb over the father, leaving just mother and child. Lifting her thumb, she looked closer at the family and noticed that they were racially ambiguous. Another principal developer, Dr. William J. Walker, an African American dentist, had emphasized that although the associates were Black, Lawless Gardens was "not a Negro project" but "a project for the people." Mom knew that this was an attempt to attract white folks. But she didn't care about whether they moved in. And grand towers, even those with blond bricks and large windows that brought the sky within reach, no longer excited her. What she wanted was stability and the rent paid. She wanted to never again feel the shame of being kicked out of a place, or having her fine china lost to storage due to nonpayment. She wanted the opportunity to breathe and not rue the jingle of her husband's keys.

When Mom went into labor early on July 8, 1968, she had erected the scaffolding of our new lives and was determined to cleave herself from her husband and child. The delivery was difficult. The baby was breech. Still, a little girl arrived just after midnight. The nurse placed my sister in Mom's arms, and when Mom saw her baby— pale, bald, with a face so much like her own—she knew without hesitation that she couldn't give her daughter up. Perhaps it was the flood of hormones, or the promise that resides in every newborn's face. But she decided to give her husband one more try. The next day, she laughed when Dad told her how Kim wailed and woke up the other babies in the nursery before falling back to sleep. It had been a long time since she laughed at anything he said. She delighted in the image of her little rabble-rouser sowing discord. Kind takes to kind.

Great-Granny Lessie believed that birthmarks were more than just routine skin maladies. She believed they resulted from something the pregnant woman unconsciously did or that was done to her. Mom was skeptical until she had me. While pregnant, she had been in a neighbor's kitchen and had seen a mouse. She jumped up on a chair, hiked up her dress, and her fingernail scratched the inside of her upper thigh. When I was born with a walnut-shaped mark, like an inkblot, on the inside of my upper thigh, she recalled her grandmother's theory and blamed herself. She was grateful that she hadn't grabbed her face. My father's birthmark was an albino lightning streak that ate into the brown color of his left leg starting at his ankle and running up a ways. Mom surmised that his mother, while pregnant with him, had been frightened by a snake. She saw that as both prescient and fitting, and later said she should have known who he was the first time he took his pants off.

After Kim was born, Mom, Granny, and Aunt Doris examined my sister's body for any abnormalities. It might have appeared that the women were counting fingers and toes. But they knew what they were looking for, and when they found nothing, that reassured Mom. She was grateful that her own fear and foreboding, anger and disappointment that had marred her pregnancy had not marked her child. Years down the road she would return to this examination. She would worry every stitch of her pregnancy, parse every detail, trying to identify what she should have done differently.

On a rainy July morning, my father helped Mom and their swaddled baby into the back seat of his cab. He drove them to the motel. Mom lowered Kim onto the bed, corralled between two pillows. And this is where my memory of my sister begins, this moment. Climbing onto the bed, I looked down at her. Black babies are often born fair-skinned, but their inner ears reveal their final color. Kim was so pale that family members took turns searching the insides of her ears, only to find that they were just as fair as the rest of her. Mom said that I poked Kim as if she were the latest addition to my collection of white dolls; as if I wondered what animated her. I wanted desperately to hold her. And when Mom finally agreed, I remember the way my sister felt in my arms, her weight leavened by my mother who only pretended to let me cradle her fully. It was the first time I truly realized that I had hands and a heartbeat. And when Kim began to howl, color pouring into her cheeks, the furrows deepening on her forehead, it was then that I fully understood I had ears. I was so unnerved by her that I didn't ask to hold her again.

From the start my sister was a great mystery to me. That would never change.

chapter three

A Caped Crusader

. . .

Until she was just over a year old, Kim had what Mom called "a smell of hair"—not enough to even clamp a barrette on. Riding down on the elevator, neighbor ladies often said, "What a handsome little man."

This boiled Mom's blood. "She's a girl," Mom seethed as she watched the numbers light up on the overhead panel. Under her breath, she added, "Blind heifers."

Initially, Mom blamed herself, saying that she had been too sick after Kim's birth to get rid of her cradle cap. But later, she would decide that Kim stayed bald simply to defy her. And in keeping with my mother's assessment, when Kim's hair did grow—when she was about eighteen months old—it did so with a vengeance. (Mom said a comb would break its neck trying to get through it; Uncle Henry told Aunt Doris that Kim always looked like she'd been holding 220-volt wires.) Kim's hair never grew long like mine. But it was beautiful: thicker, coarser. To touch it was like running your fingers across a deckled edge. Because Mom used Queen Bergamot hair grease in her unsuccessful attempts to tame Kim's locks, my sister always smelled like mint. This made some church ladies believe Kim was sweet and approachable. That is, until they tried to pick her up and she turned either firecracker red or asphyxiation blue and fought them—with a vengeance.

Kim didn't walk until, as Mom put it, "she damn well pleased."

After that, she ran and kept running. Most of the time she was in pursuit of our father, who was rarely home.

When he was around, he was sullen, enigmatic, and an introvert, which created a heaviness in the apartment even though he was never truly present. He slept during the day and worked at night. On his off days, he slept during the day and stayed up at night, watching television from our green-and-gold floral-print sofa, his feet crossed at the ankles on the coffee table. It held the latest *Ebony* magazine and glass-blown fruit and ashtrays from Granny's glass company. Dad loved watching baseball games, wrestling shows, Chicago's evening news anchor Fahey Flynn with his bow tie, and *The Road Runner Show*. I loved that show, too, because it made him laugh a deep full-bodied cackle that sounded unnatural coming from him. I stood in the bathroom mirror trying to imitate it. Long after Kim and I went to bed, he kept watching until the stations signed off. Some nights, I'd get up and see him snoring to the drone of television static.

Our father was not the disciplinarian. That job belonged to Mom and Granny. Neither was he the person who indulged us. My sister made it her singular ambition to win Dad's attention. She would climb onto the sofa to sit next to him when he watched television. He suffered her for a while and then called for Mom to come get their daughter. When Mom told Kim she had to stay in our bedroom, she slipped out and squatted next to the stereo console, peering at Dad watching the screen.

One day, when Kim was about three and I was six, Dad didn't have to work, but got up early anyway and left. He returned that evening as Kim and I had just finished our TV dinners, a rare treat because Mom said it was too hot to labor over a stove. Shirtless, Kim sat at the table exposing the tan line of her swimsuit and a necklace of mosquito bites near her collarbone. Half of her hair was unbraided and shot up as if in a salute. Dad stuck his head into the kitchen, said hi, and then continued to the bedroom to change clothes. Kim jumped up and followed him. We expected him to call Mom to come get Kim. Instead, we heard Kim scream. We bolted to the room.

Dad had draped a white towel around Kim's neck and fastened it with a couple of large safety pins left over from her diapers. He was beckoning for her to jump off the bed into his arms. Each time he returned her to the bed, he moved a step backward. And, each time, she leaped, collapsing into his chest. It was her giggles that drew Mom and me to them. It was a levity, a lightness surrounding my father that was so unfamiliar, it held us captive in the doorway.

"C'mon, Pasquale," he said. We never knew why he called Kim that. "You got it."

Kim paused, but only for a correction. "I'm Duperman," she said, taking flight.

Although Mom enjoyed her daughter's giggles, she watched with her arms folded and the corners of her lips upturned as if to hold in abeyance the belief that such a Kodak moment could last. Each time Dad stepped back and Kim jumped farther, Mom winced a bit. But she didn't doubt whether he would catch her, nor whether Duperman—face aglow, eyes bright as embers—would leap into her father's arms.

The next evening, we ate dinner together because Dad needed to leave for work early. He typically slept through dinner and left around 9 p.m. after Kim and I were in bed. But that night, after dinner, he kissed each of us on the cheek. When the door closed behind him, Mom picked up Kim and sat her on the windowsill and I stood next to them as we waited for Dad to appear from under the building and walk to the car. The streetlights over the back parking lot had just blinked on, casting a halo over the shiny hoods of the cars. The waning summer sunlight warmed the empty rooms of the abandoned brownstones and graystones beyond the parking lot, bringing them, if only momentarily, back to life. The scenery was stage set and hypnotic.

The living room windows offered Mom a sort of cinema verité and she had spent many a predawn hour over the last few years peeping behind the sheers, watching my father walk jauntily up the sidewalk toward the building, watching his long gait and the way his head tilted upward with his lips pursed, whistling. That night, she must have felt hopeful, despite everything she knew to be fact about her husband. Laws and theorems could have been applied to him, like those governing gravity or motion or the speed of light. Laws that were immutable and predictable. But hope and dramatic lighting have the power to reel you in, to pull you to places beyond your control or good sense. They encourage the worst form of trespass.

When Dad stepped from under the building, Kim sat up on her knees to make herself seen.

"Look." She pointed at him. "Turn 'round, Daddy!"

She began to wave and smile. Then I waved at Daddy. Even Mom lifted her hand. I wanted him to turn around for Kim. My sister never knew about Mom's plan to leave our father and give her to him if she were a boy. But it seemed she intuited it, and that had forged a loyalty to him and a bond that I didn't share.

"Turn 'round, Daddy," she said, pressing her face against the glass until her small nose flattened.

It was too late. He'd begun walking down the sidewalk, joined by a million other distractions. We were an afterthought.

Not long after, a few days maybe, Kim pulled one of Dad's white shirts from a hanger and tied the sleeves around her neck. If either Mom or I had seen Kim sitting on their bed, waiting for him in his shirt, now wrinkled and stained with peppermint slobber, we would have pulled her out of there. Not because we thought he would have spanked her. Mom would have said, "I just really don't want to hear his mouth." Then we would have yanked the shirt off her neck, even though she would have fought us.

But Dad saw Kim first. He grabbed her by the arm and took her into our bedroom. He sat on the queen bed we shared and slung Kim across his lap. Before I could say a word, he lifted his palm and smacked her on her behind. She scarcely flinched, although I did. She must have thought it was part of the game.

"I'm Duperman," she said, craning her neck to look up at him. She chewed her tongue. She tended to do that when she was confused.

He hit her again and she still didn't cry. He had never spanked either of us before. But now he was raising his hand a third time.

"No!" I yelled. My breath caught in my throat. "Don't!"

"I'm Duperman," Kim said to me, eyes watery but not runny.

He stood her up and she was a bit wobbly, as though she had

just stuck a landing. As she reached back and rubbed her behind, my father lifted his shirt from around her neck. And that's when she began to sob. Mighty, mighty tears. In a final villainous swoop, he had discovered a way to hurt her.

"No, Daddy," she said, jumping and clawing. "Give it back!"

Mom heard Kim crying and ran into the room. He handed Mom the shirt.

"I need you to fix this," he said. "I gotta go out later."

"For what?" Mom hissed.

"Work."

"What kind of work?"

"Work, work," he said.

He left the room. Mom turned to me. "I thought I told you to watch your sister."

In my parents' bedroom, Dad's Sunday suit had been pulled forward in the closet. On the bed lay a new pair of fake gold cuff links and an open tin of lemon drops, the kind that always tasted sweet before everything soured.

Mom rocked Kim and lay her on the bed. I stood over my sister, watching her whimper. I licked my finger to wipe grape juice splotches from the corners of her mouth. I made sure the gum she chewed earlier wasn't mashed in her hair.

"Don, I'm leaky," she whispered when Mom left our room. That was her word for having to pee, but now it applied to all over. As I took her to the bathroom, she looked warily around corners for our father. She did the same as I returned her to our bed.

"Go to sleep," I said.

For a few seconds, she looked up at me glassy-eyed and then leaned on me and conked out, as though her batteries had been touched by corrosion.

Later that night, I was awakened by loud claps of thunder coming from my parents' bedroom. I rose from bed, slid my feet into my house slippers, and patted around the bed for my robe. Every night, Mom laid both Kim's and my robes at the foot of our bed. When I felt mine, I turned on the hall light, my eyes blinking, adjusting to the glare. I opened my parents' bedroom door. My father sat on the edge of the bed leaning over my mother with his large hands wrapped around her neck. His fake gold cuff links glinted in the light. Gasping, Mom found just enough air to force out a few words: "It's okay, sweetie." She was pressing against his face with her fists. "Go back to bed."

At any other time, she would have been stern, but now her words lacked air. My eyes burned with tears as I stepped away from the door and closed it. In my bedroom, I crawled back into bed with Kim. Half asleep, my sister attempted to push me out. She thought I was the little brown baby doll she slept with every night. With its brown eyes and black tightly coiled hair, she was the first Black doll I'd ever seen, and she always began the night in Kim's arms. But because Kim slept wildly, the doll, by morning, lay sprawled on the floor. Legs kicked out, arms rigid but reaching, mouth shaped like an O, always surprised by the inevitable.

That night, I did not close my eyes. Panic swept over me as I listened to the loud bumps and thumps against the wall of the room next door. My heart hammered in my chest and I patted Kim's back to make sure she slept through it all. I'd never seen my father hit, let alone choke, my mother. In that moment, both of my parents were strangers. The woman who said "Go back to bed" didn't sound like Mom. The man with his hands around her neck bore no resemblance to Dad. The little girl standing in the doorway, robe tied fastidiously at the waist, however, was exactly me: a follower of rules, a maker of lists, a keeper of time. As I lay in the bed, I had no doubt that my sister, breathing heavily beside me, would have been exactly herself. Even as a three-year-old, she would have known instinctively that what she saw was wrong. At the very least, she would have stood there despite what Mom said. Kim would not have turned away. Over the last few months, Mom had been trying to stop me from sucking my thumb by dousing it in a cayenne pepper–flavored concoction before bed. That night, despite the sting, I placed my thumb squarely in my mouth and worked my way back to sleep.

The next morning, I awoke to Mom laughing in the living room. I jumped up without my robe or slippers and ran toward the laughter. I thought maybe I had fallen into a deep dream and gotten lost and confused. When I peeped around the corner, Mom's back was to me and she was seated in a chair, talking on the telephone. I could feel myself breathing, relieved that she sounded like Mom.

"Clara, girl, you go 'way from here." Mom's laughter filled the room. Miss Clara was the morning dispatcher at Dad's job. "No, I'm sure. Four passengers today."

As I walked up, she grabbed me close to her, entangling me in the stiff curl of the phone cord. Up close, I could feel the warmth of her cheek and hear Miss Clara's voice spilling out from the receiver. It wasn't until I pulled away from Mom that I saw her neck. A constellation of reddish-purple balloon-shaped bruises spread across her skin. Some were elongated with ribbony tails that floated into her hairline. I reached to touch them, to fit my fingers into the circles, but Mom smiled at me and gently removed my hand.

"Twenty minutes?" Mom said into the telephone. She pulled me close to her again, something she would never do on any ordinary, busy morning. "Let me think."

She buried her face into my neck.

"No, make it an hour," she said. "You have a nice day, too."

After hanging up, Mom took my hands in hers and smiled. She searched for the right words: "Your father can't live with us anymore. I told him he has to leave."

My eyes welled with tears. Not because he was leaving but because I knew then what I'd seen the night before was true.

"You understand?" Mom said.

I nodded.

"Go put on your swimsuit," she said. "We'll have one last day at the pool before my big girl starts first grade."

As I walked back to my bedroom, I saw Aunt Doris in the bathroom washing Kim's face. Aunt Doris and her family lived in a well-run housing project about a mile north of us. She'd never been in our apartment so early in the morning. A few feet away, I saw Granny. She never took a day off from work, but there she was in my parents' bedroom, shoving Dad's belongings into green duffel bags: his too-short striped pajama bottoms; his shoes, including his leather Jesus sandals; his white dress shirts. At first, she didn't notice me in the doorway.

Granny snatched up two of the bags and began to leave the bedroom. Seeing me, she said, "Don't just stand there." She peeped into the bathroom to check on Aunt Doris, who was helping Kim into her little bikini. I noticed that Kim was chewing.

Aunt Doris reached into her pocket and handed me three candy corns.

"Mom doesn't let us eat candy so early," I said, mouth watering, staring at her hand.

"Your mom's not my boss," Auntie whispered, smiling. "Besides, we big sisters have to stick together."

Granny passed the bathroom door again. "Everybody needs to get a move on," she said. Then she noticed Dad's toothbrush, the tallest of the four with the flattened bristles. She grabbed it by its neck and threw it like a javelin into the garbage can.

When it was time to leave, Aunt Doris carried two duffel bags to the service elevator and held the door open for us. Granny dragged the other two, leaving a trail in the carpeting. She despised using the service elevator, or the back stairwell or the back door off the lobby, even in a building of Black neighbors. She vividly remembered when the white folks in the downtown hotels and department stores directed her to the rear. Mom nudged Kim and me onto the elevator while writing on one of the notepads with price lists that Granny brought home from the glass company where she worked. At first, no one spoke, not even Kim, who was unaware of what was going on. In the enclosed space, I smelled Dad's scent wafting up from his things. It was a blending of cologne, exhaust fumes, gasoline, and cigarette smoke, which came from the men in the garage. In that moment, Dad was with us—in that barely there way that was most familiar.

Granny must have smelled it, too, because she grumbled, "His common ass."

Through the lobby's floor-to-ceiling windows, I saw the cab, idling. Aunt Doris flung open the back door and hefted her duffel bags onto the seat and Granny followed suit. Mom wore a khaki sundress with a tan scarf around her neck. When she leaned into the taxi's window, one of her bruises peeked out.

"This is your boss's shit," she told the driver. "Tell him not to come back. Ain't nothing left."

Mom rarely said the word "shit" in front of us, and she hated the word "ain't." She told us it wasn't a word. But the last few hours had stripped her of her defenses. When she slammed the door, the driver leaped out of his cab.

"This ain't what I was expecting," he said.

"Me either," Mom scoffed.

Mom handed the notepad with its "To Do" list to Granny, and she followed Aunt Doris back into the building. Mom picked up Kim, and we began to walk down the sidewalk through Lawless. Since we had moved in three years ago, a tall chain-link fence had been built around Lawless's perimeter. We walked through the opening at 37th Street, Lawless's southernmost border, on our way to Madden Park's pool. When we crossed the baseball field, I expected Mom to point to where Granny used to make her way through the park with her two daughters running to catch up because she walked so fast. I expected Mom to look around and complain about trash spilling from garbage cans, the growing graffiti on the benches, and how the once perfectly straight lines on the baseball diamond now looked like they had been hand-drawn by someone with the shakes. When a group of boys in swimming trunks ran past us, with one saying, "Where's my towel at?" I expected her to say, "In front of the preposition." I expected her to say, "The park never looked like this when I was a child." But this morning, she was uncharacteristically silent, and the past receded into the sound of parched grass and dandelions crunching under our feet.

While we were gone, Uncle Al, who worked odd jobs, changed the dead bolt on our front door and added a chain. Aunt Doris dialed our minister, whom we called Prophet, to tell him that Mom needed a "reading" to help her figure her way forward. Granny called her cousin who was a longtime janitor in the domestic relations division of the Cook County circuit court. He was the closest the family had to a lawyer and was well-versed in initiating divorce proceedings.

That first night, Uncle Al stayed with us. Mom told him he didn't have to, but he refused to leave us. Before tucking Kim and me in, Mom made us kneel beside our beds to say our prayers. Kim, as always, sidled next to me. My mother didn't believe in "Now I lay me down to sleep, I pray the Lord my soul to keep . . ." baby prayers. She said Black children, girls in particular, needed to speak directly to God. So she stood in the doorway as I led the Lord's Prayer with Kim as my echo. I climbed into bed, and when I couldn't sleep, I got up and peeped into the living room. Uncle Al sat on the sofa with his newspaper. At his feet was a splintered baseball bat he called his "Nigga Beater." He'd used it to teach Mom how to play baseball.

"Come here, little girl," he said after seeing me. "You doing okay?"

"Uh-huh," I said.

"Okay, then, go on back to your room. Everything will be alright."

I went to bed, but nothing felt alright.

During slavery, there was a phenomenon called "working to the coat." The overseer would loop his heavy black jacket over a post and leave. And most slaves would keep toiling just as diligently as if he hadn't stepped away. He'd instilled so much fear in them that he no longer needed to be present to keep them in line. That's how it was with Dad. Although nothing of his remained, he somehow was still there, even more there than when he had lived with us. Mom decided that she didn't want to live in the same space he'd occupied, and we needed another fresh start. It didn't help that Kim kept asking to sit in the window to look for him. Mom wouldn't let her, and in a test of wills, Kim would cry and cry.

Mom loved Lawless Gardens and being close to Granny and Uncle Al, so we moved to another apartment, one that had an identical floor plan on the eleventh floor. Initially, entering apartment 1105 felt no different to Kim and me than entering our old third-floor apartment. We immediately ran to the kitchen and then back to our new bedroom. We thought we knew where we were until we looked out the living room window. While our third-floor living room windows were nearly ground-level and overlooked the back parking lot, we now had what management called a *spectacular lake view*. About a half-mile away was Lake Michigan—vast as an ocean with a color that mimicked the mood of the sky. The only thing was that in order to see the lake, to truly appreciate it, your mind had to blot out the hunkered, brown-brick buildings of the housing project directly across the street. They were mid-rises, seven stories, and had opened in 1955. They were called the "stentions" because they were a newer extension of the Ida B. Wells Homes.

In our third-floor apartment, our bedroom had a southern view overlooking the front of the building and the turning circle; our new eleventh-floor bedroom windows faced north. Directly in front was Lawless Gardens's middle tower, an exact replica of ours, and a block away from it was James R. Doolittle Jr. Elementary, where I attended school. Mom and Aunt Doris had graduated from there. Like Lawless, *Doolittle* was yet another unfortunate name.

Mom bought Kim and me a new bedroom suite that had twin beds and pushed them close. She hung a framed silhouette cutout of my head from first grade and scattered a few stuffed animals atop a new chest of drawers and dresser with a mirror. Uncle Al had made me a wooden trunk, and I created a list of everything inside, including several books Mom had bought me and a few that I'd gotten from the Reading Is Fundamental truck that parked in front of Doolittle Elementary once a month.

Before that period in our lives, I never truly understood what it meant to lose something or someone. To my young mind, leaving was not an evanescent thing. It was simply what Mom prepared us for every night before school when she meticulously laid out our outfits on the living room sofa. In the dark, our clothes resembled two prim little girls who had nothing better to do than be still and wait for morning.

chapter four

The Principal's Office

· · ·

After my father left, my throat felt scorched all the time, like I'd swallowed flames. And I lost my appetite. It was my secret until I began to faint—first at church and then at school. The church fainting hadn't seemed too extraordinary. Parishioners at the First House of Prayer fell out all the time, having been slain by the Holy Ghost or the summer heat, whichever fell harder. The first time I fainted, a deacon whisked me to the back of the church as Mom, Granny, and Aunt Doris flew out of the choir stand to join the women in white nurses' hats who dabbed my cheeks with cool wet cloths and fanned me with cardboard funeral-home fans. The second time was in the schoolyard. I awoke in the arms of the white gym teacher, Mr. Alexander. As he ran with me, my body jostled around so much that I looped my arms around his neck and lay my head against his shoulder. I didn't open my eyes until one of my fellow second-graders exclaimed, "Look, she's smiling! She ain't sleep no more!"

"Yes, I am." Eyelids squinched, I could see kids nearly trampling one another, running alongside Mr. Alexander as though running beside a chugging train.

Mom took me to Dr. Aristomene Nicolas, our family doctor. An internist and pathologist, he was a round Haitian man whose thick accent forced Mom to squint to understand him better. His waiting room had *Highlights* and *Ebony Jr.* magazines fanned across tables; posters of haggard white women warning against the hazards of smoking and drinking; and a water cooler that belched and had a hot-water spigot. We went to Dr. Nicolas's office on most Monday afternoons for years so that Mom could get a weekly vitamin B_{12} shot to fight fatigue.

I sat swinging my legs on the examining table with Mom and the doctor facing me. Behind them, Kim had tried but failed to open a bottle of mercurochrome and was stirring her finger around in a glass jar of thermometers steeping in green alcohol. The thermometers always tasted like spearmint.

"Dawn doesn't eat," Mom said, frowning. "She doesn't sleep. I come into her room in the middle of the night and she says she hears tapping in the ceiling." She managed to sound both skeptical and sympathetic.

"I hear it," I said, mounting my defense. "Tap, tap, tap. Tap, tap, tap."

"I listen but I don't hear anything, Sugar." Mom turned to the doctor. "And she trails me to the door every time someone knocks." To me, she said, "Baby, I don't need protecting."

"Let's take a look." Dr. Nicolas picked up an instrument and breathed heavily on the glass before wiping it with the hem of his white coat. I smelled Juicy Fruit even before I saw the foil wrapper in his breast pocket.

"Divorce happens sometimes," Mom said to me. "Understand?"

I nodded as I always did. *Divorce happens sometimes* was palliative care, language used to soothe rather than heal. It was what she said before Dad picked Kim and me up every other Saturday and took us a block away to the Lake Meadows Shopping Center. There, we'd walk to Walgreens and have hamburgers and pop at the lunch counter. Kim sat between us and swiveled on the vinyl stool. Once in a while, Dad, Kim, and I walked over to Woolworths to get lined notebook paper and pencils or to Goldblatt's for gym shoes or pants. Luckily, Kim would prattle on about nothing and I only had to say, "Yes, I'm still doing well in school" and "I'm not very hungry."

Mom told Granny and Aunt Doris that I didn't sleep right or eat because I missed my father. But I didn't miss him. The truth was that I feared losing Mom. She'd begun sleeping with a glass of water beside her bed because she sometimes woke up in the middle of the night gagging. I would run into her room and she'd assure me that she was okay as she escorted me back to my bed. I was so full of dread and fear that I had no room for eating or sleeping. I knew I was supposed to do both, especially when I felt light-headed and my stomach growled, but I had lumps in my throat, as if I'd swallowed the balloon-shaped bruises I'd seen on Mom's neck. They wouldn't budge.

Dr. Nicolas placed his hands on my shoulders and looked me in the eyes. "You will be just fine," he said. To Mom, he said, "Looks like a touch of tonsillitis." He reached back to his desk for his prescription pad.

"Give her one of these at bedtime," he said, scribbling. "They're mild and will help her sleep." He turned the pad over and wrote that Mom should also prepare a raw egg and a banana in a milkshake twice a day to combat any weight loss and buy Sucrets lozenges for my throat.

Every night, Mom handed me a red pill and a cup of water before I climbed into bed. She closed our bedroom door and I listened to the noises coming through the ceiling: muffled yelling and then a little girl's sobs. Sometimes the crying would be so clear that I couldn't discern whether it was coming from overhead or from my sister in the bed a few feet away. I'd get up and stand over Kim until I was certain it wasn't her. Then I'd get back in my bed just as the medicine made my head feel light and cushiony.

The little red pills helped me sleep, but they also made me sluggish throughout the school day, and that meant I spent some afternoons catnapping in the nurse's office, which was near the principal's. The small room had a desk that overflowed with stacks of papers and a loveseat whose springs whined when I sat on it. In a nook were boxes of chalk, jars of paint and paste, and several bags of sawdust for absorbing vomit (for when the kids ate the chalk, paint, or paste). A wall poster detailed the signs of lockjaw. The air was perfumed in duplicator fluid from the nearby mimeograph machine.

Some afternoons, I peeked out the window in the nurse's door and saw Debra seated on the wooden bench designated for misfits. With her unusual amber-colored eyes and reddish-brown complexion, she was one of the prettiest girls in the school. I'd studied her over the last month, after I, and several other students, transferred into her second-grade classroom when our teacher had resigned mid–school year. Janet Sheard, my new teacher, arranged her students according to height. I was the tallest girl in the class and Debra was the shortest. Our worlds barely touched, and that was just fine with me. While I was content to view mayhem from the sidelines, she pitched herself headlong into trouble. And yet, I watched her through a narrow slit in a bathroom stall as she made faces in the mirror, holding my hand over my mouth trying not to laugh. I watched her say the Pledge of Allegiance always looking out the window at the sky instead of at the flag. During recess, she hung upside down on the monkey bars. With her cobalt-blue windbreaker, she was a spray of color on a sallow playground. On one particular morning, she jockeyed for space among our classmates and moved strategically against a press of bodies to the swings where she pumped with abandon before catapulting from the seat and sprinting over to the slide. A bully pushed her and tried to edge her out of the way, and she pushed back and elbowed harder. When she got tired, she sat on the steps of one of the two beige trailers in the center of the yard. Buttressed by cinder blocks, the trailers were throwbacks from the 1960s and called "Willis wagons." They were named after former Chicago public schools superintendent Benjamin Willis, who dealt with overcrowding at predominately Black schools by trucking in corrugated-tin classrooms rather than integrating some of the less-crowded white schools. Since the Chicago public school system had constructed a new building, which they called Doolittle West, to serve the lower grades, the trailers now were used for storage.

That day, when the end-of-recess bell rang, yard monitors and teachers began to collect us. Many students felt the tug of the bell and were inclined, at the very least, to look in the direction of the steps that returned us to class. But Debra was among those for whom bells meant little and she bolted in the opposite direction to the far reaches of the playground. Waiting in line, we watched her, a girl possessed as she clambered up the slide rather than climb the ladder a few steps away.

"Debra! I mean it," Debra's mother yelled. Mrs. Trice worked at our school as a teacher's aide. She was petite and pretty with a beauty mole over her lip and hair styled in a flip like Marlo Thomas's on television's *That Girl*. "Don't you do it!"

But Debra continued, her feet slipping and the hem of her jacket fishtailing on a spring wind. Just as Mrs. Trice arrived at the slide, Debra floated down into her mother's arms, grabbing her around her waist. Mrs. Trice brushed down Debra's bangs and pulled her close in such an effusive display of affection that it made Debra appear not only privileged but spoiled.

On another afternoon, I had finished tacking crepe-paper tulips to the bulletin board under the words "Doolittle Welcomes Spring" when Debra burst into the principal's office. Without being told, she flopped down onto the bench and folded her arms, joining two other kids: the girl resting the vomit bag on her lap, her face still smeared with the paste she'd eaten; the bully leaning forward, elbows on his knees, bored as he once again awaited his fate. However, Debra, with her perfect hair ribbons that matched her perfect outfit, was, unlike the others, neither contemplative nor contrite.

"But I didn't do anything," she insisted to the women—the school secretary and other office workers—sitting at the desks beyond the counter. When they refused to respond, Debra slapped her palm against her forehead in exaggerated frustration. She let loose a gusty, gale-force sigh. I was gawking at her, which I was accustomed to doing but without her knowing. By the time I caught myself, it was too late.

"What are *you* looking at?" she snapped.

I tried to avert my eyes, but they, like the rest of me, froze.

Then, as if something occurred to her, she said, "I wasn't chewing gum, was I? The teacher said I was chewing. Did you hear her?"

"Miss Trice," one of the women interrupted, "you're supposed to be silent."

"But if I'm silent, I can't say anything . . ."

I couldn't believe Debra was talking to me. She hadn't said one word to me the month I'd been in her class. Still, I mumbled, "No," and it was barely audible even to me and far too late. My answer hung in the air, disembodied and useless. If I weren't invisible to her before, I certainly felt so now.

"Tell them." She jerked her head toward the office staff. My nerves had thickened my tongue and I couldn't speak. Debra turned to the women. "See? She knows I wasn't chewing gum. I was swallowing it."

Mrs. Trice hurried into the office, called to rein in her daughter. Unrepentant, Debra leaped from the bench, attempting to lobby on her own behalf: "Mom, it's not what you think . . ."

Mrs. Trice ushered Debra off to the side, and all I heard was "It's not fair. It's not fair." She started to cry and then stomped her foot. Mom would have blasted me or Kim for foot-stomping.

As Debra left the office, she glared. "Stop looking at me!"

Startled, I stared up at the ceiling. This first interaction with Debra made me think of the first time I held my sister. Both Debra and Kim were loud and surly with faces that easily contorted into a kaleidoscope of expressions. Neither cared one bit about disrupting the peace and neither seemed at all friendly. I'd been reeled in by both, mesmerized by their cunning and then, bam, flooded with regret.

Spring was in full bloom the next time I was on the nurse's sofa. My throat felt like I'd swallowed a handful of needles. The nurse concluded that I needed to go home and told me to lie down in her office. Mom had gotten a new job at a downtown bank, working in wire transfers. She sometimes asked Uncle Al or one of the older neighbor girls in the building to pick me up when she couldn't. That afternoon, to my surprise, I awoke to see my father in silhouette over me. He'd never picked me up from school.

"Can you walk?" he asked gently.

I nodded. He helped me stand and grabbed my canvas book bag. He placed his arm around my shoulder as we crossed 35th Street to the shopping center and made our way to Walgreens.

Before we sat down at the lunch counter, Dad measured me against his flank.

"Every time I see you, you're growing like a weed," he said. "Everybody used to say you were tall for your age and your granny told you to tell them, 'I'm tall because my daddy is tall!' Remember that?"

"I remember," I said, my voice hoarse. I would extend my arm out in front of me, rather than over my head, trying to illustrate all of the six feet two inches that was him. Now he was the mere height of the man sitting on the edge of a bed.

This was the first time since my parents' divorce that I was with him alone, and I was angry that Mom hadn't called Uncle Al to come get me.

"Two vanilla shakes," Dad said to the man behind the counter. The name "Larry" was embroidered on his orange shirt.

To me, Dad said, "The ice cream will calm your throat. Mine used to ache like the devil when I was a boy. You got that from me. Your grandpa would wrap a poultice around my neck that smelled so bad it made me gag. But it worked, along with a helping of turpentine. He added sugar to it and lit it on fire."

"What's turpentine?"

He looked over at the ice cream. "Let's just say you're getting the better deal."

A black-and-white television played the baseball game. Although Comiskey Park, home to the Chicago White Sox, sat a few blocks down the street, just beyond Bronzeville's western edge, Dad had always rooted for the North Siders, the Chicago Cubs, because the team had Black players: Ernie Banks, Billy Williams, José Cardenal, Adolfo Phillips, Ferguson Jenkins.

Dad performed a drumroll on the counter as the man poured the milkshakes and placed them in front of us. We sipped from our long straws.

"When you drink a milkshake, you can't go easy on it," he said. "Oh, no. You have to drink it like this." He made the loudest slurping sound I'd ever heard. It was such a deviation from the man I knew that I giggled in spite of myself. He pointed at my milkshake for me to follow his lead. I slurped, but it wasn't nearly as loud. We both placed the frothy glasses back down on the counter at the same time.

When people said I looked *just* like my father, they were referring to our faces. Nobody knew about our hands. Our extra digit. We were both born with a tiny, ill-formed appendage jutting out of our baby finger near the middle knuckle. His was on his right hand and mine was on my left. When I asked Mom about mine, she said, "I told that doctor, 'That thing has got to go before we leave this hospital.'" She said the doctor wrapped suture string around the base of the tiny finger to choke off the blood supply until it could be snipped off like a faulty branch in the family tree. What remained was a small nub, smooth and round, nearly imperceptible unless you knew to look for it. Dad had a similar bump and when he lived with us, I secretly felt for it on the rare occasion when he held my hand.

He was quiet again, looking up at the game, and I concentrated on my milkshake. He must have recognized someone behind me because he raised his hand quickly to wave. Out of nowhere, I ducked and nearly fell off the stool. It scared both of us. He looked at me, horrified.

"You afraid of me?" His deep voice sounded light, weightless.

"I'm not afraid," I lied.

"What them women say about me?" he said. "Your mama, aunt, and grandmother."

I shrugged, but I locked eyes with him.

"Sometimes you have to see both sides," he said.

I know what I saw.

"Sometimes you have to step back to see what up close tends to distort."

I know what I saw: your hands around my mother's neck.

He looked at the television and then down at his watch. "Damn," he said. "Get your satchel."

We left the drugstore and hurried back to the school, where he had parked his Impala. He drove me home, although we could have walked, and when Dad pulled in front of our building, I could see Uncle Al waiting for me in the lobby. Kim was sitting at the security guard's desk, doodling.

"Your throat will feel better soon," he said.

Dad didn't get out of the car to say hi to Kim or Uncle Al. He drove off and Uncle Al opened the main door. He patted me on my head with his newspaper and then took my hand and Kim's. We boarded the elevator to the eleventh floor, and he sat with us in our apartment until Mom came home.

That night, Dad called Mom demanding she stop trying to turn his daughter against him. Mom was quiet, at times glowering at the receiver. Then she lit into him: "You must not remember that she walked in on you attacking me. You forgot about that? You knew you wouldn't have stood a chance if I'd been awake, so you went after me in my sleep!"

He hung up on her or she hung up on him.

And then Dad disappeared for several weeks. This became his pattern. My father's way of dealing with being rankled or hurt or disappointed was to extract himself from our lives. If we had an emergency, we knew to call the taxi garage. Other than that, radio silence.

Mom had moved on anyway. Mr. Ron had recently begun invading our Sunday dinners, and I didn't like it or him one bit. This wasn't his fault. I wouldn't have liked any man who came to see my mother.

Mr. Ron was of average height, with a smudge of a mustache that Granny later said put her in the mind of Hitler or Ash Wednesday. The first time Granny joined us to meet him, he pulled out a side chair at the dining table for her. She looked down her nose at it and him and then sat, as usual, at the table's head.

The moment Mom stood over him, heaping three portions of collards, three pieces of fried chicken, two buttery rolls, and an obscene amount of macaroni and cheese onto a plate that was nearly overflowing, the wishbone-shaped vein in the center of Mr. Ron's forehead appeared as though summoned by the food.

When he asked Mom why my plate looked so "puny," Granny sneered at him. "Not everyone eats like food's going out of style."

I didn't know why Granny didn't like Mr. Ron. Maybe she felt guilty that she'd championed my father and because that worked out so poorly, she wanted to be extra suspect of any other man who courted her daughter.

"Can you eat all of that?" I asked Mr. Ron, raking my fork across my plate.

"Dawn!" Mom said. "Don't be rude."

Granny laughed loudly, goading me. But it was Kim who took the cue.

"He can eat all of that?" She scrunched her face as I had.

"Young ladies, I don't turn down nothing but my collar," he said, stuffing his napkin into his dress shirt. We quickly learned that he'd still manage to dribble food down his tie. And no matter how Mom warned that the chicken was hot, he'd take a bite anyway, sloshing it around in his mouth to cool it. After dinner, we waited until the massive amount of food rendered Mr. Ron unconscious and he passed out on our sofa.

At that point, the driving lesson began. That summer, Mom had begun teaching herself how to drive using Mr. Ron's Cutlass, a two-door steel beast that swallowed us whole. Granny had never seen her daughter behind the steering wheel, but that evening she quietly folded herself into the back seat in a way that made her seem both haughty and limber.

Kim and I jumped into the front seat, and I sat next to the window. We didn't fuss about who sat where. We knew not to rile Mom. Granny, however, didn't know.

"What type of fool hands over his new car to a novice driver?" she muttered.

Mom didn't respond. She was too busy fumbling with the keys, and when she finally turned the ignition, the dashboard came alive. The Cutlass was this unwieldy machine that could bestow wings and grant her a whole new level of freedom, providing she could tame it. Mom shifted the car into reverse. The Cutlass bucked and gently scraped the car next to it. Mom paid that no never mind and continued to jerk backward out of the parking space. Shifting from reverse to drive, the car lurched forward a few paces until Mom hit her stride, moving slowly through Lawless and then outside the fence. With her hands fixed at "ten and two," she piloted the Cutlass down Rhodes Avenue, turned right at 37th Street, and drove to the light at King Drive, a busy four-lane boulevard with skilled drivers. Mom had only been on King Drive a handful of times all summer. As she always did, Kim leaned on me, straining to look out the window. I pushed her back against the seat as Mom watched the cars zoom through the busy intersection. The light changed from red to green and then red to green again. But she didn't move. Drivers behind her began to honk and yell.

"Baby," Granny said. "I think green means go."

"I know, Mom," she said, studying the traffic.

She didn't care how many drivers wagged their finger and zipped around us. Her strategy was to wait for one of the blue bulbous jitney taxicabs. From my father, she knew that cabbies were expert drivers and so her strategy was to fall in line behind one and follow like a fish in a current. But jitneys were unique in that, like buses, they picked up multiple fares simultaneously rather than one at a time and ran up and down the boulevard. Soon a jitney passed heading northbound and Mom hit the gas. The Cutlass pounced into traffic as she made a right turn. She immediately pulled up behind the cab, riding its bumper. The cab stopped for fares at 35th and 33rd Streets, and so did she, nearly slamming into it.

At 31st Street, the frustrated cabbie hopped out. "What the fuck, lady?"

"Language," Mom said calmly. "You see my daughters in here?" She stared straight ahead and kept her hands on the steering wheel.

"Why you riding my ass?" he said.

"It's a free country," Mom said.

"We can ride anybody's ass we want," Granny assured him.

The driver returned to his cab and Mom followed it to 29th Street, where she caught the slipstream of another jitney and made a left at the light, heading back south.

Mom turned right at 35th Street and Granny pointed out the Meyers Ace Hardware on the corner at Calumet Avenue. Back in the day, the building housed a nightclub that some considered Chicago's equivalent to Harlem's Cotton Club. It was one of the few racially integrated, or "black-and-tan," nightclubs in the city, and had featured the likes of Louis Armstrong, Cab Calloway, Benny Goodman.

Granny showed us the home of Muddy Waters, the father of the Chicago blues, and told us he sang "I'm Your Hoochie Coochie Man." She pointed out the church home of Thomas Dorsey, the father of gospel music, who wrote and sang "Precious Lord, Take My Hand."

This street was the one boxer Joe Louis strolled down eating butter pecan ice cream. That corner was where Gwendolyn Brooks stood, thinking her writerly thoughts, head in the clouds.

That was Bronzeville, a study in stark contrasts. And that was true way back to the Civil War, when land there had been a training ground for Union Army soldiers but wound up being a prisoner of war camp for Confederate troops instead.

And it was true of her daughters, not to mention her grand-daughters.

"Your aunt Doris never had an urge to go far away," Granny said. "She was happy to keep her feet solidly planted on the ground. She gave me fewer gray hairs."

Kim had climbed into the back seat and now she was asleep with her head in Granny's lap. Mom was so focused on driving that it might have seemed as though Granny was talking to me, but it was also to nobody in particular.

"But this woman in front of me, teaching herself—herself, mind you—how to drive. She used to stare at the maps in the back of her textbooks, tracing the continents in her mind's eye. She was always on the move even when she was sitting still."

Granny patted the headrest in front of her in lieu of touching her daughter. Having returned to Lawless, Mom pulled into the park-ing space flawlessly. We got out of the car and Mom picked up my sister's limp body. Granny had always been stingy with compliments and as we walked under the streetlights to the building, Mom's face was lit with pride. She'd been the one whom Granny had told, "Slow down." "Don't climb that." "Be still."

Now Granny's admiration fueled her daughter's desire to fly.

chapter five

Pomegranate Seeds and Little Red Pills

. . .

My third-grade teacher, Mrs. Rebecca "Becky" Love, resided with her husband in a lovely brown-brick house on the same block as the graystone once owned by Ida B. Wells. During the school year, Mrs. Love walked down 35th Street to her classroom at Doolittle Elementary. She stepped briskly, head held high, back impeccably straight with an unrelenting broad and toothy smile, except for when she whistled. Mom told Kim and me that whistling was unladylike, but Mrs. Love was most certainly a lady. She was fifty-six but you wouldn't have guessed it to look at her. She wore flouncy above-the-knee A-line skirts, showing shapely legs, and Capri pants with sleeveless tops, showing taut arms. Long shiny black hair, parted down the middle, fell in waves past her shoulders and bucked the prevailing style and social commentary of the Afros her colleagues—teachers in their twenties and thirties—were wearing.

Shortly before the new school year started, Mrs. Love had written letters to our parents telling them that her students were allowed to eat fresh fruit, vegetables, and nuts in her class. This felt subversive in an era when the only time students dared open their mouth in school was to answer questions and never out of turn. Children who disdained fruits and vegetables brought them just for the novelty of it. Mrs. Love also wrote that she had recently achieved the title master teacher of hatha yoga and we would be doing yoga poses in class "to give our brains a break."

Although our teacher definitely had an unorthodox side, I was happy to see her classroom was in many ways traditional as she welcomed us that first day. She had organized our desks in six rectangular pods of four or six desks. She'd also written our names in cursive on sturdy lined paper that she taped to the upper right-hand corners of the desks across from our readers, *Time to Wonder*.

"Okay, my darlings, find your proper places and sit down."

The majority of the third-graders now came from the Ida B. Wells housing project. Most of Lawless's parents sent their children to Catholic, private, or parochial schools. Kim and I attended Doolittle because Mom believed the education was first-rate.

"We will not be afraid of our own," she said firmly. She had said the same thing about swimming in Madden Park.

Mrs. Love arranged her students alphabetically, rather than according to height. I pulled the chair from under my desk around the same time Debra, across from me, pulled out hers. Trice across from Turner. That one change from the grade before placed me in front of the most fascinating, and frightening, girl in the school. What would I say if she told me to stop looking at her again?

Debra sat with her hands folded atop her desk.

Within a few minutes, everyone except one boy had zeroed in on his or her proper place and sat down. Sam was nine and had been held back. We deduced why when he was the last child standing and couldn't find his desk.

Debra sighed ostentatiously. "There's only one desk left."

"Shhh," Mrs. Love said. "Let him figure it out."

Debra shrugged. "What's to figure out?" She placed her elbow on the desk and cupped the side of her head with her palm.

Sam had mastered the art of the vacuous stare. He was small for his age, which he could have used to his advantage, but he didn't seem to know how *not* to bring attention to himself. Finally, he walked over to the lone empty desk. The alphabet, each upper- and lowercased letter written in cursive, spanned the chalkboard. As he sat, he regarded the letters as though they were in collusion with the ones on his nameplate, mocking him. Without saying a word, he stood and dragged the wooden desk, metal feet screeching, to the window and faced the courtyard solarium.

"You can't—" Debra said to Sam. Her eyes narrowed. She raised her hand and turned to Mrs. Love. "But he won't be able to see the blackboard."

"That's okay for now, Debra."

Mrs. Love told us that we could snack while she called the roll. I pulled my apple from my brown paper sack. Around the room, mostly everyone had the standard fare of apples, bananas, and oranges. But Debra was different. From her pink lunch box, she unveiled the strangest, most exotic piece of crimson fruit I'd ever seen. She saw me staring at it before I quickly looked away.

"It's a pomegranate," she said, plucking through white flesh. "Want some seeds?" She extended an open palm with fingertips tinted bright red. "Your braids are pretty."

I glowed from the compliment. Loretta Tyson, who sat next to me, said, "Ooh, gimme some, too!" She grabbed with fingers as if champing at the bit.

For whatever reason, Debra didn't like Loretta. When she hugged Mrs. Trice on the playground, Debra always abruptly stopped what she was doing and ran over to pull Loretta away. In addition to stealing hugs, Loretta had a reputation for brazenly leaning over her neighbor's shoulder, pilfering answers. Sitting next to her, you knew to crook your arm around your paper to block her view.

In one quick motion, Debra squeezed her hand tightly and jerked it back. Juice trickled onto my desk and all but one seed flew behind her. Loretta and I lifted up to see where the bulk of the seeds had landed.

"They're not for you," Debra growled.

Debra reached out to me again with the remaining seed. It reminded me of the little red pill that Mom placed in my palm every night before bed. Tasting the tart seed made me giggle loudly. Mrs. Love looked up, clearly surprised. My reputation preceded me as the one student with whom she'd have no trouble. Debra's reputation preceded her, too. She was unaccustomed to stifling anything—not her tears or her laughter.

Behind us, the voices answering the roll call drew closer.

"Debra Trice," Mrs. Love said in a gently chiding tone.

"Here," Debra said, still giggly.

"Dawn Turner."

I could still taste the tart. This indeed was a new grade with a teacher who flouted the rules and convention. It was an opportunity to start over. First impressions were as obstinate as knots, but if the knot never got started, I could be whoever I wanted to be.

"Dawn Turner?"

My stomach churned. "Present." I looked out the window.

"Present?" said an indignant voice from across the room.

"It's an excellent response," Mrs. Love said. "We'll be learning about synonyms."

When I looked over at Mrs. Love, she smiled her approval.

"Loretta Tyson?"

"Present," Loretta sang, once again stealing.

As Mrs. Love completed the roll, I could feel Debra's eyes on me after everyone else had moved on. But I didn't dare look at her to be sure.

At the end of the first week of school, I was walking out of the building when Debra ran over to me and grabbed my wrist. She dragged me to her mother.

"Mom, this is the girl?" Debra asked.

"Yes," Mrs. Trice said. "All summer, I tried to get you to play with her." She turned to me. "Hi, Dawn."

Debra squealed. "You're the girl! Whenever I told Mom I was bored, she told me to go play with the nice girl downstairs. I didn't know *you* were the nice girl."

Debra could see that I didn't quite understand. She placed her hands on my shoulders as if she were about to shake me awake.

"We live in the same building." Debra took a deep breath because the words were so big they needed a push. "You live under me."

Laughing, Mrs. Trice turned to me: "What Debra means is that we're in apartment 1205 and you and your family live below us in 1105. We're your neighbors."

"Oh!" I said, drawing the word out.

Debra's face flushed with equal parts wonderment and disbelief. I couldn't have stopped smiling if I tried. Mrs. Trice normally drove her sporty orange Chevy Chevelle to school. But that day she hadn't driven, so we all walked home. Debra told me that the girl walking with her mother was her older sister.

"Her name is Darlene." Debra rolled her eyes. "But don't tell her I told you. She says I tell everything."

We discovered that not only was Debra's apartment above mine but her bedroom was directly above mine. Like me, she had one sibling. Like Kim and me, they shared a bedroom. With each revelation, Debra said, "For real?" or "This is a miracle" or "I can't believe it, can you?"

Debra grabbed my hand. "Dawn, our dolls can be best friends like us!"

With the words "best friends," we skipped the rest of the way to our tower.

After dinner that night, we heard a knock at the door. I hung behind so Mom wouldn't think I was trailing her as she'd revealed to the doctor.

"Hi, I'm Dawn's friend. I'm here to visit her—um, please."

I ran up behind Mom, leaning on her, trying to see.

"Does Dawn's friend have a name?" Mom asked, smiling.

"I'm Debra," she said. She rarely seemed shy, but she did in front of my mother.

Mom didn't like "do drop-ins," but she must have felt my heartbeat. She opened the door wider and Debra saw me smiling.

"Hi, Dawn!" She walked right in, peering briefly into the kitchen. She quickly sized up our living room: our sofa and love seat; the television and stereo consoles; the dining table. I'd never given much thought to any of it until Debra.

"My father's chair is there," Debra said, pointing to an area by the north wall. "He sits in it naked in his underwear. But you'll see when we go upstairs."

She hurried to my bedroom and I followed her as if everything was new to me, too. Kim lay on the floor between our beds. Seeing Debra, Kim jumped up.

"Aren't you cute?"

Nodding, Kim stood next to me and pulled my arm away from my side, slipping herself underneath.

Debra dug into her pocket for candy. Kim opened her hand as she looked at me for approval, then took it.

My best friend saw one of my Pippi Longstocking books open on the floor.

"Are you a Thing-Finder, too?" She held up the book and cocked her head.

"Uh-huh," I said. Truthfully, it hadn't occurred to me that I could be what I read.

"We can find things together, too," she said. "Nobody ever wants to find anything with me. And we can walk along the curb, up and down, like Pippi."

Our apartments were next to the front stairwell, and after Debra toured mine, we ran up the stairs to hers. Entering apartment 1205 was like entering my own because they had the same floor plan. We were too young to know the term "déjà vu," but we couldn't escape the feeling. She led me past the kitchen, where her mother was on the phone. Debra's father was still at work, but he was present in the way my father had been when he was gone.

"This is our living room," Debra said. She flopped down on a brown leather sofa as if she were bored. She left the sofa and slid onto a brown leather recliner. "And this is Dad's chair. He doesn't like anybody sitting in it."

"So why are you sitting in it?"

"He only yells when he's here." She shrugged, matter-of-factly.

She pointed to a foldout table next to the recliner. "This is where he has a beer." Pointing to two canary-yellow love seats, she said, "Those are our pullout sleepers for guests. You're not a guest, so you can sleep with me when you spend the night."

I'd never slept over at a friend's house. I inhaled deeply, trying to tamp down my excitement as I looked at their stereo console, similar to ours with stacks of albums, including John Coltrane's *A Love Supreme*. The Trices had a bookcase of encyclopedias with a CB radio on one of the shelves. In a corner, I ran my hand along the tops of a set of bongos.

"Whose are these?"

"They're Dad's. He and his friends play music on the lakefront when he's not working. He drives a big truck, delivering food to grocery stores."

We left the living room and walked through a short hallway. In my apartment Kim and I sat in this space to eavesdrop on Mom, Granny, and Auntie. As I stood in the doorway of Debra's bedroom, my eyes grew wide. With its cotton-candy-pink walls and white furniture trimmed in pink, it seemed twice the size of Kim's and mine. Debra and her sister had bunk beds, which opened up more floor space, and legions of Debra's toy dinosaurs lay sprawled across a throw rug. Her sister's rock collection sat neatly on the dresser next to a Talking View-Master and its reels. In a corner were stacks of board games: backgammon, Sorry, Monopoly, and Operation.

A cage with two rodents rattled on the windowsill.

"These are my gerbils," Debra said. "That's Sherry. And that's Tonya."

My bedroom was practical. Hers was magical. I felt so much awe, I couldn't muster envy. Debra's bed was on the bottom bunk, but she climbed to the top to show me how she could touch the ceiling and then jump down. She picked up a dinosaur.

"My favorite is the triceratops. You know why?"

I shook my head and my braids slipped behind my shoulders.

"We have the same name," she said, pulling my braids forward.

She ripped a piece of paper from a spiral notebook, picked up a pencil, and leaned on the windowsill. Writing *TRICERATOPS* in capital letters, she underlined *TRICE*, adding a heart over the "I." She tapped her foot against the crank that opened the bottom part of the window. Tap-tap-tap. Tap-tap-tap. This was it! She was the source of the tapping! I realized, too, that meant she was the girl I'd heard crying. I looked around the room and wondered, *What in the world does she have to cry about?*

"Don't move," I said.

I ran through her apartment, down the stairwell, and to my

bedroom. I climbed up on my windowsill and tapped on the ceiling. "Can you hear me?!"

I heard her giggle. "I can hear you!"

I ran back upstairs and I'd been in Debra's bedroom for a few minutes when her father came home. Unaware that I was visiting, he undressed down to his boxers and passed Debra's bedroom en route to his lounge chair.

"Hey, Daddy," she said. "Say 'hi' to Dawn, my new best friend."

He covered himself with his *Chicago Sun-Times* and hurried back into his bedroom. A moment later, Mrs. Trice peeped into Debra's room to tell me I had to go.

"But why?" Debra grimaced. "Dawn was here first."

"Debra!" her mother demanded.

"See you later, friend," she said, head down. *Later* was only the next day, but I loved the way she made it seem an eternity.

We became inseparable. Most afternoons, we raced through our homework and, because Mom made me bring Kim along, the three of us met in the lobby and boarded the elevator to the twenty-fourth floor. If we were lucky enough to be on the elevator alone, we watched the numbers ignite as the elevator rocketed upward. Right about the twentieth floor, we crouched down and as the elevator slowed and our ears popped, we leaped into the air. We loved that feeling of flight, of being suspended even for a few seconds before the elevator stopped and our heads nearly brushed the overhead lighting. When the door swished open on the twenty-fourth floor, we hurried to the front stairwell, climbed a flight, and I sat cross-legged by the metal door that led out to the roof. Kim sat next to me. Debra always tried the doorknob even though we knew it would never be unlocked.

The afternoon Debra and I brought our diaries with us, she pulled three candy cigarettes from her shirt pocket. She handed Kim and me one each, and Debra and I wrote as my sister leaned on the metal banister, chomping on the chalky treat. Debra's diary was leafy green with a gold lock. Mine had a padded navy-blue vinyl cover. When I held it, it had the give of skin. It was perfectly fine until I saw Debra's. Mom had gotten it for me from Woolworths and given it to me as a Christmas present. She specifically chose the one with no lock because she said there were no secrets in her house. Both Debra's and my diary had a right-hand page with the inscription "This diary belongs to:" where we inked in our names.

"What's your middle name?" I asked, taking a pretend drag on my candy.

"Rachelle," Debra said, pretend exhaling.

"No way!" I said. "Mine is Michele with one L."

"They rhyme," we said in a dramatic flourish befitting yet another discovery.

Debra tore a page from the back of her diary and gave it and a pen to Kim. My sister took both as though gobbling a piece of candy and wrote her name and squiggly lines. She was a kindergartener and already a good reader.

The twenty-fourth-floor landing outside the roof was our treehouse. But the stairwell was our portal. We exited on random floors, walking through the halls from the front stairwell to the back one. We knew the rhythms of both. Twice daily, the security guards made their rounds, checking each floor by taking the stairs. We never wanted to run into them, so we listened for the rattling keys or the walkie-talkie static that usually announced their presence. In the midmorning and evening, the janitors vacuumed the halls and swept the stairs. They also checked the incinerator rooms for garbage too big for the chute. In the spirit of Pippi, Debra and I became the guardians of broken things, roaming our building in search of the perfect castoffs. Our metal tin was about the size of a cigar box and we scavenged for items that fit but did not fill: the ribbon of a broken Smith Corona; a handful of metal jacks minus the bright red ball; nuts and bolts.

Some days we walked to school together and instead of leaving our apartments and orchestrating a meeting on the elevator, we met in the stairwell and ran down the steps to the lobby. We anticipated our neighbors: the Nigerian father who laughed loudly, accompanying his children to the elevator; the community college professor who sang in a mournful falsetto while locking his door; the old man, a stroke victim, whose wheelchair, the sound of metal scraping metal, made our teeth clench.

When Debra and I arrived at school, we joined our peers lined up outside the school entrance. She walked to the front of the line with the shorter girls and I took my place in the back. Just the year before, few people would have put us together. But a couple of months into the school year, no one—not even Debra or me—could imagine us apart. Debra began volunteering with me in the principal's office. When she tired of pasting or cutting or stapling, she stretched out across the wooden bench where she used to await her fate. At lunch, we sat together at my table in the cafeteria. She had sneaked over so many times to eat with me that the Cafeteria Lady, who was also the Crossing Guard Lady and the Candy Lady, reassigned Debra's seat. (Debra had taken more pleasure in sneaking over.) At recess, we sat together on the steps of the Willis wagons, devouring *The Swiss Family Robinson* from the library. When the end-of-recess bell rang, she now only rarely answered the call of the slide. I felt so lucky to have a friend who was loyal and steadfast. That she was fearless, too, came in handy on a crisp autumn afternoon when Mrs. Love took the class outside for a lesson.

Dressed in winter coats, her third-grade students lined up, single file, girls in front of boys. I was the last girl in the line, next to Sam, the shortest boy. We walked down the stairs and just before we left the building, Sam stuck out his combat boot and tripped me. To his credit, he had warned me on the first day that he would do it. He'd leaned forward and whispered in a venom-filled drawl, "I'mma trip you." It hadn't happened so I'd become complacent, maybe cocky. For the first time in my life, I'd forgotten to be afraid. But now the day had come, and yelps of laughter hovered over me as I lay in my brown cloth coat with the fur-lined hood, arms and legs splayed, kissing asphalt. Following the ruckus, Debra barreled to the back of the line to find me. She lifted me to my feet and brushed off my coat, swiping at the dust so intently that it hurt more than the fall. No one reveled in the moment more than Sam. I turned to him.

"You . . . you tripped me," I stammered.

Without even a thought, Debra pushed him to the ground with both hands. Sam jumped up and stalked toward her, standing right in her face. It didn't seem right for Debra, a couple of inches shorter than me, to defend me alone, so I stood next to her, shaking. I'd never fought anyone before. I wished then that Uncle Al had shown me how to bob and weave like he'd taught Mom.

Debra balled up her fists and I balled up mine. I felt light-headed. The students gathered around us urging, "Fight! Fight! Fight!"

A group of clouds blanketed the schoolyard in a temporary shadow. Sam rubbed his eyes and squinted at the sky, as if this entire episode tried his patience. Just as I was sure he was going to clock one of us, Mrs. Love appeared.

"Go to your place in line," she told Debra. But she didn't move. "I said, go."

Mrs. Love twisted Sam's ear. "You come with me."

They started walking in the direction of the door closest to the principal's office while he screamed, "What did I do?! What did I do?!"

Debra escaped reprimand for avenging my honor. She was given something that might not have been offered the year before: the benefit of the doubt.

Later, in the stairwell, Debra told me that I'd looked like a flattened mouse. "I didn't laugh then." She cupped my hands in hers. "But do you mind if I laugh now?"

Ordinarily, Debra didn't ask for permission to laugh. It poured out of her, finding its own decibel: loud. I shook my head and we both cracked up as our pure joy echoed throughout the stairwell.

That night, when Mom made Kim and me say our prayers, I cast my eyes heavenward. It may have appeared that I was gazing up to God. But it was the ceiling that commanded my attention. Mom had worried that her divorce, and the reason for it, made me grow up too fast. She loved Debra because she rescued my childhood. I loved her because she rescued me. I found great comfort in having Debra in the bedroom above mine.

Even more than the tranquilizers, my new friend helped me to sleep again.

chapter six

"Death Riding on a Soda Cracker"

* * *

Kim and I wanted to watch the Saturday morning cartoons, but Mom, Granny, and Aunt Doris were holding court in the living room at the dining table. Mom sat pigeon-toed, which meant the women would be there for a while, monopolizing the space that held the apartment's only television. Mom reached for her dream book on the far side of the table. Auntie rooted around in her purse for hers and placed it, along with a small spiral notebook and a roll of Necco Wafers, next to her coffee cup. Granny's emerged dog-eared from her smock pocket. Once she removed the rubber band, pages slipped from the book's spine like leaves floating from a tree.

The books—*Dr. Pryor's Lucky Number Master Dream Book*, *The Witches' Dream Book*, and *The Three Wise Men Dream Book*—were based on numerology and assigned three- and four-digit numbers to themes and scenarios in dreams. If Mom dreamed of fish, she flicked through her book to find the number, 757, corresponding to the word "fish." The women also used the numbers to speak in code when they didn't want us to decipher their conversations. Referring to my father, Mom often said, "That man can kiss my *4712*." We teased out that one fairly easily. Assigned numbers varied depending on the dream book. That's why the women spent some Saturday mornings referencing their books and logging the best numbers for playing policy. Policy, the not-so-legal precursor to the lottery, was creed to the women. Bronzeville was called the capital of policy, but it was also played in Harlem, Detroit, and Cleveland.

Of all the women's dreams, it was the ones frequented by the dead that seemed the most instrumental in helping them unlock winning numbers. No matter the bad luck that befell them or the numbers that were close but not quite right, they were devout believers that their fortunes were always on the cusp of change.

"The other night, I dreamed about Robert, bless his soul," Granny said. Robert was her deceased older brother. "He was waiting on a train platform with his suitcase in his hand and dressed to the nines."

"Did he wave?" Aunt Doris methodically placed a pink Necco on her tongue the way Prophet did with communion wafers.

"No, not that I recall," Granny said. "But he looked clean-shaven and content."

"You didn't get on the train with him, did you?" Aunt Doris lifted an eyebrow.

"Of course not. You know I know better."

Relief registered on Aunt Doris's face. To dream of a dead loved one and then follow him on any form of transportation was a horrible omen. It meant impending death for you or someone close to you.

"Come to think of it," Aunt Doris said, "I dreamed about Mother Sadie last night."

Mother Sadie belonged to our church, the First House of Prayer. A member of the Mothers Board, she sat near the pulpit with a group of elderly women who accessorized themselves with the dead: old fox-pelt collars with tiny fox heads, mink stoles and rabbit-fur hats. Some of the women smelled of mothballs and liniments.

"She just left us." Granny nodded.

Mom patted her chest. "I believe she was diagnosed with a hole in her heart."

"So, do I look up 'heart' or 'hole'?" Stumped, Aunt Doris fiddled with a lock of hair. If this were a poker game, it would have been her tell.

"Don't know about a hole," Granny snipped. "But that heart of hers had a spot of hell on it."

"Mama, be nice," Aunt Doris said.

"The woman was foul," Granny said. "Mean as they come."

"I didn't realize she was sick," Aunt Doris said.

"You remember how frail she'd gotten," Mom offered.

"Looked like death riding on a soda cracker," Granny said. "She'd been on the sick-and-shut-in list for some time. In and out of the hospital."

I knew all about the sick-and-shut-in list. On occasion, I had stood behind the podium at church with damp palms, reading the names of church members who were ill and needed prayers. Behind me, Granny, Mom, and Aunt Doris sat together in the choir stand, teetering on the edge of their seats as if to will me to read every name correctly. What I knew about death had, in part, to do with the women and their dreams; but it also had to do with the sick-and-shut-in list.

Church was the cornerstone of my family's life. Preparations for Sunday service started on Saturday nights, with Granny filling her kitchen sink with soapy water and making Kim and me wash and then iron her handkerchiefs. In return, she hot-combed and curled our hair as we sat in her kitchen chair dragged close to the stove. It didn't matter that our church, which seated about four hundred people, had one small window in the back and became an inferno, returning our pressed hair to Afros almost instantaneously. We didn't just attend Sunday service. We were there for Sunday school and, later, Sunday dinner in a church-owned building across the street. On Tuesday evenings, we were there for choir rehearsal or church disguised as choir rehearsal because rare was the day when the choir learned a new song. They mostly slipped into old standards that were glorious and guaranteed to stir the spirit. On some Friday nights, we were there for a revival or to host a visiting church. At the end of every service, Prophet gave scriptures for home reading. This was another tool, along with the dream book, that Mom, Granny, and Aunt Doris used to guide their lottery number picks. If Prophet said, "Read Mark 9:23," the women carefully read it and then played 9-2-3 in the lottery. When they won, they tithed accordingly.

Beyond church services, we were there for funerals. I hated it when I settled in for a regular Sunday service and both of the doors in the back of the building creaked open and a couple of under-takers wheeled a casket into the sanctuary, followed by a parade of women holding flower baskets and men in white gloves guiding family members to their seats. Even with the body present, the service almost seemed like a regular Sunday morning, with singing and shouting until the time arrived for everybody to walk down the center aisle for the viewing.

That center aisle, with its cranberry-colored rug, delivered us to most of life's key moments. From the walk to the baptismal pool under the altar, to one's betrothed, to view one's final rest. We stood and rows of seats emptied in the same way they did when it was time to tithe or take communion. I grabbed my sister's hand. When we approached the casket, I told her not to look, but she never listened. She waved up at Mom, Granny, and Aunt Doris in the choir stand or at the body itself. I could never bring myself to look at the corpse, instead focusing up at the mural behind the choir stand. Shellacked and shiny, the mural showed a white Jesus with light brown hair and blond highlights, posed on a promontory, shepherding a group of lambs. The alpha and omega symbols, the beginning and the end, were painted around his wooden staff. Most often, it was the women on the Mothers Board who died. On the occasion when I did glimpse a corpse, the woman, in repose, looked just as she had in life: The same blue cottony hair and white dress. The thick pasty makeup that turned their frozen expressions a shale color. Their gnarled, deeply veined hands that lay clasped just below their stilled heart.

When all was said and done, the choir stood and sang:

It's a highway to heaven. None can walk up there, but the pure in heart . . . I am walking up the King's highway.

The clapping and the swaying made the moment a homegoing celebration. Prophet closed the casket and lay a spray of flowers atop its pewter bosom like a pinned broach. He walked ahead of the casket with the family as it was wheeled back down the center aisle.

The people who died had been on the sick-and-shut-in list and many had spent time in the hospital. When Dr. Nicolas told Mom and me that I needed my tonsils removed, I immediately imagined someone reading my name on that list one Sunday and my small body in a coffin the next. Sitting on his examination table, I cried so hard, no matter how Mom tried to console me. Although my throat didn't hurt as much in the third grade as it did the year before, now, from time to time, bacteria clusters like little white rocks formed on my tonsils. I became convinced that I would not make it through the surgery. I expected that when I died, Prophet would tell the congregation that I had gone home to be with the Lord. He would say that we preach our funeral by the way we live our lives. I kept imagining my little body in a casket, surrounded by upholstery as fine as what was on the back seat of Mr. Ron's Cutlass. Or, what I remembered of the car, since Mr. Ron was no longer Mom's boyfriend.

I hoped Kim and Debra would miss me.

My surgery was scheduled for a Monday. The Friday before it, Mrs. Love threw a going-away party for me. She wrote "tonsillectomy" on the blackboard and told the class that I had to go to the hospital and that I would return in about a week, in time for Valentine's Day. Most of the students looked bored until she told them the only thing I'd be able to eat for a week was ice cream. With this revelation, nearly every child wanted to locate his or her tonsils and figure out how theirs could be removed, too.

My teacher brought in a cake, punch, and a fruit salad. I was standing alone when she walked over and pitted an apricot.

"Have you ever tried one of these?" she asked, handing half to me.

I placed the fruit in my mouth but stared at the floor tile.

"Darling." She wrapped her arm around me. "You'll be just fine. You believe me, don't you?"

I had no reason not to believe her. We were more than halfway through the school year and she had been no less than a miracle worker, considering how many of us had changed. At least once a week, Debra sat at her desk with her hands folded, saying, "Look at me, Mrs. Love. I'm exercising self-control." Mrs. Love told Mom she was pleased with how sociable I'd become. Still, that didn't stop her from making me write "I will not talk in class" two hundred times when she caught me passing a note to Debra, who worked diligently to complete several of my pages. I was a novice with such punishments. But she was an expert and knew that Mrs. Love wouldn't examine the work closely and notice Debra's slanted handwriting, with its fanciful loops, which was so unlike mine.

"You'll be back here in no time." Mrs. Love deployed her cheeriest voice.

I wanted to believe her. And I wanted to believe Debra, too, when we met in the stairwell the night before my surgery. I still had on my church clothes.

"Don't forget to bring back your tonsils," Debra urged. "I have a big ol' jar ready for them."

We had agreed that I would ask Dr. Nicolas to return my tonsils to me so that we could include them among the things in our tin. It seemed a reasonable request since they were mine. I looked up at the fire hose on the landing above us.

"Take care of them," I said to my friend. "I'm going home to be with the Lord."

Debra looked confused. "Dawn, kids don't die. Only old people do."

The next morning, Kim was beside herself.

"I'm going, too, Mommy," Kim said when Mom placed her small lime-green Samsonite on my bed and started packing it. Mom explained to my sister that she couldn't go. But Kim adamantly added her things—her doll, her pillow, a few pairs of panties. It didn't matter how many times Mom told her that the procedure was minor as she placed Kim's belongings back on her side of the room. Kim returned them to the overnight case as soon as Mom turned her back.

I began to cry. And then Kim began to cry, as if my tears had drawn hers. When Granny arrived to watch Kim, my sister looked suspicious, but she continued on to the door with Mom and me. Then Granny tried to grab Kim's hand to stop her and Kim pulled away, hiding one arm behind her back and then the other. Granny must have picked her up as Mom closed the door. I heard Kim screaming clear to the elevator. When scooped up, she sometimes wriggled free by making her body go limp, which she must have done, because the next thing I heard was her small body thrashing against the door as though she were determined to break it down. Granny didn't suffer insolent children. The year before, when Mom told her that I was refusing to eat, my grandmother lifted her chin and said, "Go ahead, waste away, then. Who cares?" But this moment caught even Granny up short.

"Please, Granny!" The word "please" never had been packed with so many syllables nor so much dread. "Please let me go with Don."

There was something deeply unsettling about a five-year-old so desperate to get to her sister that she would try to bore a hole in a door with her whole being. It occurred to me, and obviously Kim, too, that we had never been apart for more than a few hours, let alone three nights.

"Wait for me, Mommy!" she wailed. "Please! Wait for me!"

"It's okay, child," Granny said as the elevator door opened. "Your sister is okay."

When I wouldn't step onto the elevator, Mom pushed me forward. She later told me that Kim cried herself to sleep each of the three nights I was gone. Mom let Kim sleep with her, something she would never have done had Kim not caused such a fuss. But there was nothing ordinary about that time. In the middle of my first night in the hospital, I opened my eyes to see my father seated in a chair next to my bed. I had no idea what time he arrived or what time it was when I awoke. I just knew that the rest of the hospital floor was quiet, the lights dimmed to a pale yellow. The floor hadn't been so quiet before I fell asleep. Initially, I thought he was a dream. But he sat in a cone of light created by a small lamp, reading the newspaper. I could see his silver wedding band. His new wife went to our church and, over the years, Mom had seen her in the audience but didn't know her. Betty was a couple of years older than Dad, who was about ten years older than Mom. The Sunday she introduced herself to Mom—and Granny and Auntie because they stood beside her—she told them about her split-level in the suburbs with the extra bedroom. Dad had moved in and she invited Kim and me to spend some weekends with them.

"That would be nice," Mom said, fake-smiling. As Betty walked away, Mom curled her lip. "Better her than me."

My father turned the page of his paper, unaware that I was awake.

I took a deep breath, taking in his familiar scent: gasoline and motor oil and Old Spice. It was the one time I remember feeling comforted by his presence. I dozed off again. By morning he was gone.

When I returned home from the hospital, Kim met me at the front door. "You're not dead!" she said with a happiness so genuine that she burst into tears. She slept with me for the first night, nestling into my back, sharing my slobbery, bloody pillow.

The next day, each time Debra came down to see me, Mom told her I was napping. She returned so many times that Mom finally opened the door and followed my friend to my bedroom. Debra slowly entered and looked quickly at Mom before removing Mrs. Trice's compact from the sleeve of her sweater and placing the mirror under my nose.

"What in the world? Baby, she's alive."

After about a week, I resumed class but I was a bit sluggish. During an assignment, I held my pencil motionless while staring at the page. Mrs. Love walked over to me and placed her hand atop mine. Her hand was heavy and the pencil's point snapped when it touched the paper and soon the page filled with words much darker than I would have composed. She flitted from student to student as usual, but something was off. She didn't have her usual verve and, in the days and weeks that followed, she was absent a lot from school. We had one substitute teacher after another. When she did come to school, sometimes she told us to place our heads on our desks to take a quick break. I'd look up and she'd be sitting at her desk with both hands over her eyes, crying. When the breaks were over, she would dab her face dry and the day's lesson would continue.

It was Debra who learned what was wrong, from her mother. We were looking out of my bedroom window when she told me.

"Mrs. Love's daughter is very sick," Debra explained. "Something's wrong with her kidneys."

Debra couldn't tell me what kidneys were, so we ran upstairs to her apartment to consult the Trices' encyclopedias. Mrs. Trice pulled a volume from the shelf and showed us where the kidneys were in the body and explained their function. I thought about how, just before Christmas break, Mrs. Love had stood at her desk and introduced her daughter to the class.

"Can anyone guess who this lady is?" Mrs. Love had asked.

Necks craned. Feet shifted. Silence, until a girl said, "The lady in the picture?" She pointed to Mrs. Love's desk. The framed photograph showed a young woman who looked just like Mrs. Love, with her dark hair parted down the middle, freckles, and nearly identical wide, toothy smile. Mrs. Love held the photo up for the class.

"I think you're right," she had said. "This is Miss Candy and she's a teacher like me but at another school. And she's a jazz singer. She's my little girl."

As Mrs. Love placed her arm around Miss Candy's waist, Sam raised his hand, which was shocking because we'd grown used to him talking out of turn.

"She ain't a little girl," he said brusquely. "She's taller than you."

"She will always be *my* little girl," Mrs. Love cooed.

Sometimes Miss Candy would stop by at the end of the school day and she and Mrs. Love walked to her Cadillac, laughing as they crossed the street. Mrs. Love looped her arm through her daughter's as though they were best friends. Mom had told Kim and me that right now she could be friendly with us—but she could not be our friend. She said mother-daughter relationships changed over time and she was looking forward to being friends when we were grown up. "Maybe later," she said. For Mrs. Love and Miss Candy, this was their later.

When Mrs. Love missed another day of school, the substitute led us in a prayer for Candy Love. I was used to praying at church and before bed, and I felt like an expert at it. But I looked over at Debra. I'd never seen her pray. With her head bowed and eyes squeezed shut, her lips moved as though she were reading. Wisps of sentences escaped from her: "This is Debra . . . You don't know me, but . . . Please."

Not long after, Miss Candy died. She was thirty-one.

The Griffin Funeral Home was a handsome building that looked stately with green shutters and sand-colored bricks. It was about four blocks away from our building, and Mom, Kim, and I walked there. Mom looked worried as we entered the chapel that held Miss Candy's services. She guided Kim and me to seats in the middle of the chapel. The casket was in front, surrounded by so many people who milled about that I could barely see it. I could, however, see Mrs. Love. She stood near a bouquet of flowers and in the middle of a discreet yoga pose, with her hands fastened behind her back and her chest pushed slightly forward. She'd told us that we could do yoga anywhere and anytime, and this moment was a testament to that.

I tugged on Mom's sleeve. "I want to see Miss Candy."

As we joined the viewing line, Mom held my hand and Kim's. Usually, Mom took one of Kim's hands and I took her other. But now she had both of us in a grip so tight that Kim complained.

"Ouch, Mommy!" Kim moaned. I don't know that Mom let up.

Miss Candy's corpse reminded me of Sleeping Beauty. Many times, I'd heard our church members view a body and say, "She looks just like she's sleeping." But it was never true. Although I had understood that death wasn't the sole province of old, blue-haired ladies, this was the first time that I'd known someone who had died so young. That Miss Candy was beautiful and that she indeed looked just like she was sleeping was oddly comforting. We walked over to Mrs. Love. She hugged us and introduced us to her family. During the service, Mrs. Love asked the students whom her daughter had taught to stand. She asked the musicians who had worked with Miss Candy to stand. She asked her own students to stand, and when I did, I looked around me. I saw Debra, next to her mother, and Loretta on the opposite side of the room near Sam.

During Miss Candy's funeral, I realized that it wasn't just the mother who could leave the daughter as I had feared a couple of years before. The daughter could leave the mother.

On our walk home, I asked Mom if Mrs. Love was going to be okay.

"She will be." Mom nodded, pulling me close to her.

She said parents can survive the death of a child. It's the hardest thing that any parent could do.

"Nobody ever wants to look down on her baby like that," my mother said. "I can't even imagine."

chapter seven

Miss Polaroid

I missed Debra fiercely. We vowed our friendship wouldn't change, but how could it not? For fourth grade, Mr. and Mrs. Trice transferred their two daughters to John J. Pershing Elementary School in Lake Meadows. Before the Trice family moved into Lawless a few months before we did, they had hoped to live in Lake Meadows, but the waiting list was too long. Instead, they toured Lawless Gardens, the new development south of 35th Street. Although it had billed itself as Lake Meadows's equal, it really wasn't. Since the first family moved into Lake Meadows in 1953, the development had been home to some of the city's most prominent Black doctors, lawyers, judges, engineers, and politicians who'd spend a few years there before joining the ranks of homeowners. Some of their names had been touted in the development's progress reports under "Who's Who Among Future Residents." Marketing materials invited them "to live in a park by the lake":

> For those who want the best in modern family living, Lake Meadows offers a new concept of a complete residential community where you can enjoy all of the most modern home conveniences in a park-like setting by the lakefront. There is nothing comparable to it in Chicago. In designing this community, careful thought has been given to providing sunlight and fresh air, extensive landscaped areas,

opportunity for varied family recreation, and accessibility to schools and churches, as well as a modern shopping center. The continued development of this community along these lines and the high quality of the present residents already have established Lake Meadows as the finest address on the South Side.

Mr. Trice's mother, a bigwig in state and local social welfare, had moved to Lake Meadows in the mid-1960s. The Trice family used her address to enroll their daughters in Pershing, which was about four blocks north of Doolittle and in another school district. Blessed with private-school amenities and test scores, it was the area's premier public school. (Rev. Jesse Jackson's son, Jesse Jr., would be in Debra's class that year.) All I knew at the time about Pershing and Lake Meadows was that Debra was now there for school and I wasn't. Because Mrs. Trice had always stocked the Goodwill basket in Doolittle's principal's office with so many of Debra's clothes, during recess I would see a girl across the playground wearing a cobalt-blue windbreaker or a pale pink cardigan over a white blouse with lace. It made me think of the way Debra hated leaving my apartment and always left something behind in order for her to return minutes later.

Every day, after Debra and I finished our homework, we tried to meet in the stairwell to lay out in great detail everything that happened while we were apart. Nothing was too insignificant. If we couldn't meet, rather than wait for the weekend, we left each other notes under the brown carpeting outside our apartments. We eagerly checked for new notes every day, like opening a mailbox. Sometimes, when Mom had gone to bed, I'd be in pajamas and I would quietly unlock our door, peel back the carpeting and the foam padding from the wood tacking, and find a note from Debra on the concrete floor. I returned the carpeting to its proper place, stomped lightly on it so that everything appeared undisturbed, and double-locked our door. I would run back to my bedroom to gobble up the tale of the day.

The first note Debra ever left was about her first recess at Pershing. She described how she and Darlene stood together on the school playground under a tree watching the students and their cliques, already formed since most of them had been together since kindergarten. Debra's love of running helped her make friends when she saw a group of fourth-graders racing one another. She joined in and began beating everyone in sight. The exception was a boy named Joseph. Their race ended in a tie. She had found her place in her new school. But the most important part of her note wasn't about school but a discovery after classes ended. Debra and her sister walked to their grandmother's Lake Meadows apartment to maintain the charade that they lived in the community. Mrs. Trice picked them up later. During the ride home, Debra saw a windowless mechanical building that abutted a small hill.

It can be our love spot, she wrote.

What's a love spot? I wrote back, folding the note and leaving it.

A place where we can sit and read or talk and nobody will bother us.

A few days later, Debra, Kim, and I ran through Lawless Gardens on our way to check out the meeting place Debra had scoped for us. Getting to it meant going beyond the fence, which Mom told us not to do, and crossing the four-lane 35th Street. Debra and I took Kim's hands and looked to our left and then ran to the median strip, where we looked to our right and crossed over.

When we arrived, I wasn't impressed. The facade of the mechanical building was unassuming, but inside was an underground room with gigantic boilers and other equipment that made it both brain and heartbeat of an adjacent tower. Steam billowed from vents as we climbed a small hill. I made Kim sit by a tree as Debra and I stepped gingerly out onto the roof, sitting on its ledge. Behind us, a short ivy-lined wall shed leaves as we leaned against it. Anyone in the housing project, Lawless Gardens, or anywhere else in the city could shop at the Lake Meadows Shopping Center. Its apartment complex, however, seemed more off-limits and so much farther away. The development stood just to the east and north of the shopping center's parking lot but was buffered by trees and shrubbery and spectacularly manicured lawns, the emerald green of Oz or Eden. Although Mom had driven through the complex at night while learning to drive, I'd never seen it during the day and never on foot. The land was mostly flat, but the slightest contours gave it the feel of an elite golf course.

"What should we be when we grow up, Dawn?" Debra said, as if inspired by the white towers, the way they absorbed light and reflected it, appearing luminous.

"We should be . . ." I thought for a moment. There was no shouting or loud music. No honking horns. No blaring sirens. "We should be doctors."

"Okay, then. That's what we will be." Debra lifted up to speak to Kim, who was digging in the dirt around the tree. "What do you want to be when you grow up, Kim?"

"Umm." Slowly, she pondered the sky and leaves. "A teacher?"

"Okay, then."

While I was doing well in the fourth grade, earning all "E"s for "Excellent," Kim's first-grade marks were less than stellar, mostly "S"s for "Satisfactory." Missing assignments had dragged down her grades. This surprised the teacher because Kim was one of her smartest students. She always had the answer whenever called on, though she rarely volunteered. Kim had already instigated a couple of playground fights. Mom had to come up to the school because Kim refused to apologize. When the teacher uncovered Kim's missing work, completed and crumpled, in Kim's desk, Mom was livid and lit into her daughter: "I've been up to that school more in the little time you've been at Doolittle than all the years your sister has been there!"

They were in the living room and Kim sat quietly on the sofa, listening. We knew when Mom got that way what followed was a lecture about how she was sick and tired and the only person more sick and tired was Fannie Lou Hamer, who had coined the phrase. Mom said she refused to be taken for granted anymore and called Kim ungrateful. Why Mom's ire turned to Kim's laundry, I'm not exactly sure, but she made Kim separate her dirty clothes from the others and do her own "damn laundry." Mom told me that I had to go to the laundry room with her, which meant I had to do all the work.

"But I get good grades."

She shot me a look and stormed into her bedroom, slamming the door.

The laundry room was on the first floor just beyond the service elevator and had a wall of floor-to-ceiling windows. It was dusk and there was nothing and no one outside to see. The clothes had been loaded into the washing machine and Kim was stretched out across the three chairs near the large sink basins. When I bent down to tie my gym shoelaces, I spotted something sandwiched between two washing machines. I got a clothes hanger from the folding table and took my time fishing out a yellowing and tattered white envelope. Inside was a Polaroid of a woman, buck naked. I was so stunned that I didn't examine it closely and I definitely didn't want Kim to see it. When we were done with the laundry, I left a note under the carpet in front of Debra's door. I told her she had to meet me in the stairwell the next day after school.

Pacing along the twelfth-floor landing, I could hardly stop my heart from racing as I waited for Debra. When she opened the door, I carefully pulled the fraying envelope from my pocket and handed it to her.

"I call her Miss Polaroid."

Debra opened the envelope slowly so it wouldn't rip further. She gasped, covering her mouth, her shoulders rising and falling with laughter.

The woman in the photo was sitting on a credenza with one leg up, exposing her—as Granny would later put it "natural ass." It wasn't the first time Debra and I had seen a vagina. We'd paged through the *Playboy* her father kept in a shoebox in the back of his bedroom closet. But those photos were of white women—women whose bodies were different from ours and our mothers'; women with whom we felt only the slightest connection. Miss Polaroid, with her deep brown skin, was the first naked Black woman we'd ever seen. Her dark areoles. Her slight paunch. Her chipped toenail polish. The way her toes on the foot resting on the credenza curled under. The way she leaned back on her haunches, staring out at us with righteous aplomb. Her only outfit, if we chose to dress her, was the worn envelope, a dingy, fraying white slip of a thing.

Miss Polaroid spent one night wedged behind the fire hose in the stairwell where we'd once hidden our tin before we moved it to the ledge. But we decided she was too precious a find to chance a nosy janitor or security guard happening upon her. So we took turns tucking her under the carpeting in front of our doors, but farther back. One or both of us checked on her every evening for about a week, caring for her as though she were a prized possession, a plant or pet that needed tending.

A few days before Thanksgiving break, Mrs. Trice knocked hard on our apartment door. I opened it and immediately homed in on Debra's bloodshot eyes. Without any pleasantries, Mrs. Trice asked to speak with Mom. I had no idea what was going on. When Mom came to the door, Mrs. Trice handed Mom the battered envelope and I swallowed hard. Mrs. Trice wanted to know if I knew anything about it.

"I didn't say Dawn knew anything," Debra sniffed. Mrs. Trice ignored her and watched Mom open the envelope. "I keep telling you, I found it all by myself."

Mom looked at Miss Polaroid. "What the hell?" She looked at me.

Mrs. Trice explained that Debra had taken Miss Polaroid to school. She said that during class, Debra was passing the envelope to a friend when the photo fell out, faceup on the floor. Debra's fourth-grade teacher, whom Debra despised, was walking nearby and saw it. I imagined that the expression on the teacher's face as she picked up Miss Polaroid must not have been too different from the one on ours when we first saw her. The teacher demanded Debra go to the principal's office, where her parents were called for the first time since she'd been at Pershing.

"You know anything about this?" Mom asked me.

The vagina had been the one part of my sister's and my anatomy that Mom repeatedly told us not to look at, touch, or discuss. And, if Kim or I stumbled on the other in the bathroom attempting to examine the space between our legs, we policed each other with warnings: "Oooh, I'm gonna tell Mama." Shame and our mother's wrath were deterrents of equal standing.

In the past, when talking to Kim and me about our privates, Mom had always referred to our vaginas as our "pocketbooks." But her favorite purse, an old leather number with a chipped Lucite buckle—and a ripped inner lining that made the purse an abyss—didn't exactly exemplify cleanliness and chastity. For that, she relied on a palm-sized, heavy rubber coin pouch she received, along with the annual calendar, from the Supreme Life Insurance man. The coin pouch was shiny, blue, and oval with a slit down the center. Most people squeezed the ends together, opening it to deposit coins. Mom squeezed it open to demonstrate proper hygiene and then clamped it shut to explain why it needed to remain that way until after marriage.

She pleaded with Kim and me to travel and see the world before we had children; to understand who we were and who our husbands were, first. She squeezed the coin pouch to a pucker and told us to imagine how unbelievably painful it was for a baby to spring forth from an opening that small. She told us that babies would nail our feet to the ground. They would limit what we could do and who we could become. They would reconfigure not only our bodies but our goals and ambitions, too.

"Just wait," she begged us. And it was the only time she begged.

Staring at me, Mom returned Miss Polaroid to her envelope. "I asked you a question. Do you know anything about this?"

I considered lying, but I was horrible at it. I had no poker face, no ability to think quickly on my feet. My mouth hung open.

"That little red flag there," Mom said, gesturing at my tongue. "How it normally waves and waves. But now, nothing. I can look at you and tell you're lying."

"But she hasn't said anything," Debra said.

Mom and Mrs. Trice formed a united front and glared at Debra.

"I'll take care of this," Mom said to Mrs. Trice. As Mom closed the door, Debra mouthed, "I'm sorry."

Mom snatched me up by my collar and dragged me to my bedroom. She didn't spank me often, but I knew this would warrant one. Kim had been eavesdropping and I glimpsed her as she slipped around the corner ahead of us. Mom had an old leather belt of Uncle Al's that she kept on a hook on the back of her bedroom door. She looked for it and it was gone.

"Where is it?"

Her tone ripped through me.

"Where's my belt?"

"I don't know," I groaned.

"Kim!" Mom yelled. "You got my property?"

My sister didn't answer. Mom looked at me. "I'm going into the kitchen to turn off my pots. If that strap isn't in its proper place by the time I return, it's going to be too bad, too sad for both of you."

Mom left and I peeked under my bed and Kim's. I ran into Mom's bedroom and looked under hers. Then I opened her closet. Kim had a secret hiding place way in the back behind Mom's white church dresses. When I slid the dresses out of the way, Kim waved at me and then placed her finger up to her mouth. "Shhhh!" She held the belt coiled around her fist.

"You're just making her madder."

I knew Kim was trying to save me, but I also knew that Mom was relentless. We might as well get it over with. I looked at my sister. She was pleased with herself.

"Mom!" My voice quivered. Disbelief filled Kim's eyes. "Here she is."

I lay across my bed and pulled down my pants. Mom said she didn't believe in spanking clothes.

"Please, Mom," I begged. "Please." She swung the strap three times. I was crying before the first blow. The only thing Kim hated more than hearing me beg was watching me get hit. She looked away as if seeing my naked behind was too much, even though she'd seen it many times.

When it was Kim's turn, Mom struck her once. She told Granny that hitting Kim was like striking iron. Kim hardly squirmed. She made no noise, not even a murmur.

We heard Debra screaming as she was getting spanked. We each looked up at the ceiling.

Debra and I would never see Miss Polaroid again. For embarrassing ourselves and our families by taking pornography to school, we were banned from seeing each other for a month. That felt far worse than the spanking.

Knowing I couldn't see Debra, I spent some afternoons doing my homework in Granny's apartment. With its glass menagerie, her living room sparkled like the showroom where she worked. She brought home discounted high-end items that were slightly damaged and unsellable, items she never could have afforded had they been whole. A glass robin had a chipped wing and a fluted vase couldn't hold water because of a notch on the bottom. A porcelain ballerina had two nicked feet. Granny had positioned her figurines so that their scars and defects were artfully disguised. Throughout the day, pieces refracted sunlight and cast little rainbows on white walls and her cream-colored furniture, sheathed in plastic.

Most days, I left before Granny came home from work, but one day I lost track of time. She came in, took off her coat and scarf.

"I'll see you later, Granny," I said, gathering my things.

"No, stay. I've been meaning to talk to you," she said. "I'll be right back."

She headed to her bedroom and returned in her floral house dress and slippers. "Your mother told me that Mr. Malone sent your writing to *Ebony Jr.*"

Mr. Malone was my fourth-grade teacher. He had told the class to write a short story, and mine was about two girls on an elevator that mysteriously rockets them past the twenty-fourth floor in their building to the moon. He said he'd been impressed by my use of language and my imagination.

"But they didn't publish it." I hung my head. "They said maybe next time."

"Oh, you think your teacher sends every student's writing to a big-time children's magazine? And you think they read everybody's papers just to say yea or nay?"

"No?" I said, unsure exactly how to answer.

"He sees something in you, child. That magazine thought enough to read your work. *Maybe next time* is what they said. So, write something else." She studied her hands. "Your mother told me about that nasty photograph."

My chest tightened.

"You need to leave that little girl, that Debra, alone. Giving you pictures of naked women. She's fast and will bring you worse trouble."

"She's not a fast girl. And she didn't—"

"You see, Debra is pretty and enough things will come to her so easily that she'll expect it. You're smart. You have a lot going for you."

"But—" I stared into my lap. "What if it wasn't Debra who found it?"

Disappointment washed across my grandmother's face.

"Some people don't mean us one bit of good," she said. "Your mama doesn't feel like I do about Debra. But you should find a friend who better suits you."

I won't ever have a better friend.

The Saturday our punishments ended, I knew I was defying my grandmother when Debra and I met in the stairwell. Starved of each other's company, we hugged with rapturous delight. We were dressed in T-shirts and jeans and we shot down the steps to the lobby. An autumn wind held open the door for us, but we didn't care about the chill as we made our way to our ledge. At 35th Street, Debra grabbed my arm.

"I didn't tell on you, Dawn. I swear to God. I would never do that."

"I know. I believe you."

At the ledge, we pulled our arms inside our T-shirts to ward off the wind. Behind us, the ivy had shed its leaves and the branches felt like welts against our backs. We had hidden our tin of things in a tangle of leaves and it was now partially exposed.

"My teacher asked me if I know why I do the things that get me into trouble," Debra said. "I told her, 'How do I know? I just do them.'"

"You just do them," I agreed, and shrugged.

Being together that afternoon felt like we were back in our proper places, like the world had righted itself. We lay flat on our backs, head to head, staring at an overhang of trees and a dapple of sky. Every now and then, the wind revealed the upper floors and balconies of a nearby tower. Our weekends unfolded that way until snow and ice accumulated on the ledge, at which point we spent some Saturdays ice skating instead. A temporary rink had been set up on one of Lake Meadows's lawns. The first time we went, Mrs. Trice drove us to the rink and as soon as we stepped out of the car, I stood there captivated by the scenery. Snow coated the bare branches on the trees. White Christmas lights swayed above the rink. Music played over the loudspeakers. When the Jackson 5's "Santa Claus Is Coming to Town" came on, teenagers dropped everything to return to the ice and skate to the beat. But when Bing Crosby launched into "I'm dreaming of a white Christmas," the kids relinquished the ice to the adults, many of whom skated hand in hand.

Debra led the way to a group of kids lacing up skates and yelled over the music, "Hey, everybody! This is my friend Dawn! The smart girl I've been telling you about!"

They chimed, "Hi, Dawn!"

One girl walked up to us. "That's where you rent skates," she said, pointing to a tent. "And you can get hot cocoa from that building."

I'd met a handful of Debra's classmates, girls and boys we'd seen walking by the ledge. They were not at all as perfect as I'd imagined Lake Meadows's kids would be. Some were nerdy and needed braces and had thick glasses.

Debra and I rented our skates and sat on a rubber mat to slip them on. As soon as our blades touched the ice, we fell. We helped each other up and fell again. Then we held hands until we got our bearings, and when we did, we skated with our legs and arms stiff as boards. After a while, Debra asked me whether I minded if she rested on the sidelines with her friends. I told her I didn't. I skated around and around by myself, my fingertips and toes growing numb.

More than how pretty everything was that night, it was the effortless feeling I got gliding on the ice. I tried to take in everything. The falling snow shrouding the buildings in a celebration of white confetti. A father chasing his son on the ice. Another dancing with his daughter. A mother snapping so many pictures from her Instamatic that the bench behind her holding the used flashcubes appeared studded. The main attraction, however, was a woman who swooshed past me elegantly, twirling like a ballerina, taking flight like a swan. She wore white pants and a plush white sweater and white earmuffs. She was brown like me with a long braid. Each time she passed, I wanted to skate like her, defy gravity like her. In my mind, I was her. I was soaring. I skated around and around, like on a carousel, with each revolution revealing something new—about Lake Meadows, about me.

To paraphrase the theme song from the television sitcom *The Jeffersons*, Lake Meadows residents had indeed moved on up and gotten their piece of the pie. In my view, it was a piece of the sky.

As I skated that evening, if someone asked me, "Can you imagine living in this type of world?" I would have shouted, as though from one of the balconies:

"Yes. I most certainly can."

chapter eight

Roots and Good Times

. . .

It was during the evening rush hour when Granny stood on a downtown "L" platform, staring at a man who looked familiar. When he walked past her, she looked him up and down. "Oh, I'd know those slue feet anywhere, Andrew McDonald!"

Mom had met Andrew on a blind date in the early 1960s, a couple of years before she met Dad. They had fallen in love but had what Mom called a "silly little spat" that torpedoed their relationship. He had gone bowling on a night when he was supposed to have taken her out on a date. She considered Andrew "the one who got away." Granny felt that way, too, because he was smart and the type of guy who never met a stranger. It didn't hurt that he looked a lot like the famed Harlem congressman Adam Clayton Powell Jr. but without the ego.

Several trains came and went as Andrew filled Granny in on his life. He was twice divorced with three children—two daughters and a son—who lived with their mothers. He worked as an overnight security guard in the Chicago Public Library's main building downtown.

Granny told him that Mom was divorced with two daughters and worked downtown, too. "Not far from the library," she said slyly. "She'd love to see you."

They exchanged telephone numbers, and Mom and Andrew began dating.

He asked Mom for a list of Kim's and my favorite books, and when he came over for the first time, he brought me a Trixie Belden mystery and Kim a science book. We liked him immediately, in part because he admired Mom's rule that if Kim and I were reading, we didn't have to do chores. So that we could stay immersed in our books, he sometimes washed the dishes or threw out the garbage for us. Once, on his off day, he took Kim and me downtown to the library. We both marveled at such a behemoth of a building, lavishly ornate and filled with old, briny-smelling books.

Debra liked Andrew, too. He was visiting when one of her gerbils escaped its cage and scampered down a pipe into our apartment. He scooped it up before Mom, who was still terribly afraid of rodents, saw it. He and I walked up the steps to deliver the furry animal safely to its owner. Grateful, Debra hugged Andrew around his waist.

Less than a year after Mom and Andrew's reunion, as the Bicentennial dawned, Mom sat Kim and me down in the living room to tell us that she and Andrew had decided to marry. He would be moving in with us.

"That means"—she wagged her finger at Kim, then me—"you will no longer be able to walk around here bare-assed, like you've just stepped out of a *National Geographic*."

A month later, Mom and Andrew went down to City Hall and wed. Granny was their witness. Andrew became an integral part of our family, cooking meals, hosting get-togethers. When the miniseries *Roots* aired, he insisted that Granny and Uncle Al join us to watch it. He asked them to come early for his smothered pork chops topped with pineapple slices, and mashed potatoes and green beans. At the table, he poured himself his customary glass of wine. This always felt odd, like a special occasion, because like Mom and Dad, neither Granny nor Uncle Al indulged.

After dinner, we gathered in front of the television. Granny, Uncle Al, and Kim sat on the sofa. Mom sat on the love seat with Andrew. I lay on the floor in front of the cocktail table a few feet away from the set. Concealed under my sweater was my Archie comic book that I planned to secretly read while the show aired.

But from the opening scene with Kunta Kinte running away

from his captors, I was mesmerized. I, like millions of other viewers, was rapt. The show depicted images—positive images—of Black folks that I'd never seen before on television or at the movies: Black love, Black ingenuity, Black resilience. Before *Roots*, I'd thought of slavery mostly in terms of Mrs. Patterson, the old woman Mom knew. It was abstract and distant, but now I saw myself and my history. When the episode ended, Andrew talked about how he had grown up in the Jim Crow South in the late 1930s and how his fair skin and straight, curly-on-the-ends hair afforded him an array of privileges that were denied his darker siblings, how his family moved north searching for heaven and, instead, found segregated communities that were resourced differently, cleaned differently, and policed differently. A perfect example was right across the street.

"We like to look at the squalor and say Black people don't keep stuff clean," he said. "But downtown didn't do what was required to sustain a healthy, functioning community. The entire deck has always been stacked favoring everyone but us."

It was freezing outside and the heat from the room had frosted the windows and the glass held polka-dot circles where Mom had scratched at the ice crystals whenever police sirens blared in the housing project or someone leaned on his horn. As the Ida B. Wells Homes deteriorated, the fence around Lawless began its evolution. New, massive, padlocked gates had been added, cordoning off four of Lawless's six entrances. Only the two northernmost entrances, near 35th Street, remained open. Before the gates, nonresidents could walk through Lawless to go anywhere. Now they had to walk around.

I was quietly sitting on the floor. Kim was leaning on Uncle Al, feigning sleep. I could tell by the way her eyelids gently fluttered. Mom had already told Kim that at eight, she was too old to be picked up and taken to bed. Still, she tried it anyway.

Andrew looked at my sister and then at me. "Do you know who Ida B. Wells was?" he said. "Can you tell me why a housing project is named after her?"

Self-conscious, I was quiet for a second.

"Granny told us she used to live in the neighborhood."

"Okay, fair enough," Andrew said. "But I'm wondering about her, not where she lived."

I shook my head.

"I bet you can tell me everything about *The Six Million Dollar Man*, though," he gently chided. "I've seen you run home, leave Debra behind, to watch it."

He was right. Once a week, I recited the introduction as the credits rolled: "Steve Austin, astronaut, a man barely alive. Gentlemen, we can rebuild him. We have the technology. We have the capability to make the world's first bionic man."

"Ida B. Wells-Barnett was a journalist," Andrew said. "She wrote about Black people getting lynched in the South. She was brave."

After *Roots* aired, Andrew no longer brought me books about white girls and I no longer requested them. He brought home Carter G. Woodson's *The Mis-Education of the Negro* and bookmarked the page that contained: "When you control a man's thinking you do not have to worry about his actions. . . . He will find his 'proper place' and will stay in it. You do not need to send him to the back door. He will go without being told. In fact, if there is no back door, he will cut one for his special benefit. His education makes it necessary."

He added Langston Hughes's poem "Harlem," which asked *What happens to a dream deferred*, and Richard Wright's *Native Son*, set in a Chicago ghetto. Both men had spent time in Bronzeville.

Andrew read Gwendolyn Brooks's poems to Mom, Kim, and me. They told stories about the seven-year-old Black girl "cut from a chocolate bar." And the "charity children" and the man with "patent leather hair."

I came home from school one day to find Andrew sitting on the living room sofa reading St. Clair Drake and Horace R. Cayton Jr.'s *Black Metropolis: A Study of Negro Life in a Northern City*, published in 1945. I asked him what it was about and he read me an excerpt from Richard Wright's introduction: "Will the Negro, in the language of André Malraux, find meaning in his humiliation, make his slums and his sweat-shops his modern cathedrals out of which will be born a new consciousness that can guide him toward freedom? Or will he continue, as he does today, saying Job-like to the society that crushes him: Though it slays me, yet will I trust in it?"

I looked confused.

"It's about self-determination," Andrew said. "We can't wait for others to do what we must do for ourselves. And yet we can't do it alone."

I still watched *The Six Million Dollar Man*, but by spring I'd written the names of eight books on a sheet of notebook paper that I taped to the wall by my bed. I'd color-coded the list and included a legend at the bottom. The titles of the books that I read alone were written in red. The four I'd read with Andrew were in green. And the books from which he had excerpted chapters or passages, I wrote their titles in blue.

The end-of-school bell rang, heralding the weekend and, instead of joining the trickle of students heading home to Lawless Gardens, I followed the roaring mass en route to the housing project. A classmate named Pamela had missed school and I was delivering homework to her. She lived in one of the seven-story extension buildings. Since *Roots* aired, I'd begun reading the scripts that our sixth-grade teacher wrote for me to introduce short films for assemblies. Sometimes Pamela worked the projector and we had become friends. Most of Lawless's parents told their children not to venture into the project. But Mom never forbade me, so I'd been to Pamela's apartment several times.

At Pamela's building that afternoon, young men congregated along the steps leading to the main doors. Pamela had just turned twelve and was already curvy. When we were together, I'd seen her handle catcallers by offering them her middle finger or rolling her eyes. On that day, I could feel my body tensing as I walked past the guys. Still, I tried to blend in with a few other students entering the building. Inside, I passed the lone elevator with the spasmodic light. I didn't dare board it. Nobody did. The elevators were prone to getting stuck between floors. I entered the stairwell and the acrid smell of urine accosted me. Graffiti littered the walls and it was always dark because blown-out light bulbs were rarely replaced. At night, residents used matches and lighters to walk up and down the stairs. I knew that I only had to make it to the third floor, so I ran up quickly. In the housing project, the incinerator chutes were in the open hallways—not in closed-off rooms like in Lawless and Lake Meadows. The chutes spewed smoke and seemed to regurgitate whatever was shoved inside them. The smell of urine yielded only to that of putrefying garbage.

I knocked on Pamela's door. Although the building was in such disrepair, her apartment was always neat and tidy. I thought about how her mother and father greeted me with kindness, asking about my grades and my family, even though they had never met them. They reminded me of the Evans family in the sitcom *Good Times*. Her father worked hard at a plant and hated the notion of welfare. Pamela had told me that her family was trying to move because a year before, they had been robbed at gunpoint in the middle of the night. Her older sister came in late and two men rammed in behind her. Pamela still had difficulty sleeping. I knocked again, and when no one answered I pushed the homework under the door and headed for the stairs. It would take them seven more years, but they would buy a new townhouse on the South Side.

By the time I exited the building, my eyes strained against the light. I saw my tower across the street. I saw the grassy berm on the edge of our parking lot and the rows of cars that sat between perfectly straight white lines on black asphalt that shimmered. Standing in the housing project felt like standing at the base of a mountain where the wind had swept everything bad downhill. Before Lawless's new gates, I could have just crossed the street to my building. But now I had to run north along the fence to the opening, and once inside Lawless, I ran all the way south, home.

The last assembly of the school year highlighted the Jim Crow South and featured Emmett Till, the Chicago boy whose brutal Mississippi murder Rev. Jesse Jackson would later describe as "the big bang" of the civil rights movement. It followed assemblies on the Middle Passage and the Underground Railroad and was such a big production that several classes from the lower grades were invited to join in, Kim's included.

I sat in the school's auditorium in a seat marked "Reserved." I looked around the auditorium at the standing-room-only crowd and saw Kim leaning over the balcony. She waved vigorously. My heartbeat pulsed in my ears. When the lights dimmed, the sound of the clacking projector filled my chest as I leaned toward the microphone, looked down at the illuminated page, and began reading the script.

The film ended and teachers complimented me on how mature I sounded. I had never excelled at much beyond academics. But I felt totally at home in front of an audience. Language was music to me. Reading even required a bit of theatrics during which I stepped outside myself and into the written word. I found a refuge beside a machine that animated a flat white screen. And it was in the dark that I began to find my voice. Some of my peers actually appreciated my skills. A couple commented with "Good job" and "I didn't know you could read like that." The knucklehead boys whom I was sure would have ridiculed me didn't. Their silence alone was a compliment.

After the assembly, Kim ran up to me. "I saw you, Dawn," she said, out of breath. "I told everybody, 'That's my big sister.' Did you hear me clapping?"

I couldn't help but smile.

At home, I ran upstairs to read the script to Debra. Later, she slipped a folded piece of lined notebook paper under my door rather than leave it under the carpeting. This spoke to her sense of urgency.

"Dawn," she wrote, "why do you sound white? We are Black."

chapter nine

The Violation.
The Maiming

. . .

Before Debra and I became best friends in the third grade, we had never seen each other in all of Lawless. Afterward, we somehow crossed paths all the time. I'd be on the elevator and the door would swing open onto the lobby with Debra waiting to board. We'd hug with our eyes closed as though we hadn't seen each other in years. Our families passed in the parking lot or in the playground or the laundry room. Debra and I thought it was nothing short of a miracle that our timing was so impeccable. We never viewed ourselves as moving in opposite directions. We never imagined we wouldn't be in each other's orbit. But the summer between sixth and seventh grades, we began to want different things. Debra's friends were a faster, edgier crowd, and she liked hanging out with a group.

I preferred being with one person, and increasingly that person was a boy named Thomas who lived in Lawless in the tower closest to 35th Street. A top student, he pushed me to achieve. He was also the only boy Mom allowed in my bedroom. Thomas was gay during a time when most kids didn't have the language for it. He had long fingernails and he dressed neatly with meticulously creased pants and perfectly tucked polos. He did not run amok on the playground like the other boys or gossip about which girls had the biggest breasts or ass. He did not try to touch us or berate us about our bodies or make us feel small.

I took Thomas to the ledge in Lake Meadows.

"How come you don't play with Carl?" I asked as we walked up the short hill.

Carl was the other boy in our class who was *different*, like Thomas, but far more effeminate.

"I don't like Carl," Thomas said, sitting on the grass where Kim used to sit rather than on the overhang. I still sat there but one foot was on the hill near him.

"He's bossy but he's not that bad," I said.

"He dresses loudly and talks loudly and he's just plain boorish."

Boorish. Thomas was fearless when it came to unusual words. That is, fearless when it was just the two of us. Neither of us dared speak that way among our peers.

Although I spent most of my time with Thomas, there were milestones only Debra and I could share. With her bedroom door closed, we stood in front of the mirror on her dresser, daubing Noxzema on our faces. Seemingly overnight, puberty recontoured our bodies and we surveyed the changes at length with our T-shirts and training bras raised, staring at the growing mounds of flesh on our chests. Most of all, we tried to discern what boys saw when they saw us. Debra's body was the kind they salivated over. She had shapely legs leading to well-defined hips, a thin waist, and breasts like perfectly symmetrical grapefruits. She embodied the "brick house" the Commodores crooned about: "Thirty-six, twenty-four, thirty-six, oh what a winning hand!" I was not a brick house. My legs resembled reeds and made my gait storky. I had no hips and was just a hedge above flat-chested. My breasts started to bud around the same time I got braces, and the two seemed to cancel each other out.

When Debra and I walked down the street or took the bus to the downtown movie theaters or to the museums, boys flocked to us because of her. I often stepped back to let them fawn unimpeded. But Debra always pulled me forward, looped her arm through mine, eager to deflect and share the attention.

"Say hello to Dawn, too," she'd say. "She's my friend."

Over the years, I had come to expect everyone, even adults who had just met Debra, to say, "What beautiful eyes you have" or "You're such a pretty girl."

Although neither of us was planning to lose our virginity any time soon, we continued to experiment with our sexuality. We met a couple of boys downtown and they followed us onto the bus, walking to the back row, and we kissed them. We met some boys while in the Lake Meadows Shopping Center and took them back to a vacant eighteenth-floor apartment in Lawless. The boy I was with was afraid of heights and, as he kissed me, mouth pinched tight as a snare drum, he kept his eyes open, looking out the window.

We were still new to our bodies the summer between seventh and eighth grade when we planned to take a walk along the lakefront. We had been warned that we had to be careful. Granny had told Kim and me plainly, "Old men might try to snatch you from yourself, take what's not theirs to have." Debra's father had told his daughters, "You're little and you will need to know how to fight." He had a brown belt in karate and sometimes moved the living room furniture out of the way so he could spar with them, showing them how to kick a man in his groin or disengage from a chokehold.

All of that was preparation for a moment we all hoped would never come, a moment that, unfortunately, too often does. What we hadn't been told is that there are degrees of the violation, the maiming. It's the difference between a blush and a bruise, the depth of a scar and an amputation; of being consumed all at once or forced to watch yourself be picked apart.

Debra and I began that afternoon on our way to the lakefront in Debra's bedroom, dabbing on her mother's rouge and then the eye shadow and lip gloss we'd bought from Woolworths.

"Smack your lips like this," Debra said, pressing her lips together and releasing.

I did and then she did again. We wore hot pants and sandals and tube tops with talcum sprinkled on our cleavage. We stood in a fog of hairspray to protect our curls against the humidity.

Outside, we passed through Lawless on our way to the 35th Street bridge to the lakefront. We crossed and were making our way to a gravel path when a man rode up behind us on his bike. He hopped off and started talking to us. I noticed his large nose and moles, and the patches of whiskers around his chin like metal filings responding to a magnet. He walked alongside us in a heavy, lumbering way, his gym shoes tied so tight the tongues looked squeezed. He asked us whether we knew how pretty we were. Debra and I laughed, trying to appear charming and mature. When his hand brushed across my behind, I shook it off as a mistake, an innocent accident.

We continued on the path that wound along the embankment where fishermen sometimes sat with their rods planted like flags in the concrete cracks. No fishermen were out that day, nor people crowding around grills for barbecues. No one was around at all. It was almost like the man and I noticed that the lakefront was deserted at the same time. Suddenly he shoved his hand inside the back of my shorts and tunneled his finger inside me. One quick motion that left me motionless and limp-bodied. I tried to scream, but the sound burrowed down into my throat. He grabbed my arm with one hand and held on to his bike with the other. As he wrenched me toward him, Debra realized what was happening and fixed on my other arm in a tug-of-war.

"Let go!" she screamed, then spotted a police cruiser. "Help! Police!" The words peeled from her like a screeching car.

The man jumped on his bike and Debra reached down, scooped a handful of gravel, and flung it at him as he sped away. The police car rushed toward us from the parking lot, jumped on the path, and slowed. Pointing, Debra said to the two officers, "That man was going to rape her."

The driver flipped on swirling blue lights and the siren blared as they began chasing him.

Debra gripped my hand, her fingers laced tightly through mine. "You okay, Dawn?" She seethed with anger.

"I'm okay," I said. My chest heaved and Debra clasped my hand tighter. We waited a few minutes and then began walking back to the bridge. We were still on the path when we heard a siren. The police car pulled up beside us and the man, minus his bike, was handcuffed and slumped in the back seat. Blades of grass stuck to the side of his face and a small patch of skin had been scraped bloody and raw.

"This the guy?" The officer jerked his head toward the back seat. I nodded.

"That's him," Debra said.

I couldn't look at him. Instead, I focused on my friend. Her eyes were wild and her face red. She was angrier than I'd ever seen her, staring in a scathing way. It was too soon for me to hate him. My brain and body were still processing what had happened. But Debra's hate for him was immediate and primal. The officers told us to wait for a second police car that would take us home. As they sped off, Debra brushed off the back of my shorts and noticed that my period had come. I'd had it for about a year, since I was twelve, but wasn't expecting it now.

"Don't worry, Dawn," she said. "I'll stand behind you. Nobody will know."

Later, at the police station, Mom and I sat at a table in a small room with her arm fastened around me. A policewoman talked to us and took notes as Mom gave her our address and told her that I was thirteen and about to enter the eighth grade, emphasizing I was a straight-A student.

The officer asked me to recount what happened, which I did, my voice shaky.

"And now this is delicate and I'm sorry I have to ask this, Dawn," she said. "Can you tell me where he touched you?"

"Yes," I said. "Down in my shorts."

"Now, once again, I'm sorry I have to ask: Did his finger go inside your vagina?"

"Yes. I mean no," I said. "My rear."

I could feel my mother's body shudder.

"You've done very well," the lady officer said.

Looking at Mom and then at me, the officer asked if I'd be able to identify him in court. Mom bit her lip. The officer told us to think about it. But if I did go, it would be best if I wore my hair in braids rather than down the way it was now. She said I should dress in long pants and a long-sleeve shirt.

On the way home, Mom said, "It's not necessary to tell your sister. No need in worrying her. And we will not tell your father. He will kill that man and no need in his ass going to prison."

A few months later, I sat in court with Andrew and Mom in a long-sleeve sweater, my hair parted down the middle and in braids. I saw the man enter the courtroom handcuffed, though I didn't—couldn't—look at his face for very long. Although much of the proceeding was a blur, I recall one of the attorneys saying that the man had been on parole. He was a serial child molester. And that he'd ridden his bike so fast to elude police that they had to speed to catch him. The man returned to prison.

Mom was so shaken by it all that she hardly let me out of her sight. She preferred I stay within the fence, but she wanted me to report to her if I left. Her fear magnified my own. Inside the fence or out, I saw his face on every man with brown skin and a similar body type. I never knew I thought I was invincible until I realized I wasn't. My body felt ill-fitting, like it no longer fully belonged to me.

For a long time, I did not wear my hair down.

chapter ten

A Cleaving

▪ ▪ ▪

Sometimes when Thomas and I were in my bedroom, I could hear Debra and her friends upstairs in her bedroom. I could hear her unbridled, full-bellied laugh that had become my lifeline, that had allowed me to sleep and had saved me.

The summer before high school, our lives had veered in different directions, and Debra and I hardly saw each other. But as our freshman year was about to begin, she tapped on her floor to ask me to meet her in the stairwell. She wanted to walk to our ledge, which I found curious because we hadn't been there together in ages. As we walked, we caught up on each other's lives. I told her that I'd been accepted at Hyde Park Academy, a magnet school, not far from the University of Chicago. I told her that Andrew had attended my eighth-grade graduation plastered, and that Mom had said all that reading he did about white folks had made him a drunk. What bothered me most was that he hadn't brought home many of the library books I'd requested from my freshman English reading list. I didn't know if it was because of his drinking or him disapproving that the majority of the authors on the list were old dead white men.

"Last week he came home without one of his shoes," I yammered on as Debra and I crossed 35th Street. "Mom made him leave and spend a week with his brother."

"For real?" Debra said flatly. She was distracted, and that unnerved me even more about our impromptu trip to the ledge. I'd never had a need for yammering with her because she'd been the talker. She'd often led the way.

At the ledge, we sat down, our legs swinging over the side, and almost instinctively, Debra felt around for our metal box, which for years we'd kept hidden in a tangle of leaves and vines and tucked out of sight. The vines had been pruned and the box was gone. We both knew that, but that didn't stop her from feeling the barren space.

"I have news, too." She paused, peering down at the asphalt and sighing. "We're moving, Dawn, to corny ol' Indianapolis."

"Why?" I suddenly felt like I was freefalling.

"Dad thinks I've been getting into too much trouble here."

"Trouble? What kind of trouble?"

"Smoking weed. Too many fights. He thinks it will be quieter in Indianapolis compared to Chicago. My grandmother has a duplex and we'll live next door."

Her grandmother had left Lake Meadows a few years before and bought the property, where Debra and her family had been spending part of their summers.

"I'm going to just die of boredom." Again, she exhaled gustily. "You can come see me, though, okay? And we'll write every week and call each other. We'll still be friends."

Endings sometimes return you to the beginning. The way she said "We'll still be friends" was as though we were seven and eight again and just starting out. Trying to imagine Debra's bedroom not being above mine was like trying to picture Kim's bed moved to a place far, far away. I did not need to hang out with my sister every day to know that if she left me, there would be a cleaving and a vital part of me would be gone.

"I'm afra—" The word lodged in my throat.

"You're tough, Dawn," she said. "You promise me you will be even tougher."

"I promise," I said.

But we did not cross our hearts. We did not hope to die.

"Don't forget about little ol' me." Debra grabbed my hand, staring down beyond our knobby knees and sandaled feet. She let go of my hand.

"We should jump," she said.

Kim and I were at Dad's house on Debra's moving day. I didn't see the movers carrying her family's furniture to the service elevator and down into the truck, or Debra trying to orchestrate the movers' every move. I didn't see the Trice family walk through the apartment one last time before their car pulled off, leaving Lawless Gardens for good. When Dad brought Kim and me home, my world had been upended without me.

I was in the hallway outside our apartment when I heard workers upstairs milling about. I walked up the steps as I had countless times for nearly five years. The janitors had propped open the door so that a cross-breeze could help dry the freshly painted walls. I entered and the empty apartment felt completely different. As I walked through the living room, my memory re-created where the furniture had been, the bookcase that held the encyclopedias and her father's CB radio. In Debra's bedroom, the throw rugs had been removed, exposing the brown tile floor. Her dinosaurs and gerbils were gone. The workers had not yet painted the room and holes pockmarked the walls where art once hung. At the window, I looked down and noticed the nicks and scratches on the floor. Over the years, while I'd stood on the concrete windowsill in my bedroom tapping on my ceiling, she had tapped and scratched the tiles.

Before I knew Debra, I knew the sound of her. The sound of her tapping against the window crank. The sound of her feet hitting the floor as she jumped down from her sister's top bunk. The sound of her mother yelling at her to hurry up and get ready for school. The sound of Debra protesting, trying, as always, to bend the universe to her will. Now I felt a void.

All of it and all of her were gone.

part two

chapter eleven

A Rabbit-Assed Mind

■ ■ ■

Once again, Mom was tired. Scratch that. "Sick and tired."
Tired of her husband, who, after a week in exile, still hadn't devised a sufficient plan to stop drinking. Tired of her younger daughter, who was using her mattress, via a slit in it, as a repository for a couple of letters about missing homework her fifth-grade teacher had sent home. The start of high school was a few days away and now Mom was sick and tired of me, too.

I was lying across my bed looking over my class schedule when she entered the room. I had washed my hair earlier that day and as it air-dried, it had begun to look like an old, matted wig, long and wild, curly in some places, kinky in others. Mom asked me when I was going to press my hair.

"I'm not," I said, scanning my class schedule. "I'm going natural."

Her eyes held me in contempt. "You must be out of your rabid-assed mind."

For years, I thought she was saying "rabbit-assed mind," but I'd just read the rabid dog scene in *To Kill a Mockingbird* and finally understood. It was one of the few books from my summer reading list that Andrew had brought me.

"But, Mom . . ." I stood so she could see how earnest I was.

"You're not living in my house looking like that."

I began what I believed was a discussion about how beautiful

Black hair was in its natural state and continued on about white standards of beauty. We both knew that it was an argument Andrew would have appreciated.

Mom whirled toward me in a lather and stood in the hollow between the beds. Kim appeared in the doorway, shocked by my rare display of defiance.

"Either press your damn hair or get the hell out. Looking like you've just been released from a mental institution."

"But, Mom, you're adhering to white standards."

She grabbed me by my collar. It didn't matter that I was several inches taller than her. "This isn't about white standards. This is about my music. Dance or leave."

"Okay, fine." I gathered my things: my keys, my shoes. We had reached an impasse. I was frustrated and angry and hurt. Debra was gone. Andrew was, too. Was he coming back? That was unclear. Who would read with me? Everything felt like it was in tatters.

"You can take your shoes," Mom said. She, like Kim, expected me to acquiesce, to cower. "Leave everything else. I paid for it. It's mine."

She turned to Kim and waved her hand over the mound of clothes on her bed. "I thought I told you to clean up this mess. You can leave, too, if you like. You ingrates."

As Mom left our bedroom, Kim scrambled around in the pile, exchanging the shorts she was wearing for a pair of jeans.

"You don't have to come with me," I said, trying not to sound sniveling.

"I know. I *want* to come."

My sister's decision was an act of loyalty. But, more than that, she reveled in being involved in shit as much as she relished starting it. I never doubted whether she'd leave with me. Would I have joined her? Absolutely. The difference was that I would have tried to talk her out of it first.

We took the elevator down to Granny's apartment. The only reason I left was because I knew if ever there was a cool head, it was hers. She opened the door and then blocked it when I started to walk in.

"Your mother is exhausted," she said, as if rendering a verdict.

"She works very hard and she just called down and told me not to let you in."

Granny attempted to close the door and I shoved my foot on the plastic runner that led to the kitchen. Other runners crisscrossed her living room.

"Please, Granny."

Kim yanked the back of my shirt.

"Just go press your hair," Granny said. "And don't even think about going to your aunt's place. It's not safe outside at night for girls. Now move your foot."

"Please."

Kim whispered, "Girl, don't beg. Let's just go."

As my sister walked over to the elevator and pushed the down button, I backed up a few steps. Granny closed the door. Her peephole darkened.

While Kim and I walked through Lawless to 35th Street I couldn't help thinking that if Debra still lived in the building, we could have had a sleepover in her apartment and been nearby when Mom came to her senses.

A car alarm whooped in a staccato rant in the housing project, and Kim and I jumped.

"I wish a nigga would try something." Kim punched her palm.

Yet another crazy person.

Despite Granny's warning, we headed to Aunt Doris's place, about a mile north on King Drive. I was certain she'd take us in.

The sun had gone down and the sky was dark and splotchy, like navy-blue paint peeling. In the distance, we could hear the squeals of the "L" train and farther still, a white halo balanced above Comiskey Park, the light from a night baseball game.

At 35th Street and King Drive, the clock on the Supreme Life building showed a few minutes before nine.

"Let's go to Alco's first and get cupcakes and Twinkies," Kim said.

"You got money?"

"I don't need money."

"You should go back home if you're thinking about stealing."

Kim began to walk a few steps ahead, ignoring me.

We crossed the street to the store, passing the Victory Monument, a statue that stood in the middle of King Drive. It was created to honor a Black unit of the Illinois National Guard but now it honored the drunks who collapsed along its base and the pigeons that did their thing on its bronze relief panels.

Although Alco Drugs stocked some items that qualified as food and others as drugs, it was most popular for being a twenty-four-hour liquor store. During the day, the lights on its marquee competed with the sun. But after dark, they were a beacon. That night, a bare-chested man, completely out of his head, stood under the marquee fanning it with his shirt, attempting to put it out. As an instinct, I reached for Kim's hand, but she stepped away from me. I wanted to hurry past him, but she wanted to linger.

"Look at his puffy hands," Kim said. "He's a dope fiend."

"I don't need to see his hands to know that. How do *you* know?"

"I just know." She winked at me. "I know a lot of things."

My sister entered Alco's. The pungent scent of garbage and alcohol hung in the air. Street vendors, unaffiliated with the stores, sometimes set up shop outside them, inviting passersby to check out their wares: incense, irregular tube socks and pantyhose, hand lotions. By far, the loudest salesmen were the street preachers who hawked salvation behind a microphone that spit out static and feedback along with warnings of hellfire and eternal damnation. Most of the other vendors had made their peace with eternal damnation—since their present hell was sharing the sidewalk with preachers who harangued them.

When Kim came out, she slowed to listen, but I pulled her away.

"Come on. Let's go to Auntie's."

We were about a block away and passing the Griffin Funeral Home, where Candy Love's services had been held, when Kim extracted a Twinkie from inside her jeans.

"I thought I told you not to steal."

"I've got one mother," Kim said, biting open the wrapper. "One father. I don't need another."

"It's not like you listen to them."

"But it's their job to try," she said. "Not yours, big sister."

As soon as Aunt Doris opened her apartment door with tears in her eyes, I knew that Mom had called her, too. Still, I tried: "Can we please spend the night?"

She shook her head. "I'm sorry." Her voice wavered. When we were little, and Auntie would spank us—tap us on our butts, really—she would cry so much that we would feel sorry for her. I knew that Mom had to talk Aunt Doris into shutting the door on us. I was certain she pushed back because it wasn't in her to turn her nieces away.

Slowly, she closed the door.

Kim and I walked back to King Drive to the bus stop. The No. 3 King Drive bus would take us the six miles south to 80th Street and let us off directly in front of the taxi station where Dad worked. We had no other options. Somehow, I'd had the presence of mind to take my new bus pass with me when I left the apartment. I'd gotten it because I'd be riding the bus to high school. But I had no money for Kim. When the bus came, I pleaded with the driver to let her on for free. I told him that we'd been put out by a deranged woman and we needed help getting to our father's job, the Jiffy Cab Company.

"We can run in and get him to pay you, I promise," I said. "The bus will let us off directly in front of the taxi garage."

"I know where it is," the driver said gruffly.

Because the drivers tended to have an edge, I was certain that my tale of woe would fall flat. But as I spoke, the driver's eyes left me for my sister. And when I looked at her, I did a double take. With her downcast eyes and trembling bottom lip, her hands clasped as if in prayer, she could have won an Oscar.

The driver jerked his head toward the back. "Y'all holding up my damn bus."

We sat and Kim wiped her face.

The route was straight down King Drive to our father. I settled into a window seat as the city flicked by in a glittering blaze. At 65th Street and King Drive, we passed a motel and although it wasn't the one we'd lived in during Mom's pregnancy with Kim, that was where it once stood. Kim got up and sat in the seat in front of me, head lolling against the window. I stared at her reflection. What our mother didn't know about the letters Kim had squirreled away was that I had seen an earlier one about her fighting. We both had mailbox keys and when I saw the school's stationery, I opened the letter and confronted Kim about it. I'd gotten in her face and she'd shoved me, and I shoved her back. When she began to cry, I sat on the edge of my bed, pulled a pen from my book bag, and signed our mother's name with a short note: "My daughter understands what she did was wrong. She will not do it again." I knew that was a lie. But Kim had melted me with her watery eyes, as she had just done with the bus driver.

At 80th Street, the bus stopped in front of a muscular beige-brick building with cranberry trim. The taxi company sat surrounded by neat houses and, from the outside, appeared rather modest, especially at night. What stood out were the lights flashing around the red, white, and yellow sign: "Jiffy Taxi Cabs." Because the red garage door was always open, it was only at night that the drivers waiting around for calls could be seen sitting in front of a television set.

By the time Kim and I got off the bus, I'd forgotten the promise I'd made to the driver and maybe he had, too, because he opened the rear doors, let us out, and pulled off. We saw Dad sitting at the metal desk in the dispatcher's office, and Kim sprinted to him, pushing open the door and planting herself next to him. As the night manager, he wore a navy-blue smock with his initials embroidered on his breast pocket, which held several pencils that he sometimes sharpened with a switchblade. Although he dispatched cabs when the late-night dispatcher went on break, he spent the bulk of his night tending to the needs and complaints of drivers. He also had to manage the people, from businessmen to junkies, who wandered in from the street looking for a ride or just a way station. Rarely did my father sit down.

I stood at the window but didn't go inside. Dad was on a call, speaking into the base-station microphone and writing in a ledger.

"Ma'am, would you repeat your address?" His voice was deep and slightly muffled by the glass.

Kim stood beside him, so eager for him to hang up that she ripped a piece of paper from the ledger to write him a note. Behind them, a large, frayed map of the South Side was tacked to the wall. In front of them, four chairs lined the wall with the window. They were for walk-ins or drivers who just wanted to gossip.

When he got off the call, Kim greeted him as she usually did, by tackling him.

"Hey, Daddy!" she said, still holding on to his neck. "Guess what Mom did."

"You're a little ripe," he laughed, and twisted his nose. It always seemed as though he were fighting to hold in his laughter, but his daughter wheedled it out of him.

She sniffed her armpits. "No, I'm not," she giggled. "I washed."

Whether she had or not was always questionable.

I left the window to give my sister and father their moment and wandered to the garage area with its lingering smell of exhaust fumes and paint. The boss's office was on the left. But straight ahead, cast in superhero comic-book colors, was a cavernous receptacle where old red-and-yellow cabs and equally old cabdrivers came to rest. The men gathered in mismatched chairs in front of a black-and-white television mounted on the wall above a locker.

Dad walked toward me with Kim attached to him like an ornament.

"What's this I hear about your mama putting you out?"

"I told him," Kim said to me. "Mom's done lost her mind." My sister tended to mirror our father, taking long strides like him with her hands in her pockets, adopting his southern accent.

"She put me out because I wouldn't press my hair," I said.

"I had to come with her," Kim boasted.

"You didn't *have* to." I cut my eyes at my sister.

"What the hell?" he said, under his breath. He nodded toward the men. "The fellas would want you to say hi to them."

We walked up behind them. A man named Mr. Hayes was center stage and Dad didn't want to interrupt him.

"Li'l Johnnie said to me, 'Pops, you gotta help me move again.'" Mr. Hayes shook his head for emphasis. "I told that boy, 'Son, I've been at that college five times helping you change dorms. I'm done. I ain't lifting nothing heavier than my dick, you hear me?'"

"Hayes!" Dad exclaimed. "Don't you see my daughters right here?"

Mr. Hayes looked startled. "Oh, Lord, you know I ain't seen them girls."

Dad peeled my sister off him and trudged over to the boss's office, shutting the door. The office had large windows and I saw him sit behind the desk in the handsome leather chair. The first call clearly was to Betty. As Dad spoke, he slowly nodded and his gestures were of a cajoling, somewhat pleading variety. He was asking her to drive all the way into the city to pick us up and take us back to their house. Betty had been our stepmother for about seven years, and I knew Dad didn't have to plead. She loved us and, truth be told, we loved her, too.

Dad placed the phone down and yelled out, "She's on her way. Y'all be ready when she gets here."

The second call was to Mom. Elbow on the desk, he held the phone to his ear, bracing for an onslaught. His demeanor quickly changed. He shook his head a lot. I heard, "But . . . But . . ." a lot. She must have told him the same thing she told Granny and Auntie—to let us fend for ourselves—because the next thing I heard was, "Do you know it's almost midnight?"

Several times, he removed the phone from his ear and looked up toward the tin ceiling, kneading his forehead, gnashing his teeth.

The next morning Betty brought us back to the garage. Suffused with sunlight, the garage looked dull, less vibrant. Dad's shift had ended, and he sat in his car, waiting to take us to Lawless. Kim dove into the front seat. I climbed into the back. I looked at the clock on his dash and I knew Mom had already left for work. I wondered what might happen when she arrived home. Mom was known to nurse a grudge. Kim didn't care. Prattling on about nothing, she rode with her hand out the window, grabbing air.

Later that evening, when I heard Mom's keys in the door lock, I was in the kitchen with the hot comb on the stove, putting the finishing touches on my hair. I just wanted to put the entire matter to rest. Mom nodded when she saw me and said "Hello" in a formal, almost aristocratic way. She didn't mention what had happened the night before, not one single word. With her purse still dangling from her wrist, she washed her hands and began pulling pots from the cabinets and food from the refrigerator. After filling a pot of water at the sink, she turned on a burner and placed the pot on top. She then leaned against the counter waiting for the water to boil.

chapter twelve

The Academy Rewards

* * *

(Take One)

Thomas and I began our mornings riding three Chicago Transit Authority buses to Hyde Park Academy. Over the summer, he'd gotten his hair relaxed and cut into a feathery pompadour. He'd grown out his nails and when he pointed to a car he liked or waved at a driver he thought was handsome, the clear polish caught the light and made his hands look magnificent. High school was a new start and he was determined to inhabit his true self fully.

"I want to see the world," he said as we got off one bus and stood in front of a storefront that sold Polish sausages but had begun selling gyros.

"Some kids backpack through Europe while in college," I said. I touched his arm. "You and I are going to backpack through Europe. I think I want to be a writer."

"Not a doctor?" he asked.

"I don't know," I said, placing my head on his shoulder.

On the bus, Thomas and I never felt compelled to talk during the hour-long commute. We were content looking out the window or reading or daydreaming, the morning sun painting our eyelids orange. My biggest distraction was the teenaged girls who heaved themselves onto the 47th Street bus on their way to one of the city's public schools for pregnant students. During the early weeks of the school year, they sat scattered throughout the bus. But as they got to know one another, I marveled at how they clustered in the back rows, chatting and laughing as though their futures hadn't suffered a major blow. Thomas paid the girls no mind. But I eavesdropped on their conversations about their boyfriends, birth plans, and even baby showers, celebrations that were antithetical to Mom's warnings that a teen pregnancy would hobble Kim and me and be akin to a heavy curtain descending over our future. When the girls got off at their stop, I watched them file across the street, book bags jouncing against their backs, babies rounding out their bellies. The girls were saddled coming and going. Mom emphasized that the two loads could not coexist. I believed her and was determined to remain a virgin.

Hyde Park Academy, with its limestone facade and Grecian columns, spanned nearly the length of 62nd Street along Stony Island Avenue. Thomas and I were not in the same homeroom, and although as freshmen we took the same core classes—among them, English, algebra, and biology—the only period we shared was lunch. We were sitting in the cafeteria, eating from each other's plates, when a boy at the table next to ours started performing rudimentary magic tricks.

"Pick a card, any card," he said, fanning the deck like one of those Three-card Monte guys on the bus. Students stood around him, fixating on his hands.

I didn't have classes with him, but I'd seen him in the halls, running from one place to another, scooting past people saying, "Excuse me. Excuse me." He wasn't as handsome as one of my crushes, who cruised the hallways in his football jersey, or as debonair as another, who was tall and slightly bowlegged and had a smile that caught your words in your throat. No, this boy was lanky and wore pants that were a hair too short. He had light skin, a narrow face, and a ski-slope nose under a thick Afro.

"Who is that guy?" I asked Thomas. "He looks like a nerd but acts like a jock."

"Last week, a teacher called him obnoxious," Thomas said. "That's David Trice."

"Trice with a T, like Debra Trice?"

"Oh, yeah," he said in an "aha" way. Debra had left Doolittle before Thomas had gotten to know her well. But he knew her mother. "Yes, Trice—like Trice."

As the school year wore on, I continued to see David in the cafeteria. Maybe it was because of his last name that I watched him the way I'd watched Debra all those years ago. He was witty with a corny sense of humor and could expertly return an insult. When a girl who had an ample nose said his clothes looked like Garanimals, he shot back, calling her nose a two-flat apartment building. "How much for rent?"

Watching him reminded me that I hadn't heard from Debra. She had promised to call me to give me her new telephone number and address. I'd written her several letters, but they remained in my dresser drawer because I hadn't heard from her yet. In one letter, I wrote that Andrew had come home and was sober for about a month but then returned to his old ways. Mom told him she was done, and he left on a Sunday while Mom, Kim, and I were at church. He left a note apologizing to us. I was sad, but the good thing was that his leaving wasn't a surprise. I knew I just had to wait for the sadness to wash away. In another letter, I told Debra that Granny and Uncle Al had left Lawless and moved into a two-flat Andrew owned. (The building would remain in his name, but Mom would care for it.) It was located on a street called Normal and that's what we called it: *Normal*.

I was a week outside Christmas break and hunkered down in my bedroom working on a biology project when the phone rang. I answered it and heard, "Is this my long-lost friend?" Debra laughed, and I met her laughter with a scream.

"I can't talk long, Dawn," she said. "So much has happened."

"I thought you forgot about me," I said. The sentence escaped from me like a feather from a pillow. I hadn't planned to say it but suddenly my heart overflowed with joy. "How do you like corny ol' Indianapolis?"

"Well, it ain't so corny after all. When we got here, all everybody was talking about was the consent decree to desegregate the schools. We were bussed, Dawn, across town to Northwest High School."

"As in bussed to a white neighborhood school?"

"Yes, ma'am. On the first day, angry white folks with picket signs were waiting for us. The bus driver had to drive us to the back of the school, and we had to run inside."

"You had to have been scared to death."

"Girl, I'm from Chicago. I was ready for their asses."

Debra and I caught up on our families and all that we didn't say we promised to include in letters. When she gave me her telephone number and address, I wrote both in my biology book. But I didn't want to forget one thing: "There's a guy at school whose name is David Trice. Is he related to you? Trice isn't a common name."

"I don't think we have a David in our family but hold on." In a muffled voice, I heard her asking her father. "We don't know David Trice. But call me soon, okay? And ask David Trice if he's related to me."

"I will."

Throughout freshman year, I saw David sporadically. I didn't have any classes with him, and he was a blur, always hurrying through the halls with his friends. It never seemed the right time to ask him: *Are you related to my best friend?*

At the beginning of sophomore year, Thomas told me he'd been accepted into the Pilot Enrichment Program at the University of Chicago. It was a special program for college-bound students who came from high schools throughout the city. Students took classes at the university two days a week and attended their magnet courses at their home school the rest of the week. If Thomas had gotten in because he was smart, I knew I belonged there, too. David was also enrolled. Hyde Park Academy was a mile from the university, and I walked to Mandel Hall, one of the university's many austere Gothic buildings. Mandel housed the program and I'd arrived on a day when its students were taking classes.

When the school day ended, Thomas showed me around campus, beginning with the Midway Plaisance, where white students were playing soccer and baseball. We passed the buildings where Enrico Fermi led his Manhattan Project team; where Milton Friedman honed his free-market theories; and where a visiting Langston Hughes taught poetry to the university's laboratory students. The campus stood as an island of crenellated rooftops and white privilege that had cordoned itself off from the surrounding Black neighborhood. A long-standing tension had simmered between the two. The program was one of the university's attempts to smooth things over.

I filled out the application, had Mom sign it, and then ferried it between Hyde Park and the university to get all the other requisite signatures. When my homeroom teacher told me I'd been accepted, I found Thomas by his locker and we hugged. In addition to taking college-level courses, we would spend our Saturdays practicing college entrance exams and attending tutoring sessions.

That spring, David and I were paired to work together on an assignment crafting two macabre poems in the spirit of Edgar Allan Poe. David was smart, the type of student who aced midterms and finals. But he never turned in homework and that dragged down his grades. He also never took notes. I sat beside him in several classes and watched him draw. I kept pushing him to get going on his part of the assignment and he finally invited me to his house on a Saturday after class to work on it.

He lived in Chicago's Beverly neighborhood, sometimes called Beverly Hills because it was one of the few areas of the city where the ground had even the slightest undulation. On Sundays when Andrew didn't have to work, he had driven Mom, Kim, and me around to see different neighborhoods. We'd come here and slowed down, ogling the stately Longwood Drive mansions sitting on hills. Andrew had said they were owned by white folks with old and new money. The neighborhood was also home to a healthy portion of City of Chicago workers who had to reside in the city. They lived in the more-than-comfortable, suburban-like homes. Seeing Beverly by car was nothing like seeing it on foot.

As David and I walked to his house from the bus stop, I only caught fragments of what he said. I was enraptured by the pumpkins and cornstalks adorning the front porches and stoops. The white children diving in and out of piles of raked leaves. The gingerbread-like homes that seemed to come straight out of a fairy tale.

"Here we are," David said. We had arrived at a beige-brick Georgian on a corner lot. He jogged up a few steps and opened the front door.

Entering the foyer, my chest swelled as I scanned the large living room to my left and dining room to the right. Straight ahead was a staircase leading to the second floor. Beside the stairs was a quaint nook with a desk and chair.

"How long have you lived here?" I asked, trying to restrain my gawking.

"We moved in last year," he said, draping my coat across the desk.

A fair-skinned man, taller than any human I'd ever seen up close, came from around a corner with a kitchen towel flung over his shoulder. "Dawn-O!" he bellowed, extending his hand.

"Wow, how tall—" I started.

"Six foot seven," David said, accustomed to being quizzed on his father's height.

"I hear you live in Lawless Gardens," Mr. Trice said. "I have friends at Supreme Life." David had told me that his father was a vice president at the Chicago branch of the Atlanta Life Insurance Company. "I lived in your neighborhood when I came up to Chicago from Paducah, Kentucky, in the late 1940s, before Lawless was built." He motioned for us to follow him. "I fixed a pot of chili just for you."

"He makes chili almost every weekend," David said, correcting the record.

In the kitchen, a built-in table held four place settings. The bowls and glasses were huge. Mr. Trice pulled out a chair so that I could sit. A pinball machine was on the sun porch across from the kitchen and I'd never seen one in someone's home.

"What if she doesn't like chili?" Mrs. Trice said, entering the kitchen. She wore her hair in a short press-and-curl. David looked like her and was about her height, five foot eight. Because I was sitting, she bent down to hug me.

"I like chili," I said with a nod.

"Have you started thinking about college?" she asked, sitting next to me.

"I like Berkeley." It sounded more like a question.

"I went to Lincoln University in Missouri and Jim went to Winston-Salem State University in North Carolina. Our two older boys are at Morris Brown. It's in Atlanta. They're all HBCUs."

My confusion must have shown on my face.

"Historically Black colleges and universities," she said.

"Oh, I see." I never knew they existed.

"She won't tell you she has a master's degree in social work from the University of Chicago," Mr. Trice added proudly. "It ain't an HBCU, but it's impressive enough."

We finished lunch and David and I worked in the dining room for a few hours on our poem. As it started to get dark, I told him that I had to leave because I didn't like being on the bus so late by myself. He said that his father had planned to take me home. Once inside Mr. Trice's Cadillac, I gushed about how beautiful their home and the neighborhood were.

"I wish I lived in a place like this," I said, still starry-eyed. "It's just perfect."

Mr. Trice was quiet. Instead of driving toward the expressway, he detoured to a nearby park and stopped in front of a basketball court.

"What's wrong with those basketball hoops?" he asked me.

Light pooled in a couple of places around the court and it took me a few seconds to detect the problem. "There are no nets."

"A month after we moved in, David and three other Black kids who live here were playing basketball when a bunch of white boys jumped them. The next day the nets were cut down. They'd rather not play themselves than allow us to play."

As if to save face, David said, "I fought as best I could."

"My son had just turned fourteen. When I was fourteen in 1939, my friends and I would go to the park and steal a swig from the 'Whites Only' water fountain. We'd take off running." He laughed at the memory. "I was taller than the other boys, gangling, and the police would see me loping off and report me to my mother. My father passed away when I was seven. Mom told me I only had one, maybe two more summers before they'd do more than warn me." Mr. Trice grew quiet, his face fading in and out of the light. "You said you wish you could live in a place like this. I believe you will one day. I only wish by then nobody will be trying to run you out."

chapter thirteen

The Academy Rewards

* * *

(Take Two)

Someone was banging on our door. Kim didn't hear it at first. Wearing headphones, she was plunking on the keyboard set Mom had gotten her. Kim's sixth-grade teacher had recommended that Mom buy Kim a musical instrument, hoping it might help my sister focus and inspire her academically. What it inspired was Kim spending hours teaching herself how to play, rather than completing homework.

I motioned for Kim to remove her headphones. "Can you get that?" I was lying down, having just come in from my summer job answering phones and sanitizing instruments for our family dentist.

Kim went to the door and stayed for a few minutes. When she returned, she said, "It's for you." She sat back down on the keyboard's bench and slid on her headphones.

"Who is it?"

"Some old lady. I think she's from our church. She doesn't hear well."

Annoyed, I hurried to the door.

"Hello?" I said, peering out of the peephole. I didn't see anyone. Slowly, I opened the door and looked down the hall. I still didn't see anyone, but I noticed the door to the stairwell was open. "Hello?" I said, walking toward it. I saw Debra, her back against the door with one eye open, the other pinched shut like a kid playing hide-and-seek in the middle of a playground. We hugged and screamed so loud that two neighbors opened their doors.

"Everything's okay," Debra chortled. "We haven't seen one another in—"

"Two whole years," I said to the neighbors as they closed their doors.

Kim smiled from our doorframe. I realized that although she hadn't known who was knocking, she and Debra had quickly conspired to surprise me.

"Look at you, Dawn!" Debra said. "Look at your hair!"

It was pulled back into a braid and pinned up to be professional. Debra, being Debra, plucked the two bobby pins holding it up, allowing the braid to shimmy down my back.

The only thing that seemed different about Debra was her hair, which was cut into a chic bob. She wore tight Jordache jeans and a plain black T-shirt. Watching her walk into the apartment felt surreal.

"Everything looks the same," she said, as the three of us passed through the living room to our bedroom. "I miss Lawless, Dawn. I miss you guys!"

Kim sat on the bench while Debra stretched out across my bed.

"Why are you in town?" I said, sitting at the foot of the bed and crossing my legs.

"To party," she said. "I rode up with a couple of girlfriends. They're a bit older."

Debra crawled to the head of the bed to look out the window.

"On our last night here, Mom and Dad allowed us to stay outside well after dark to say our goodbyes," she said. "Later that night, I got up and saw all the boxes with my dinosaurs and comic books and I walked over to my window and cried uncontrollably."

It occurred to me that I had no idea who lived in apartment 1205. It still felt empty, like a sealed-off room in a large house no one ever disturbed.

"How do you feel about the move now?" Kim asked, her headphones resting on her neck.

"We still have a few racial flare-ups at the school and at this burger joint down the street, but nobody bothers me." She looked at her watch. "Why don't both of you come with me to my uncle's apartment? My friends are waiting for me downstairs."

"I'll get dressed," I said, happy to spend more time with her.

"I'm good," Kim said. "I've got things to do."

Debra looked at me, surprised. I shrugged. "She has her own friends now."

I picked through my closet and found a casual navy-blue dress and held it in front of me. Debra shook her head. I retrieved a pair of Levi's and a tank top and held them up. Debra and I both nodded.

A hatchback was idling in front of the building. Debra opened the back door and got in. I followed. She introduced me to Keesha, the driver, and Bunny, in the passenger seat. They had clear complexions and straight hair, the type of girls who, no doubt, were not just pretty but popular.

As we left Lawless, en route to downtown, Debra cooed at Doolittle, despite its new graffiti-scarred facade and chipped concrete steps.

"That's where Dawn and I met," she said, patting my hand. "You remember we used to make fake fingernails by pouring Elmer's glue into oval shapes on the inside of our desks. We let them dry overnight and then glued them to our nails."

I laughed. "Mrs. Love called us creative before making us take them off."

Debra instructed Keesha on a detour, pointing out every right and left turn until we arrived in Lake Meadows at our ledge. The sun had tucked behind the building and the ledge was barely visible.

"There it is!" Debra said. "When Dawn and I were kids, we came here all the time. We called it our love spot."

"Why a love spot?" Bunny asked, pretending to care about a panorama only Debra and I could see.

Debra looked perplexed. "Dawn, why did we call it that?"

"I have no idea," I said. I stared at the area. The streetlight had come on and we could see the concrete shelf.

Debra told Keesha to head north and showed them Pershing Elementary, which, unlike Doolittle, was still well-maintained and manicured.

When we arrived at Debra's uncle's eighth-floor apartment, he was in the kitchen styling a woman's hair. The apartment was appointed in pastels and smelled of weed and cigarette smoke. Debra and her friends sat on the sofa and fired up their own joint.

"Wanna hit?" Debra asked.

"No, I'm good," I said. I had tried marijuana, but I hated the way it made my head feel. I didn't like not being in control.

Diana Ross's "I'm Coming Out" filled the room and we all got up to dance, arms swaying, hips gyrating. Debra and her friends passed around another joint and I walked over to the window, looking out onto a downtown studded with lights.

An hour passed and I pulled Debra to the side. "Girl," I said. "You know Mom."

"You've got to go," Debra said. "Mrs. Turner doesn't play."

I waved goodbye to everyone and Debra walked me to the door.

"I'll see you next time, friend, okay?" she said.

"You'd better call me." We hugged for a long time before letting go.

On the bus home, I thought about the pregnant girls who boarded along my commute to and from Hyde Park. Like them, Debra and her friends scared me. They were another cautionary tale. I didn't want to judge them so much as outrun them.

During senior year, I took a slew of advanced-placement courses at Hyde Park and continued my instruction at the University of Chicago. On weekends, we learned classical music, along with dances from other countries, and watched artsy foreign-language films. I wrote Debra, telling her that I'd applied to three universities: Northwestern University, where Thomas also had applied; the University of Chicago; and the University of Illinois at Urbana. Although Northwestern and the University of Chicago were private schools and highly selective, I wanted to go to the University of Illinois. The state's flagship public school, it was far away enough that my family would think twice before dropping by and close enough that I could easily come home in an emergency. Although David's mother had encouraged me to apply to an HBCU, there were none in Illinois and I worried that I wouldn't be able to afford out-of-state tuition. What I didn't tell Debra was that before I dropped each envelope in the mailbox, I'd recited the scripture that ended every Sunday service at my church: *In all thy ways acknowledge God and he will direct thy path.*

She called to tell me she'd received my letter.

"Have you decided what college you're going to?" I asked her.

"I'm going to hold off a year," she replied.

I couldn't fathom delaying college. Waiting to hear back about my applications consumed me. It was all I thought about in school, in church as I swayed in the choir, at David's house. Every day, after school, I entered the lobby and went directly to our mailbox. Sometimes Kim got the mail and it perturbed me that I had to wait until I got upstairs to see what she left on the dining table. The letter from the University of Chicago came first. It was thin, a rejection letter. That was fine. It was too close to home anyway. But when Northwestern's rejection came, I worried that I'd been too confident.

In the middle of the night, Mom peeped into our bedroom and saw me staring at the ceiling in the dark. "You're about to worry yourself into a stroke," she said. "You know they run in your family on your father's side."

After Christmas break, I opened the mailbox and saw a large, thick envelope wedged inside. I used both hands to pull it out, and when I did, I smiled at its heft. I ripped it open there in the lobby. With the word "Congratulations," I jumped up and down and then went upstairs to call Mom at work.

"I got into the University of Illinois!"

"Praise the Lord! Baby, you just hit the lottery!"

My high school graduation was to be held downtown on a June evening at Orchestra Hall. Each graduate received six tickets, two each for seats on the first, second, and third levels. There was no question regarding where Mom would sit—on the first floor—next to Granny. My plan was for Dad and Betty to take the second-floor tickets and for Kim and Aunt Doris to be on the third floor. But when I called Dad from the kitchen phone to explain the seating arrangement, he got quiet. I could hear *Nightline* in the background and anchorman Ted Koppel's voice.

"The seats are just fine on the second floor," I tried to assure him.

"If I'm not on the first floor, you all can go on without me," he said sternly.

Mom was sitting up in her bed when I entered her room and told her. She looked me squarely in the eye: "Under no circumstances will I sit next to that man."

I didn't bother calling Dad back and trying to persuade him, but the next day I drove Mom's car to the taxi garage in the middle of the afternoon and left an envelope with two tickets on the dispatcher's desk with his name on it. I hoped he would do the right thing, but my gut knew he wouldn't show up and that meant Betty wouldn't either. And yet, that didn't stop me from looking for them as I stood in an aisle in Orchestra Hall waiting to cross the stage. I searched the seats in the balcony trying to see beyond the blinding stage lights, knowing deep down there was no need to look.

After the ceremony, I picked my way through the crowd on the sidewalk until I saw Mom, Granny, Aunt Doris, and Kim, each dressed as though it were Sunday morning. My graduation gown folded over my arm, I stood with them in my tea-length, cream-colored lace dress. Granny had seen me gaping at a similar one in her Neiman Marcus catalogue and asked her cousin, a seamstress, to make it for me.

"The University of Illinois at Urbana," Mom said, hugging me. "Here she comes."

"My nigga," Kim whispered in my ear. "If you don't get no bigga . . ."

David and his family found us, and we all squeezed together, posing for pictures. When David put his arm around my waist, Aunt Doris nudged Mom. David and I had shared our first kiss on prom night, and we'd decided to date, though it would be long distance. He was heading to his mother's alma mater, Lincoln University.

Thomas, who was on his way to Northwestern, joined us in photos as well.

I watched Mom talk to my teachers and Mr. and Mrs. Trice on a sidewalk that shimmered under the streetlights.

Later that night, as Kim and I stood in our bedroom undressing, she grabbed my arm. "I hate your father," she said. He belonged to me when he did something wrong. "I thought for sure he would change his mind and come, didn't you?"

"You don't have to hate—"

"I hate him," she said emphatically. "I'm never speaking to him again."

Mom surprised us, entering our bedroom and sitting at the foot of Kim's bed, which she never did. Looking at the mess on Kim's side of the room, Mom had begun saying she needed a tetanus shot before touching anything.

"In elementary school, I skipped two grades," she said. Kim plopped down next to her. "That's why I graduated high school at sixteen, the same year your aunt graduated. This burned her ass. Your grandmother asked us if we wanted to go to college and Doris's exact words were: 'Mama, don't waste money on me. I barely made it out of high school.'"

I wondered where this story was going because Mom had told us this before.

"But me? I leapt at the chance. I enrolled in Woodrow Wilson Junior College and because Doris and I slept on a let-out couch in the living room, I studied in the bathroom. Doris got a job at a hospital on the cleaning staff. Two years later, I graduated cum laude with my associate's degree in business administration." She laughed at herself. "All I wound up doing with it was minding other people's business."

I wondered if our mother might be considering returning to school. Over the years, countless half-completed applications to local universities lay on the dining room table collecting dust. But she looked at me with her hands folded in her lap.

"Tonight, three of your teachers came up to me and said you told them that you were the first in your immediate family to go to college. Baby, you are not the first to go."

Shame burned across my face. "Mom, I'm so sorry. I only meant I was the first to go to a four-year institution."

She nodded, patting my knee. "I know, baby."

Then she turned to Kim and smiled. "That brain of yours would be a waste if you don't go to a four-year institution, too. I never want either of you to get to where you have far more regrets than wants and your dreams no longer matter."

She stood and pointed to my graduation gown.

"Now, don't forget to hang that up."

chapter fourteen

"Pray for Your Sister"

. . .

I knew immediately something was wrong. I came home from my summer job at the dentist's office and Granny was sitting on our living room sofa. Since she moved, Mom, Kim, and I typically visited her at Normal.

"Come in and sit down," she said, patting the sofa cushion.

"Is everything okay?" I sat, quickly surveying the living room for a clue.

"Your mother just learned that Miss Kim hasn't been going to school right and lying, saying her mother was sick," Granny said. "Her grades are fair to middlin'. She's in the bedroom with your sister right now, tearing it up."

Mom had been conducting random searches of our bedroom ever since she discovered the letters in Kim's mattress. And if she found something untoward, she left it on the dining table so that it greeted us when we came home. A couple of times when Andrew was with us, empty bottles of Smirnoff and Tanqueray lined the table. Now it held a wallet and a makeup bag. My sister had completed her freshman year at Hyde Park Academy. She was not in the magnet program, although she could have been if she applied herself. I'd hardly seen Kim at school, but I'd been so focused on my senior year that I never thought much about it.

"I know the plan is for you to leave for college in a couple of months," Granny said. She patted her foot the way she'd always done while sitting at the table. "But your mother can't afford it. I want you to take the bus downtown to Carson's and apply for a job as a saleswoman."

I already had my financial-aid package, which included grants, loans, and work-study. But Granny didn't know that. It was easier to just say, "I understand."

Mom came out from the back, her face scrunched in anger.

"I took that heifer's mailbox key away from her," she said, slamming four letters onto the dining table. She turned to me: "Has she been using your key?"

"No," I said. "Absolutely not." Then it occurred to me that I often left my keys on the hook beside my bed. She certainly had access to them. But I didn't tell Mom.

"They're all addressed to your father," Mom said. "*Excessive truancies* is what the woman wrote. That girl is wearing a hole in my patience."

Why Kim hadn't tossed the letters made absolutely no sense. Why the letters were addressed to Dad is another story. My sister recognized early on from the meetings Dad attended at Doolittle that teachers loved fathers who were involved in their children's lives. Not many came up to the school, and teachers tended to give students with dads who advocated for their kids more latitude, believing problems would be solved at home.

When Mom called the school and asked why no one thought to call her, Kim's counselor assured her that he had tried but apparently Kim had intercepted the calls.

Mom picked up the wallet and pulled out an ID. "You see this?" She walked over and handed me the card. "It's fake. What the hell does she need with it if not for mischief?"

The Kim in the picture looked very different from the fifteen-year-old we knew, who hadn't grown out of being a disheveled tomboy. She and I had a similar body type, tall and thin with no hips. But, unlike me, she had huge breasts, which she concealed under baggy sweatshirts. Also, unlike me, she had a jiggly butt, and when Mom noticed it, she clucked: "Girl, you need to get some law and order about your ass."

Kim rarely wore makeup or her hair down. But in the photograph on the ID, she looked like a younger version of Mom, beautiful with her mauve lip gloss and shimmery eyeshadow and her hair in curls. This woman, a stranger, was born in 1962, making her twenty-one. Her name was "Kandie Turner."

"I just told your father about her grades." Mom sighed loudly. "He told me that a few months ago, one of his drivers saw Kim on 43rd Street at a pool hall during school hours. Your father talked to her about it and she promised him she wouldn't go back. He doesn't know his way around a promise—why does he think she would?" Mom sniffed the air. "She *promised*."

When I entered our bedroom, Kim was sweeping her side of the room. You could always tell how much trouble she was in based on her sudden commitment to tidiness. When she saw it was me and not Mom or Granny, she propped the broom against the wall. I walked up to her.

"You want to mess up?" I whispered, pissed off. "You go right ahead. But your grandmother is talking about me not going to college because of you."

"Girl, you know Granny goes nuclear," Kim said, looking at me utterly carefree. "And, I've said before, I only have two parents, sister."

This was the fundamental difference between my sister and me. If I did something I wasn't supposed to do, I didn't want to get caught, therefore I didn't do it for long. I didn't want to be punished but, most of all, I did not want to disappoint Mom. Kim didn't care about any of that. The moment mattered most. She knew whatever punishment Mom meted out had a shelf life. Afterward, she could resume business as usual.

Kim spent the next couple of months following Mom's rules to the letter, staying close to home and accounting for her whereabouts when she was away. Mom told Aunt Doris that Kim was "an outdoor cat pretending to be a model citizen."

That summer, I worked during the week and hung out with David on the weekend. When he came to our apartment, he treated the model citizen as an equal rather than a little sister. He invited her to walk to the lake with us or to Alco's for a snack. July flew past and by mid-August, my sister seemed to be thriving. I was relieved because it was time for me to leave for college and I didn't want to have to worry about her.

In our bedroom, my side of the room was now sparse. My trunk and several boxes of my things cluttered the living room. The night before I left, Kim lay in her bed as I sat on mine folding clothes and packing. She got up and edged in next to me, both of us feeling unmoored. We were about to be separated for longer than we'd ever been.

"When I'm gone, don't touch my shit," I teased her.

She leaned against me. "You ain't got no shit. Now everything in this piece is mine." She kissed my cheek, got back in her bed, and faced the wall.

"Be like that, then," I said. "Like I care."

Dad wanted to be at the university before the noon check-in. He told Mom, Aunt Doris, Granny, and me to be ready by 8:30. At 8:25, he was ringing the intercom. Kim was still in bed and her back was to me. I jumped on her bed.

"I'm outta here." She didn't respond. "I know you're not asleep."

When she still didn't respond, I started dragging my things to the elevator. One of the janitors was waiting to help me carry boxes downstairs because Mom wouldn't allow Dad to come up. After loading everything in the car, I returned to our room one last time. I placed my head on my sister's.

Finally, she sat up and wrapped her arms around my neck. But she didn't open her eyes. "Don't leave me with that woman. When she's old and crazy, how will we know?"

"We'll know." Feeling her chest quake, I pulled back and saw that she was crying through closed eyes. I started to cry, too. "Are you going to look at me?"

"I can't stand to see you leave me. Just go. Please."

I left our bedroom and it hit me that for the first time in my life, my roommate wouldn't be my sister. Going to college meant I had to leave her and home. Until that day, both had seemed like minor sacrifices on the way to my future. But now I felt ripped apart.

The elevator reached the lobby and the doors opened to a small but cheering crowd, people who had watched me grow up: the janitor who had told Mom when he saw me in the hall during her work

hours with friends instead of doing my homework; the little old ladies who often asked me about my grades and told me they were
praying for me; men who reprimanded me if I failed to say "Good
morning" while boarding the elevator. These neighbors, in their
own ways, had helped raise me and were invested in my success.
They wanted nothing more than for me to thrive.

Mom, Dad, Granny, and Aunt Doris stood near the windows,
watching residents clap me on my shoulder or pat my back as I
passed. A few people pressed folded $5 or $10 bills in my hand.

"Knock their socks off," one of the janitors said.

Beaming, I couldn't have felt prouder or thanked everyone
enough.

When Dad finished loading his and Mom's cars, I jumped into
the back seat of Mom's. Granny was in the front seat. Aunt Doris
rode with my father. Dad had given me a maroon Chevy Caprice, a
refurbished taxi, and the plan was for me to drive it back to school
after Christmas break. As we made our way around the turning circle and then to the 35th Street opening, I got on my knees and looked
out the back window, up at my bedroom. Sure enough, Kim was
standing there. I waved at her. She lifted her hand and then stepped
out of sight.

During the drive to Urbana, I got lost in the monotonous landscape along Interstate 57. I had come down for orientation and
learned that the University of Illinois at Urbana had 34,500 students
and African Americans made up only 3.4 percent of the student
body. I entered on the early wave of affirmative action through the
university's Educational Opportunities Program. All I knew of my
white peers was what I'd gleaned from *The Brady Bunch*. I was sure
that what they knew of Black folks, they'd seen on their late-night
newscasts.

When we arrived at Blaisdell Hall, Dad got a dolly and Mom,
Granny, and Aunt Doris checked out the room and the floor, watching young white women passing down the hallway.

"Not many Colored," Granny said, peeping her head out of my
door.

My family stayed for a couple of hours, helping me settle in, and Dad looked down at his watch. "I've got to get on back," he said. "I work tonight."

"I guess it's time for us to go," Mom said, rolling her eyes.

I walked the four of them down to their cars. When I hugged Dad, he slipped me fifty dollars. I walked back to Mom and hugged her and Granny. When I hugged Auntie, she started to cry.

"Good Lord," Mom said to her sister. "She'll be home for Thanksgiving."

"I know," Aunt Doris said. "Don't forget to be good or to call home."

I watched both cars until I couldn't see them anymore, then I walked the four blocks to the open house being held at the Afro-American Cultural Center. It was a two-story Dutch Colonial Revival just east of the quad. As soon as I entered, I saw a mural of two Black girls on the wall a few feet away. Imagining they were sisters, I immediately felt homesick. The wall partitioned the lounge into two areas. A few students sat on a couple of sofas. But mostly everyone—about fifty students—were either sitting in folding chairs or milling about when a man, balding with a scraggly beard, commanded the floor. He introduced himself as Bruce Nesbitt, the center's executive director.

"Look at the people around you," he said. "You all belong here. You might think someone did you a favor by letting you in. It's okay to be grateful. But you earned a spot and you do have a responsibility to do your best."

Mr. Nesbitt encouraged us to sit in the front rows of the lecture halls and not be shy about asking and answering questions. He urged us to acknowledge one another with a head nod while passing along the quad.

"And sit together in the cafeteria if you want. They do it. Why can't you?"

When he finished speaking, I walked over to a glass case that held flyers and old issues of the *Griot*, the cultural center's newspaper. I picked up the March-April issue: "Washington Bids to Become Chicago's First Black Mayor." The story had been published before the April election because Harold Washington won. This was no small task in a city so riven and racially polarized that the *Wall Street Journal*, in a few months, would call Chicago "Beirut on the Lake."

I started reading and a young man walked over, introducing himself as Taylor Fuller III.

"Are you interested in writing for us? I'm the new editor."

"I've never written a news article before."

"It's my job to help."

My first assignment was to cover the commemoration of the twentieth anniversary of the March on Washington. It was being held in Douglass Park in the neighboring town's African American community. Taylor walked up to me and pointed out a white woman wearing a red T-shirt with the Delta Sigma Theta sorority letters and crest.

"A white woman who belongs to a Black sorority," he said. "Go interview her."

No one in my immediate family had been in a sorority or fraternity, so I didn't know that Delta Sigma Theta was founded in 1913 at Howard University. That a white woman was a member made her both an anomaly and a minority. But the story really wasn't about her, it was about the march. I quoted participants talking about the need for peace and jobs and better education. The article appeared on the front page of the *Griot*'s September-October 1983 issue and included a photo of me interviewing the white Delta woman. Rev. Martin Luther King Jr. called seeing one's name in print "the vitamin A to our ego." My inaugural story was just that for me. I loved talking to people I didn't know, collecting their stories and laying it out in my own words.

The cultural center served as my respite, the one place on campus where I didn't stand out because I was Black. I had a job at a clothing store to earn extra money and my class schedule seemed manageable. My transition into college life felt seamless until I was in the lounge area of my residence hall one evening, studying with four white classmates. I was wearing shorts and I noticed one of them staring at my bare legs.

I stared back at her. "What?"

She was sheepish. "I'm just wondering: Do Black girls not shave their legs?"

"I don't shave mine."

Seeing the shock and awe on their faces, I realized that Mom had never mentioned one word about shaving my legs. She was a general when it came to hygiene, which she made clear with her Supreme Life Insurance Company coin purse prop. Regarding the hair under my arms, all she said was, "You're really hairy and you don't want to be funky, so put on a lot of deodorant."

Another girl said, "My mother would kill me if I didn't shave."

Annoyed to be under scrutiny like a lab rat, I asked if we could return to studying. Suddenly self-conscious, I kept looking down at my legs.

Yet another thing I didn't know.

During my weekly call home, I didn't tell Mom about this. However, I did tell her that my rhetoric professor gave the class an assignment to interview someone we met on the street. I wanted to return to the area where the March on Washington commemoration had been held, so I called the bus information line.

"I told him I wanted the best route to get to Douglass Park and he got quiet," I said. "He then asked me, 'Are you sure you want to go to the Colored part of town?' I told him, 'Sir, I am *Colored*.'"

"Bastard," Mom laughed. "You answered right, baby."

Ordinarily, Mom was greedy for details about my college experience. When she didn't follow up with a barrage of questions, I could tell she was distracted.

"How's your other daughter?" I knew that the model citizen had begun to falter early in the new school year.

"She's doing better," Mom said weakly.

I didn't believe her. "How is she really, Mom?"

"Kim's being Kim."

Mom said that my sister had been skipping school and staying out later and later. Mom gave her ultimatum after ultimatum, but nothing was working. Kim would cry and apologize and say that she lost track of time or she was with someone who had a flat tire, or she tried to call but got a busy signal. Her excuses were limitless. My mother was desperate. The only thing she hated more than feeling desperate was showing it. She started driving around the neighborhood looking for Kim. More and more Mom ended our conversations with "Pray for your sister."

"I always do, Mom," I said.

"Pray I don't kill her."

That Thanksgiving, when I returned home for the first time, I was worried that Mom *would* kill Kim.

I rode home with a friend, and she dropped me off in front of the building. I was surprised to see Mom waiting in the lobby. I entered the first door and Mom opened the second. It hurt me to see how much her eyelids drooped and how much weight she'd lost. Her coat hung off her shoulders and she looked like she'd been emptied out.

"That's my baby." I dropped my bags and she took me in her arms. Pulling away, she said, "You've made it safely and now I'm going somewhere. I'll be back."

"Going to look for Kim?"

"You mind your business and I'll mind mine." She tried to sound lighthearted.

"I'll take my things upstairs and I'll be right back. I'll ride with you."

"You're the one who's been up late cramming for tests."

"Nope," I said as I boarded the elevator. "I'm fine. Don't move."

When I returned to the lobby, Mom was in her car in front of the building. She had told me that Lawless's chain-link fence had been torn down and replaced by a sturdier black wrought-iron one, yet another symbol that the housing project was deteriorating. We left Lawless and, as we drove along the new fence, I got to see it up close. Outside the development, I was surprised by how different the neighborhood looked or, rather, how I saw Bronzeville differently. Everybody tells you about the "freshman 15," those extra pounds that stick to you from chowing down on cafeteria food. But my transformation was of another kind. I wasn't prepared for returning home and feeling like my community was not the place I remembered. It occurred to me that if I'd sketched a portrait of my neighborhood before I left and another when I returned, it would have seemed as though two different people had seen two different places. As Mom drove through the housing project, the decay—"blight" was the word one professor had used—seemed far more pronounced.

"Forced to live like dogs," Mom said. "How do you expect people to act?"

It wasn't that she didn't know what was going on. Sentinel-like, Mom watched the project from our living room window: The new generation of nuns from Holy Angels passing through groups of young toughs, parting bodies. The young women who held their children tightly. The others who allowed toddlers to dart into the street or play in what Mom called the patchy I'm-trying-as-hard-as-I-can-goddamn-it grass below.

That night, when a young boy with a clothesline lassoed something protruding from the bricks and began to swing from it, she said, "That's that bad little boy who's always climbing things. He'd tear Jesus off the cross."

I looked at the way Mom angled close to the steering wheel, head on a swivel. It hurt to see her like that.

"Mom, maybe it's time you put your foot down." I regretted the words as they shot out of my mouth. "I don't mean—"

"You think I haven't?" she said. "Your sister is fifteen years old and should be too old to be spanked. I've punished her. I've threatened to put her out. Your father has talked to her."

"I'm sorry," I said. "I know you're doing the best you can."

After driving around for an hour, we gave up on finding Kim and returned home.

Lawless had installed a closed-circuit video system and whenever someone buzzed the intercom, residents could turn to a designated television channel to see a grainy black-and-white image of the person in the lobby. That night, Mom kept it on, just staring at it, despite the poor resolution, hoping to see Kim entering the building. Mom didn't believe Kim was on drugs, but nobody could understand the rebellion.

The next night, around midnight, Mom was asleep, and I was sitting in the living room when I heard keys in the locks. I ran to the door, wedging my foot against it.

"Do you still live here?" I said. I could feel Kim trying to push the door open.

"What up, Sis!" Kim said cheerfully. "Welcome home."

"This isn't your home."

She got quiet, then began to push harder. "Girl, open the fucking door!"

"Why? You've got Mom looking like shit, worried about you!" I yelled.

Gathering her robe, Mom hurried up behind me. She yanked me away and when Kim crossed the threshold, grabbed her by the collar.

"Get your ass in here," Mom said in a raspy voice. She looked at me. "Both of you, waking up the neighbors."

She guided Kim to the living room and Kim jerked away. Mom walked up on Kim. My sister and I had long been taller than our mother, but she'd never been shy about getting in our faces. To defuse the situation, we were always expected to look away or step back. But Kim did neither. She stood flat-footed, glaring at Mom with a scalding intensity. It was a flagrant test of wills that I'd never seen before. Her arms dangled at her side, but I was shocked to see that she'd balled up her fists. The moment felt combustible and my sister seemed to be on the brink of something that until now had been inconceivable. I thought Kim could actually strike our mother.

I felt a spasm of rage as I ran into the kitchen and dialed the police.

"My sister is causing a disturbance," I spoke loudly so Kim could hear me. I wanted to teach her a lesson. "Yes, please come."

I hung up and returned to the living room. Mom and Kim looked stunned.

"You called the police on me?" Kim's face twitched with anger.

By the time the two officers—one Black, the other white—knocked on our door, the situation had calmed down. Mom and Kim sat in the living room talking. I stood in the hallway explaining to the officers what had transpired. I felt horrible when they still asked to speak to Kim. I called her, and both she and Mom came to the door.

The Black officer beckoned my sister to him and said, "Let's go downstairs."

"What the hell for?" Mom grabbed Kim's wrist, trying to hem her in.

"Ma'am, we're just going to have a conversation," the white officer said.

He took Kim by the elbow. Mom and I stood in the doorway as Kim looked over her shoulder at us. She and the two officers began walking down the hall and my sister complied even though now I, however irrational, didn't want her to. As they reached the elevator, Mom snatched her coat from the closet and put it on over her robe. We followed behind them. Downstairs, my mother and I watched from the lobby window as Kim slouched in the back seat of the squad car for about fifteen minutes. The interior lights shone brightly, and we could see Kim nodding. I recognized her look of fake contrition as the Black officer wagged his finger. Later, she told us that the men lectured her about the dangers of breaking curfew and not going to school. It was a sort of *Scared Straight* exercise that would have been utterly humiliating to each of us if it hadn't been the middle of the night. Now it was just plain ol' humiliating. Mom nursed a low-grade contempt for the security guards because she said they sometimes saw her struggling with grocery bags and wouldn't press the button on the side of the desk to buzz her in. The worst ones mimed sliding a key in the lock and turning it.

Now the security guard rose from his desk to join us at the window. "What y'all looking at?" he asked nicely.

"None of your goddamn business!" Mom snapped.

He sat down. Mom's face was doleful, and she had her hands in her coat pockets. I imagined they were balled into fists. She did that when she was angry or disappointed, sad or dispirited. She was each of those things in that moment.

On the elevator ride back to our apartment, I pushed the button to the eleventh floor while my mother and sister stood as far away from me as possible in such a confined space. In calling the police, I'd not only been disloyal, I had crossed a line. Mom held her coat collar cinched around her neck as she stared up at the number panel. Kim stared at it, too, but tears began to fall. These were real tears. Not the ones she would have manufactured for the police, if needed. As she angrily flicked them away, my heart sank. I was a traitorous, sanctimonious know-it-all. They didn't speak to each other, but they were united by my act of betrayal.

chapter fifteen

Humble Pie

. . .

Shortly after my freshman year ended, I was back home at Law-less standing in the lobby by the mailboxes holding two letters from the University of Illinois. The base of my neck tightened and my hands had never shaken so much in my life. Had Mom been anywhere near me, she would have said, "You look like you have the palsy."

My sister's life was in disarray, but I didn't tell anybody that mine was, too. After my fall semester, I was home during Christmas break when I had gotten a letter *informing* me that I was on academic probation. Surely the school administrators were mistaken, I had thought. I'd never had problems with my grades in my life. The letter had said I needed to have a strong spring semester, or I'd have to leave the university for at least a year.

I leaned against the wall. I couldn't open either envelope. Mom was already stressed out from Kim's behavior. She didn't need me adding to it. Besides, college had meant everything to me. It was my ticket out of Bronzeville to a new life and I had squandered it. Now I was standing in the same lobby where neighbors had applauded as I left for college nearly a year ago. That pride had morphed into full-on shame.

It was afternoon and the only other person in the lobby was the guard. Munching on chips, he was watching *All My Children* on a small television on top of his desk.

I inhaled deeply and opened the first envelope. It held my grades. I had two Ds, a C, and an S for satisfactory. Most people would have known the contents of the second letter. But I prayed as I ripped it open. *Please, God. I need a miracle.*

The first word I saw was "Regretfully . . ." The dean of students was informing me that I had failed to meet the requirements to get off academic probation. I would not be able to return for the 1984–85 school year. I'd have to attend another college, bring up my grades, and then be reassessed. There were other criteria, but I couldn't read them. Time had stopped around me. My brain felt wadded with cotton.

I folded the letters and stuffed them into my pocket. Mom was at work and Kim was upstairs. The only way to broach any subject with Mom was to make sure I had a solution.

Later that evening I drove to the Trices'. David had told me that his parents wanted to help me figure out what to do next.

David greeted me with a hug, and I could already feel some of the weight lifting. He led me to his mother waiting in the living room. His father, having heard the doorbell, hurried up from the basement.

"How's my girl?" he said, sitting in a nearby chair.

"Not good," I said into my hands. I was trying not to cry.

"I know you think you're special," Mrs. Trice said, smiling and patting my back. "But you're not the first person to have a rocky start."

"Forget about sitting out a year." Mr. Trice clapped his palms together. "How about I get you and your mom, and we'll all take a trip to Spelman? You can transfer."

"Dad, that's not what she wants."

I wasn't sure why Mr. Trice believed I'd be accepted at Spelman with my grades. "I started at the University of Illinois," I said. "I want to graduate from there."

"That makes sense," Mr. Trice said. "You want to sit out a whole year?"

"No," I said.

"Then you'll have to plead your case."

"But the letter said their decision was final and nonnegotiable."

"Everything is negotiable, Dawn-O. Are you willing to fight?"

The next morning, I dialed Dean Robert Copeland, an African American dean known for helping Black students do what was needed to earn their degrees. He was strict but fair and did not suffer fools.

His assistant announced that he didn't have time for me. I called the next day and she said he was about to leave campus. I called a third time and he picked up.

"Miss Turner, are you going to waste my time if I meet with you?"

"Absolutely not, sir." My face felt hot.

He was quiet. I could hear him shuffling papers on his desk. When he spoke again, he said, "I'll see you in two days. Come with a plan."

"A plan?"

"Your plan to earn your degree from the University of Illinois."

D avid drove me back to campus to meet with the dean. The whole ride, I practiced what I was going to say: "I promise to make school my first priority by studying hard. I will meet regularly with my professors, participate in class, and attend every tutorial offered."

Dean Copeland's office was in Lincoln Hall. I climbed the steps to the third floor. Copeland sported a goatee and tinted glasses that made him look both patrician and like a Black Panther. When I entered his office, he mostly looked angry.

"Have a seat," he said, pointing to a chair in front of his desk. On the wall behind him hung a poster of that iconic photo of Tommie Smith and John Carlos during the 1968 Olympics medal ceremony, standing on the podium giving the Black Power salute.

"You flunked out and now you're coming to me crying about it."

"Yes, sir," I said, surprisingly dry-eyed.

"Did we make a wrong decision bringing you here in the first place? Is the work too challenging? Did you spend your time partying?"

"No, sir. I did some anti-apartheid protesting. I wrote for the

Griot and read the news on WBML. I just didn't work hard enough on my classwork."

I saw the disappointment on his face. I noticed the framed photo of his wife and son on his desk, and for some reason it made me feel worse as I delivered my rehearsed spiel. "I promise to work hard next time. Please let me return in the fall."

"Those things in your plan—isn't that what we talked about at orientation?"

"Yes, sir."

He flipped through a manila folder. "Your GPA for this semester is 1.33. Having to claw your way back is sometimes tougher than getting accepted in the first place."

"It won't happen again. I've learned my lesson. I promise."

"Alright, then." He exhaled and pushed back from his desk.

I saw this as a glimmer of hope that I could stay and began gathering my things.

"Sit out for one semester and, if you meet the terms of your academic probation, you can return in the spring of your sophomore year."

"I still have to sit out?" My legs went liquid. "But I thought—"

"You get to work your plan at a community college," he said. "Make sure you attend one whose credits transfer here. Hopefully, we'll see you in the spring."

I couldn't move.

"Good afternoon, Miss Turner. Stick to your plan. I wish you well."

Seeing David sitting on the quad tossed me into full breakdown mode. He met me halfway and wrapped both arms around me. We had said "I love you" in letters that we'd sent during freshman year. We'd said it after long phone calls. That he had convened his family for me and had driven me down to school to help save my college career made me feel cared for and understood and safe.

"It will be okay," he said as I sobbed.

We were silent for much of the ride back, with me staring out the window at cornfields zipping past in a hypnotic whip. I needed to break the news to Mom. I was too embarrassed to stay in Lawless, so I would ask Dad and Betty if I could stay with them during the fall semester and attend a suburban community college near their house.

That night, Mom was in her bedroom when I sat down on her bed, confessed everything, and told her how I was going to fix it.

"Okay. I know you'll make it work."

Whether she actually knew or was too exhausted to press, I don't know. But the disappointment in her eyes made me even more determined.

I was midway through the fall semester at Thornton Community College when Debra called one evening as I was getting ready for class. She'd gotten Dad's telephone number from Mom. Debra and I hadn't talked for a while and I was happy to hear from her.

"Dawn, you wouldn't believe it, so I'm just going to tell you. I enlisted in the air force a few months ago. I was in San Antonio, Texas. But I'm back home now."

"Wait, what? The air force? You've never mentioned wanting to join the military."

"After high school, I felt stuck. I spent the year working for a Steak 'n Shake in Indianapolis while living at home. Daddy and I weren't getting along, so I had to leave."

I sat on the bed, placing my American national government book in my bag. On the dresser, I left the textbooks for my other classes: general biology; composition and research; calculus and analytic geometry.

"When I told Daddy that I was enlisting, he was against it. He said the military was too regimented, but I knew in my bones that I needed the structure."

"How long were you there?"

"Just two months. I didn't make it past airman basic training. I've got fallen arches and everything I did was so painful. The doctors said, in order for me to stay I'd need to have surgery. I called Daddy and he told me to just come home."

Betty liked *Wheel of Fortune* and I heard her trying to solve a puzzle. I usually left for class before the show came on. I was running late.

"The trip back to Indianapolis was just miserable," Debra said. "All the while, I thought about my flight marching and something kept telling me that I'd made a wrong decision. I still have this feeling of foreboding, Dawn—when you know a moment can change your life, but you don't know how to stop it."

"What will you do next?"

"I'm not going to just hang out and party all the time. I'm going to school like you. Just wait and see. I know you're doing well, friend."

I rolled my eyes up to the ceiling. "Girl, I'm so sorry." Worse than being ashamed was being a hypocrite. "Can we talk later? I'm going to be late for class."

"Yes, go. Later is fine."

As soon as I hung up, I regretted not telling Debra that I'd flunked out of college and that my drive home had felt as awful as her flight home. I wished I'd told her that I, too, had stumbled. At least she had a legitimate health reason. I wished I'd said that I was running late for my government class at the community college, where I sat next to a gray-haired white hippie who had been making me cassette tapes of Tina Turner's music. He'd told me that I looked like her, which I didn't, and asked me if we were related.

I didn't tell Debra any of this because of my shame. But I also didn't want to tarnish my image as the one who did things the right way, who knew the path and the rules and fell in line. I had not only burnished that as my image, but it was my identity and, having faltered, the part of me that I was so desperate to reclaim.

chapter sixteen

Three Miracle Candles

...

Having run up three flights of stairs, I abruptly came to a halt just shy of Dean Copeland's office. His assistant wasn't at her desk, so I caught my breath and tapped on his door.

"Come in." He looked at me over his glasses. I could tell he was trying not to smile. "Do you have an appointment, Miss Turner?"

"No. I just want you to know I made it back."

"I know you're back. Telling me something I already know. Now you must graduate. Nothing is more important than that."

He was right and I felt like I needed every advantage. While I had respectfully pooh-poohed the scriptures and the blessed items Mom, Granny, and Aunt Doris had sent me during freshman year, when I returned I eagerly read every chapter and verse they recited and accepted every item Prophet had prayed over: a blessed handkerchief, a bottle of holy oil, a yarmulke that Granny instructed I bobby pin to my hair and wear under a hat during tests. I absolutely did.

I didn't hear from Dean Copeland again until the semester ended and I was back home and went to the mailbox. I got a manila envelope from the university and my chest felt like it was going to explode. I ripped open the envelope and pulled out the paper. I had made "the Dean's List for academic excellence." A paper-clipped note from Dean Copeland read: "Now you're back."

Days before Kim's senior year started, I told her that I wanted to go up to Hyde Park with her so that we could meet with her guidance counselors. Mom had been up there so many times, she was tired.

Although Kim wasn't ditching school as much, her grades were barely average. It had been nearly a year since I'd talked with Dean Copeland to devise a plan to return to the university and I wanted to use that as a model to get my sister back on track. I was beginning my junior year at the university and had worked hard to get one of the highly coveted positions as a resident adviser. RAs didn't have to pay for housing. I also had a job in the admissions office as a "peer recruiter," encouraging more African Americans to attend the university, which still had painfully few Black students. Earlier that year, I'd applied to the College of Communications but had been rejected because my grade point average still suffered from my freshman-year stumble. My goal that semester was to make sure I kept my grades up so that I could win admission.

Before the semester got too busy, I drove home and picked Kim up. When we walked into Hyde Park's main office, some of the staff members recognized me immediately. But I didn't stop long to converse with anyone. I was determined to make this day about Kim. We entered Kim's counselor's office and my sister immediately seemed sincere.

"Do you want to go to college?" the counselor asked Kim.

"Absolutely," I blurted out.

They both looked at me.

"I'm sorry."

"Yes, ma'am," Kim said.

"You'll have to go to a community college to improve your grades," the counselor said. "But you first have to graduate high school. Are you willing to buckle down?"

"Yes, ma'am."

I watched my sister take notes, listing the classes she'd need to retake in summer school. She said, "Yes, ma'am," which I'd never heard her say. She sat up straight, and by the time we walked out of the school we had a plan. We were on the same page. Onward.

I drove back to school patting myself on the back.

And then, not four weeks later, Mom called. Her voice trembled so I eased down on my bed.

"Your sister and I spent the day in the emergency room."

No matter how I resisted, I could feel my body descending into panic mode.

"She was lethargic and throwing up. I told the doctor that Kim had been studying and working hard and her resistance was low. I thought she had the flu."

I began to get irritated. "Mom, just call the school and tell them that she's sick and needs to miss some classes."

"I'm not done. When the doctor suggested Kim take a pregnancy test, I was offended. I was sure that was his conclusion for all Black teenage girls. Besides, I'd asked Kim if she could be pregnant and she swore up and down she wasn't. The doctor took the test, came back in, and said, 'You're going to be a mother.'"

I laid back on my bed. Because I was an RA, I had a room to myself with its own bathroom. I felt sick. Mom said she told the doctor to redo the pregnancy test. Not only was this the second time in her life that she had asked this of a doctor, but it was the second time a test came back positive.

"I could have sunk through the damn floor." Mom's voice was filled with hurt and fury. "That girl had the nerve to look surprised. I wanted to just slap her."

"Do you think she knew? All this time, I've been calling her to check up on her to see if she's following the plan. Do you think—"

"She may have been in denial." Mom knew what it felt like to know but not want to know.

I held the phone. My mother had been strict and unequivocal when it came to her daughters and unwanted pregnancies. While I was in high school, she'd pivoted from telling me to wait until marriage to have sex to begging me to protect myself. "Don't bring me no here-afters," she'd said. During the first semester of my freshman year, she kept asking me whether David and I were having sex. I finally vowed that I would tell her when I was ready. After I returned to school from Thanksgiving break that year, I went to the infirmary to be fitted for a diaphragm. David and I had planned to have our first sexual encounter while we were home during Christmas break. I told Mom, as I'd promised, and when I wasn't sure I'd put my diaphragm in correctly, she had me lie down on my bed and helped me.

"How many times have I told you both to wait?" she asked me now. "How many times did I beg you? She's only seventeen years old."

"How far along is she, Mom?"

"Eighteen weeks." Her voice flattened.

"That's four and a half months."

"She wears those baggy-ass sweatshirts. I've got to find a place to take care of it. She can't have a baby right now."

My mother had a kitchen drawer filled with rusted things. It was the first place she searched for items that she said were in her possession and yet simultaneously lost forever. I could hear the jangle from her rummaging through it now. Mom despised crying and, I suppose, had to do something else with her eyes. She ended the phone call in a way I'd come to expect: "Don't let this worry you, baby. I'll figure it out."

Of course, I was worried and I was driving home. That weekend, I entered the apartment and hugged Mom for a long time even though she tried to push me away.

"Girl, I'm okay." The bags under her eyes suggested otherwise.

Mom kept several miracle candles that she'd gotten from Prophet in the linen closet. Whenever she received bad news, she would place one in the bathtub and light it. I saw the flickering shadows of an unprecedented three candles on the bathroom door as I turned the corner to my bedroom.

"Your mother is not happy," I said to Kim as I entered.

I looked around the room and she tried to distract me by hugging me from behind so that I wouldn't complain about the dirty clothes on the floor, the bedsheets that hadn't been changed in ages, or the empty fast-food containers stacked on the dresser.

"I know she told you," my sister said. "It's like she reports to you."

I could feel her protruding abdomen under her baggy sweatshirt. I'd seen her a month before. *Was she showing then?* Now her thick hair looked even fuller and her skin was indeed luminous.

"Shouldn't you be in school?" she asked.

"Shouldn't you?" I jabbed back, and yet I couldn't resist palming her stomach.

"I know, right? But don't worry. This is a good thing. I promise." She smiled down at her midsection. "This baby flip-flops all the time and tickles me."

"But you have options," I pressed. "Children change your life."

"I know that's what your mother has always said."

"Then, please—" I could hear myself begging. "Don't do this."

"My baby is what makes me laugh, Dawn. She's going to help me get my life in order. She'll force me to grow the hell up. I'm going back to school and everything."

"She?"

"Oh, it's a girl," Kim said, puttering around the room, picking up clothes. "Mother's intuition."

She faced the mirror. "You know what *your* mother had the nerve to say?"

"No, what?"

"She said I look like a big pair of titties with a girl standing behind them."

During the drive from Urbana to Lawless, my heart had felt so heavy for my sister. But in that moment, we laughed together so hard, it hurt.

A couple of weeks later, I was in my dorm room and decided to skip my last class and drive home. I didn't call ahead. I'd bought a pink bunny for my niece, and I shoved it into my book bag. Its head poked out of the top. I tore down the highway, riding a rush of optimism. I'd been thinking about Kim so much, wondering how to help her. And I'd just come to the conclusion that we were simply going to make it work. Turn it—Kim's daughter—into a positive. *Kim can still have a future. Other women have had babies young and have succeeded.* Kim had said she was ready to be more responsible, more accountable. One child didn't have to be the life sentence Mom often made it seem. Pumped up on a hot surge of adrenaline, I drove so fast north on Interstate Highway 57 I got a speeding ticket.

I arrived home just after noon. The apartment was still. I dropped my book bag in the living room and walked to the back. Mom was at work and her bedroom door was always closed, but I was surprised to find Kim's and mine closed, too. I heard snoring. *Good Lord, my little niece is causing Kim to sound like a man.* I opened the door. The shades were drawn. The dark room smelled of funk and stale cigarette smoke. I flipped the light switch and saw my sister and a man asleep, our beds pushed together.

"Kim, what the fuck?! Who the hell is this?"

Cigarette butts spilled from an ashtray on the nightstand. A vibrating pager flashed red. A smoky film hung in the air.

"Oh, hey," Kim said, bleary-eyed. "Give us a minute, okay?"

"Hey," the man said, coughing. "You must be Big Sis, the bigtime college student."

"Kim, does Mom know you've got someone here?"

"Give me a minute, okay?" She had the nerve to sound annoyed.

I seethed as I walked to the living room. I noticed the man's jacket hanging on the dining chair. Videocassettes lay on the cocktail table. Kim loved *Mahogany* and *Lady Sings the Blues*, Diana Ross as both model and addict. Mom had amassed a library of movies that she watched as she waited up late for Kim.

I sat down at the dining table. I thought about when Kim and I were young and would sit under the table and she would, out of the blue, start reaching to touch Granny's bunions. Kim was a con, skilled at divining a soft spot, even one calloused over. The blownglass ashtray that Granny had given Mom that for years was a decorative art piece now overflowed with cigarette butts like the ashtray in the bedroom.

After a few minutes, Kim slinked out first. She wore a pink quilted robe with a dusting of lace around the princess collar. I had one in lilac. Mom had gotten them a few years before on sale at Carson's.

"What the fuck are you doing?" I asked her.

Kim thought I was looking at the ashtray. "Oh, I'm not smoking."

"I don't care about that. Mom says you hang out with gangbangers. Do you have a gangbanger in this apartment? Is that the baby's father?"

"Can you not start? You don't even live here anymore."

"Is he?"

"He may be affiliated," she said calmly.

She saw the pink bunny peeking out of my book bag.

"You got something for me?" She smiled.

"Something more than contempt? I thought this baby was making you better."

The man strolled out from the back, naked under my lilac robe, wiping sleep from his eyes and hawking to clear his throat. He looked to be in his early twenties.

"Excuse me," he said, pounding his chest with the flat of his hand. "Girl, your little sister is so proud of you." He placed his arm around Kim. "Other than this baby, you're all she talks about. Dawn this. Dawn that."

"Why are you wearing my shit?" Locking eyes with my *little* sister, I yanked the bunny from my book bag, tossed it at her, and left.

I had no idea what to do next.

Later that night, Mom called me to explain: "He was only there for the night, Sugar. They were watching a movie and it got late."

"Mom, since when is that okay with you?"

"Listen to me. His mother had been nice enough to let Kim stay at their house. That's where Kim had been when she would disappear. I talked to the woman and she thought Kim was much older and she apologized. I just let him stay."

"Okay, Mom. Everything will be fine."

What hurt more than any of this was that she had been so desperate to know where her daughter was that she was allowing Kim and her boyfriend to shack up in our apartment. Kim had not only worn Mom down to the nub but had turned them both into two people completely unrecognizable to me.

I decided to live my life. As the dean said, I had to graduate, and nothing was more important. Especially not my sister's shit. I put my head down and worked. I talked to David every night, and a couple of weekends after my drive home, he and I met in St. Louis, midway between Urbana and Jefferson City. We found a cheap motel and spent the majority of the weekend in bed, leaving only to find meals. David was on pace to graduate the following spring, in three years. He hadn't wanted to go to college but because his parents forced him, he decided to *show them* by graduating a year early.

The weekend was fantastic, and my week unfolded as normal. I tried not to think about my sister. But by midweek, I opened the door to my room and stepped on a bunch of yellow slips of paper, messages from the residence hall's office secretary. Mom wanted me to call home immediately.

She told me that Kim had been cramping and in so much pain that Mom took her to the emergency room. She was twenty-two weeks pregnant and the doctors seemed to think everything was fine, so they sent her home.

"Kim got back in bed, but the pain wouldn't let up," Mom said, speaking low so that Kim couldn't hear. "A few minutes later she yelled, 'Mom, I think you're going to have to take me back.'

"I was exhausted, but I told her okay. Kim got up and walked back to the bathroom. I helped her sit on the toilet and then walked away, hoping to lie down for a few minutes before returning to the emergency room. But Kim yelled, 'Mom, something's coming out!' I hurried to the bathroom in time to see Kim catching the baby just before it hit the water. I held the baby in a towel while helping her back to her bed. His tiny chest fluttered. He was fully formed but his facial features were cloudy. Like seeing him from a distance or submerged in water."

Mom's voice pitched unusually high and nervous.

"When the paramedics came, one tried to revive the baby while the other tended to Kim. They rushed them both back to the hospital. He didn't make it, poor thing. He lived for about an hour. He was no bigger than a minute and he never cried."

"It's going to be okay, Mom." I had my hand over my mouth and didn't realize it until my voice came out muffled.

"The nurse asked me if I wanted the hospital to take care of the remains. I said, 'Yes.' What did I know? I thought it was the right thing to do."

"It was," I said, trying to sound confident.

"But Kim just asked me, 'Mom, what do you think they did with my baby?' I couldn't answer her."

"Don't worry. We'll figure this out."

When I arrived home a couple of days later, Mom repeated that the baby had come too soon. Only now she showed me her fingernails as she described his and she extended the palm of her hand to demonstrate his size.

As I walked toward the bedroom, Mom sat at the table and placed her head in her hands, trying to hold everything together. No miracle candles burned in the bathtub.

In the bedroom, Kim was sitting, shoulders slouched, withering on the edge of the bed, looking as though she'd been lying down but had sat up when she heard I was there. The twin beds had been separated and returned to their proper places. The room was clean. I didn't know if Mom had cleaned it or if Granny had when she sat with Kim or if Aunt Doris had when she arrived. Or maybe Kim herself had been nesting and it didn't matter that the baby was gone.

"What can I do for you?" I kneeled in front of her, rubbing her thighs.

Rheumy-eyed and hair storm-tossed, she resembled a battered doll, all staring and no blinking, threadbare and fading.

"Nothing," she said, slowly shaking her head. "I named him Brandon. Did Mom tell you?" Kim didn't wait for my answer. "I had to give him a name for the death certificate." Her eyes pooled. "I thought he was a girl. I didn't know him."

"You were going to know him."

"Remember I told you"—she swallowed hard and inhaled deeply—"Brandon tickled my belly?"

I smiled, nodding.

"I think he did it because he had wings."

I nearly burst into tears.

Kim wore a nightgown, something she never wore, that had wet circles around her nipples from her milk coming down. And she wore socks, which I was certain either Granny, Mom, or Auntie had forced on her. They had always made us wear socks when we were on our period, explaining that it was the time when our bodies were the most open and susceptible to catching a cold. Kim could never be more susceptible than now. And yet I removed those silly socks one at a time. I hugged her and peered into her face. She looked depleted, as if the baby had taken the bulk of her with it.

I should say *him*.

I spent most of the weekend sitting on my bed watching my

sister. She was quiet and compliant and had never looked so unlike herself. At one point, I went into the bathroom, wet a face towel, and returned to our room to wash her face. I held the back of her head in my hand as I traced the contours of her eyes, cheeks, and nose.

"I'm so sorry, but you can start over," I said. "This is your second chance."

As soon as I said it, I knew it was selfish and insensitive, me wanting her to have the life I'd imagined for her. She bit her lip and nodded, struggling to hold back tears.

That night, in the middle of the night, she jumped out of her bed and turned on the light. Adjusting my eyes, I saw her raising her gown. Without the baby, her body now looked disfigured.

"I don't have stretch marks. How will I know Brandon was there?"

Mom had told us that during Kim's birth, a woman laboring in the maternity ward kept yelling: "Somebody! Somebody come get this pain up off me!" My sister didn't utter those words but I knew she felt that way.

I got up and placed my arm around Kim. Returning her to bed, I tucked her in and lay with her. My sister's body convulsed as she cried and I held her tightly, nestling my body against hers as if I, her sister—who had known her all her life—could fill in the missing space.

"It was my fault. I had one thing to do and I messed that up. He was supposed to be safe inside me and he wasn't."

"It wasn't your fault." I held her tightly and she still felt like she was slipping away.

The next afternoon as I was making my bed and throwing a few things into my book bag, about to return to school, Kim said, "Don't worry about me. I'll be okay."

She was not okay, but I believed she would be. She lifted her T-shirt to scratch her stomach. She had a paunch that, although we could not see it, had begun the process of flattening. And there would be no stretch marks.

"What do you think they did with Brandon's remains?"

Her voice was nearly inaudible and the pain inside it sliced through me like shards.

"I wish I knew." I stopped smoothing out my bed's comforter and picked up my book bag. "I'm so sorry I don't."

"Okay." She smiled but I could see the despair in her eyes. Turning her back to me, she said, "You know I can't stand to see you leave me. Just go."

As I left our bedroom, I expected that my sister would mourn for a while, and then eventually heal. That was what happened when someone died. At the same time, I knew that something had ruptured inside her, deep in a place where we could neither see nor understand and where no amount of scar tissue could ever adequately cover.

chapter seventeen

A Baby-Blue Aspirator

. . .

My mother and Kim had their secrets. Sometimes I felt as though they were accomplices, co-conspirators, and I was the outsider. They told me only what they wanted or needed me to know. After I returned to the university, I talked to Kim nearly every night. Although she sounded strong—making plans to return to school—she hadn't. And she never mentioned that she'd decided to move into the first-floor unit in Normal. Mom had planned to live there—one day. We couldn't quite tell what was keeping her at Lawless, but for now the place was empty except for the appliances and furnishings she was slowly amassing. Much of them remained wrapped in manufacturer's plastic.

"It's only temporary," Mom had said of Kim's move. "Your sister needed a change of scenery, and I gave her the keys."

It had been a month since Kim lost the baby when I left campus and drove to the building. The neighborhood had once been solidly working-class—"respectably rough" was how Mom described it—but now disinvestment and neglect had continued to gnaw at it the same way they had in the city's public housing projects.

I walked up the porch steps and rang the doorbell. The main door was primarily glass and behind it were a vestibule and two more doors. One on the right led to the first-floor apartment, where Kim was staying, and the other to the steps to Granny's upstairs apartment. Those doors were wooden with frosted glass. I could see

Kim's silhouette before she opened the door. Seeing me, she jumped up and down as she unlocked the deadbolt to the outside door.

"What up, Sis?!" She wore a T-shirt and sweatpants and was barefoot. She folded her arms against the chill. "It's cold. Come on in."

We hugged and she held my hand as she led me past the small living room and the dining room. My sister took me into her bedroom, off the kitchen. I lay on her bed near the headboard and she lay across the foot. I tucked my feet under her flank. The television sat atop an armoire and was on but muted.

"How long you plan to be here?" The air was thick with cigarette smoke, but I didn't say anything.

"Umm, let me think." She stared at the ceiling and thumped her temple. "Not long. Maybe another week or two."

"And you moved in because?"

"Mom's never going to move in here."

"Why do you think that?"

"It's no longer the life she expected. Andrew is gone. This neighborhood is going to hell. It's like you make plans and life knocks you off your square!"

Whether Kim intentionally touched her stomach, I don't know. I didn't ask her about Brandon. Instead, I said, "You're pretty perceptive these days."

"Yeah, for a high school dropout."

On the drive up, I'd promised myself I wasn't going to be the know-it-all who always interfered. But I couldn't resist. "You should consider—just consider—getting a GED." I expected her to tell me she only had two parents.

"You know, my counselor suggested that route. I like the idea."

"There's a community college not far from here."

"Yup. I'm on it."

She unmuted the television and we watched the five o'clock news with Kim nodding off until she fell hard, snoring. As she slept, I looked at her stained pillowcase. Smudged mascara and lipstick had drawn her visage in avant-garde. A Crown Royal bag on the floor next to the radiator overflowed with silver dollars. A pack of cigarettes and matches sat on the dresser next to pink foam rollers.

It was growing dark outside and I needed to head back to school. But I didn't want to leave. I wanted us to stay just like that—in the bed together like old times, so that I could watch over her as she slept and know that she was safe.

I placed my hand on her back, rousing her. "I've got to go, but don't move. Uncle Al will lock up."

"No, don't go," she said, eyes closed, swatting sleepily for my hand and missing.

"I'm sorry. I have to." I stood and slipped into my shoes.

She plunged her nose with the heel of her hand and hawked.

"You're still gross," I said, laughing.

"Hey, did Mom ever tell you that Debra stopped by?"

"No," I said, shocked. "When?"

"Maybe about a week ago? Mom said the intercom rang in the middle of the night and she turned the television on to see who it was. She saw this young woman dressed in jeans and a T-shirt with her hair pulled back. She thought it was me."

"The resolution is so bad that everybody always looks like they're standing in a fog," I said.

"Mom said it was Debra and her eyes were glassy and red, and her hair was messed up. She looked strung out on some hard shit."

"I'm not surprised. She's always dabbling in something."

"Mom said she rested in your bed for an hour and left all of a sudden."

"Damn. No, Mom hasn't said a thing."

"She probably forgot. You know she's got her hands full with yours truly." My sister's self-awareness never ceased to amaze me.

Slipping on a sweater, she slid her feet into a pair of gym shoes and walked me to the door—beyond which, my car was parked right out front.

"Call me when you get to campus," she said.

"You ain't my mama," I joked.

She grabbed me around my waist, lifting me. I held her tightly, laughing. Then I stepped out onto the porch, watching her vanish behind the door and its opaque glass like a ghost.

When I got back to my dorm, it was too late to call Debra, but I tried her over the next several days during breaks from studying. Though I talked to her mother, I couldn't reach Debra. And then work and school dominated my life and soon the story of her coming by and whether she was or wasn't doing drugs left my radar until she called me the following March.

She said "Hey, Dawn" in such a flat, resigned way that I knew something was wrong. "Daddy's gone."

"Oh, no. I'm so sorry."

"He died of kidney failure from diabetes, one week before his forty-fourth birthday. We've already had the funeral, but I just wanted you to know."

She was quiet for a moment. I got the feeling that she was trying not to sound like she was still grieving.

"You know what I remember?" I said. "I'd be in your apartment and he'd come home from work and I'd have to leave."

"Boy, I hated that," she laughed. "I remember when you and I looked up kidneys in the encyclopedia because of Mrs. Love's daughter. That was the first time I heard the word." She hesitated. "Dad said I was stubborn like him. We butted heads, but I know he loved me."

We held the line in silence because there really wasn't much else to say. Although I still wanted to know why she visited Mom a few months before, I didn't ask. Nor did I engage in what had become a carefully choreographed dance about what she was doing with her life. Neither seemed appropriate.

After we said our goodbyes, I thought about my father. I didn't butt heads with him as Debra had with hers and I didn't fawn over him as Kim had with ours. What I did was replace him—and Andrew—with Black men who were father figures.

Bruce Nesbitt was a father figure. Later that fall, I sat in his office as he helped me apply for a summer journalism internship for minorities out of New York University. He told me to write out my résumé and then he swiveled around in his squeaky chair to his typewriter, inserted an embossed sheet of paper, and pecked with his two pointer fingers for about an hour. He left a space at the top and then meticulously stenciled in my name in a blocky font.

When I got the letter saying that I was among a handful of college students throughout the country chosen to spend the summer taking a class at the university and interning at one of their partner businesses, I was thrilled. I ran from my dorm to the cultural center and up the stairs to his office to tell him. He congratulated me and shook my hand. And when I returned in the fall, I told him how I'd lived in a Greenwich Village apartment, a few blocks from Washington Square; had toured Harlem; and that my NYU professor, A. Peter Bailey, was a journalist who had worked closely with Malcolm X.

I considered Dean Copeland to be a father figure, too. The College of Communications was in Gregory Hall, next door to Lincoln Hall and Dean Copeland's office. On most days, I was too busy working through my senior classes to think about him as I crossed the quad. But on the day that I took my last final, I scaled the three flights to his office without an appointment to let him know that I was graduating.

His door was open, and he was on the phone. Seeing me, he said, "Let me call you right back. I have a student here."

"I did it," I said, breathless.

"You haven't gotten your final grades," he said. "How can you be so confident?"

"I just aced my last final," I said with a smile.

He walked to a file cabinet near his desk and retrieved a folder.

"Let's see. This semester you took an economics class on poverty and income maintenance. A social and cultural geography class. Two journalism classes. And matrix theory?" He looked at me over his glasses. "What journalism student takes a math class as an elective in her final semester?"

I shrugged. "I like math."

"So, what's next, Dawn?"

"I have a summer internship at the *Chicago Sun-Times* and then I'll look for a more permanent position. I haven't ruled out graduate school."

"Good luck to you," he said, smiling. "Despite your freshman year fiasco, you did it in four years. I'm proud of you."

He extended his hand, but my entire being overflowed with

gratitude. I hugged him for believing in me and giving me a second chance to prove myself.

"Thank you," I said. "Thank you for everything."

A live to the moment, I spent the next few days walking around campus saying goodbye to professors and friends. On the night before graduation, I sat on the quad reflecting on the eighteen-year-old who arrived and the twenty-two-year-old who was leaving. I felt triumphant until I returned to my dorm and found a message to call my father. When I did, he told me that he wouldn't be able to make the graduation. He said something came up at work and nobody was able to fill in for him. I dialed David. He had graduated the year before and was living in Michigan, working as a sales representative for Shell Oil.

"He's not coming." I hated that my voice sounded shaky. "He drove me down here four years ago. He allowed me to stay with him when I flunked out. Why wouldn't he want to see me graduate?"

"He wants to be there. I don't think he knows how," David said. "Your world is different from his. Maybe he doesn't know how to be a part of it."

"He's always been like this."

"Well, we're going to have a celebration tomorrow, with or without him. Deal?"

"Deal," I said, smiling.

I made calls to Mom, Granny, Aunt Doris, and Kim. Each was furious when I told them about Dad.

Mr. Trice called. "Dawn-O, this is what we're going to do. Instead of Sarah, David, and me riding down in a separate car, I'm going to rent a van. I'll get your mother, Kim, and everybody. We'll make chili with what's in the kitchen."

"That sounds fantastic." I tried to stop my voice from breaking.

Emotionally spent, I made one last call that night. To Debra. We hadn't spoken in months.

"Guess who's graduating tomorrow?" were my first words when she picked up. I lay across my bed, staring at the ceiling.

"Dawn!" she screamed. "Congratulations! Send me pictures, okay?"

"I will. Mom, Kim, Granny, Aunt Doris will be here, along with David and his family—"

"So, David's still around!" She sang the words. "Your very own substitute Trice."

"What are you doing these days, friend?"

"I'm dancing, Dawn," she said, giggly.

"Dancing? I didn't know you danced."

"I'm dancing topless. Can you believe it?"

"Topless?" I sat straight up. "What the fuck, girl?"

"I know it sounds bad, but it's not. I'm only doing it until I can pay for nursing school. I make a lot of money."

"C'mon, Debra. This ain't for you. Those places are dangerous."

"Oh, it's not seedy. And I don't let anybody fuck with me, Dawn."

I placed my hand on my forehead. "Are you doing drugs?"

"Girl, nothing hard. Mostly weed and I love my beer."

By the time we said goodbye, I was sitting awkwardly on the edge of my bed realizing that the conversation had been fairly futile. Maybe because Debra and I started out together, I nursed a fantasy that we would both be standing at the same place at the same time. But we were on different trajectories. I decided I couldn't worry about her. I had enough on my plate fretting about Kim. Debra had a strong family and was, in her words, a wild child. Maybe she'd have to hit a wall or find a passion. I didn't know. But I trusted she would somehow find her way.

I wasn't certain if Kim was finding her way, but she seemed to be. I saw it the next day when she ran out of the van with a bouquet of flowers and hugged me. I saw it as she applauded during the ceremony, standing and clapping louder than anyone when I crossed the stage. I saw it a few weeks later when I invited her downtown to have lunch with me at my internship and I introduced her to the *Sun-Times* movie critic Roger Ebert and other reporters and editors. I watched my sister in her yellow sundress shake hands and smile in a way that made her seem like a confident nineteen-year-old.

I had moved back into our old bedroom, planning to use the summer to figure out my next move. Every time I looked over at my sister's perfectly made bed, I thought of her. Every time someone dropped something in the apartment above, I thought of Debra. I was searching through drawers for an old T-shirt to sleep in one night when I found what felt like a deflated small ball wrapped in a scarf. I unfurled it and discovered a tiny blue aspirator. I assumed it was the one paramedics used on baby Brandon. I didn't know if Kim had asked for it or if, in their haste, they had left it behind. I held it up to the light and it was still covered in mucus that had dried over time. I wasn't certain exactly what it meant that Kim had kept the aspirator. But I wondered if somewhere inside my sister was a young mother still trying to bring herself and her son back to life. I wrapped the aspirator in the scarf and pushed it back into the far reaches of the drawer.

I had returned home to this place where ghosts and spirits and dreams had always meant something to the women in our family. Death no longer hovered over Kim and me at the dining room table, a figment of the women's conversations. For Kim, death had a distinct presence, a tiny one, in our bedroom. She didn't move out because she felt she had a choice. My sister—once fearless, intrepid, daring—had been forced out by a beautiful little phantom who lay in ambush in every corner of that room.

chapter eighteen

Choices

. . .

D avid and I were sitting on the futon in the living room of his new condo, about four miles from his parents' home. We were watching *Saturday Night Live* and sharing a bowl of chocolate ice cream. During a commercial, he placed the bowl on the futon—because he hadn't yet bought a coffee table—and got down on one knee. He took my left hand and my right flew over my mouth.

After my *Sun-Times* internship, I'd spent a year working at a newspaper in Florida and David had returned from Michigan. That night, I had been back in Chicago for about six months. I'd gotten a position as a low-level editor at the *Chicago Tribune*, the *Sun-Times*'s rival. Because I worked Sunday through Thursday and David had a normal workweek, we spent our Saturdays together.

"I've known you since we were fourteen," he said. "That's ten long years." He stretched out the word *"long"* and I laughed. "I don't want to spend my life with anyone else. Will you marry me?"

Every time his mother had asked me when her son and I were going to wed, I'd told her that I wanted to buy my own condo and find my footing at work. Mom had allowed me to move back into Lawless so that I could save money for a down payment. And yet, my answer now was clear.

"Yes," I nodded, throwing my arms around his neck.

We dialed Mom first, standing cheek to cheek, holding the receiver between us.

"Hallelujah!" She cupped the phone. "Dawn's getting married!"

"To who?" Kim shouted. During the year while I was gone, she'd gotten her GED and enrolled in a community college. Although she still was living in Normal, she often stopped by the apartment. She picked up the phone. "Do I know this guy?"

"You're not funny," David said. "I know where you live."

"Congratulations! I've always wanted a big brother."

We said goodbye. I knew Mom would tell Granny and Aunt Doris and tell them to sound surprised when I called.

David dialed his parents next. When Mrs. Trice picked up, he asked her to have his dad get on the extension.

"Dawn has agreed to marry me!"

"Finally," Mrs. Trice said. "Dawn, I guess you should now call us Sarah and Jim."

Mr. Trice let out a robust laugh. "Welcome to the family, Dawn-O!"

By the time we'd made all the calls we needed, including one to my father because David was old fashioned and wanted to formally ask for my hand, *Saturday Night Live* had ended. We went to bed and celebrated by making love.

We agreed on an inexpensive wedding to save the bulk of our money for the down payment on a house. I had friends whose nuptials had cost a small mint and one couple was still paying for theirs after they filed for divorce. We decided on an August wedding, which would give us three months to plan. There would be no honeymoon. And I didn't want an extravagant ring. That Monday, we met downtown at a jewelry store and I selected a modest band with a small ruby and diamond that I loved. I only wanted two bridesmaids: Kim and our cousin Lila, Aunt Doris's daughter. I found two pink, three-quarter-length cocktail dresses for twenty dollars each at a boutique that was going out of business. Pink suddenly became my color theme.

A month later, David and I were in his bed on a Sunday morning looking through the *Tribune*'s real estate section. I felt queasy. I had no idea why. I spent the week trying to work and not hurl and by Friday, my day off, I couldn't keep anything down. I didn't want to bother Mom at the bank, so I called Kim. She had gotten a job at a nursing home, and I asked her to stop by when her shift ended to bring me some soup. She arrived not long after Mom did. I was in the bedroom and she placed the soup on the nightstand and then asked me to follow her into the bathroom. After locking the door, she pulled a pregnancy test from under her shirt and handed it to me.

"Oh, I'm not pregnant," I whispered.

Mom tapped on the door. "What are you two doing?"

"Nothing, Mom!" we shouted in unison, having relied on those words over the years to collude and cover up so many secrets.

Kim sat on the edge of the tub, unwrapped the test, and handed it to me. I peed on the stick and returned it to her. She made a face as she held it away from her body.

"I can't be pregnant," I mumbled, still perched on the toilet. Anxiety roiled in me and I felt on the verge of throwing up. I thought about what Mom drilled into us: *When you have kids, even with the most helpful husband, you will be the one who tamps down her dreams, shaves off parts of yourself because you will care more about that child being whole than you.*

"You've always guarded your gate," Kim said, saluting.

"I've never slipped up." I sighed. "I've never been impulsive. One time the condom did break and it was a nightmare waiting for my period."

"Did I ever tell you that when you left for college, I got in this shower and cried."

I looked up at her. "No, you didn't."

"I cried because I couldn't imagine my life without you because you've always had my back. Just like I've got yours."

As she handed me the stick, I didn't look at it. Her half-smile told me everything I needed to know. All my life, I'd planned and set goals, some delayed by detours, but I wasn't ready to be a mother.

"This can be our secret or a celebration." She walked over to the toilet and hugged me. "I promise to help you if you decide to keep going."

"I'm not telling Mom," I said. "I'll tell David. He should know. But I can't have a baby right now. I'm not ready."

"Okay," she said. "Then we know what we have to do."

As I walked back to the bedroom, I felt awful burdening my

sister with this. It had been nearly four years since she lost Brandon. Although we never talked about him, she was still healing.

"Please go home," I said, getting into the bed.

"You get some rest." She sat on the bed next to me.

I awoke in the middle of the night to see her sitting at the keyboard, wearing headphones. Hearing just the thumping—such an elegiac, percussive sound unaccompanied by music and melody—was disconcerting. That night, I watched my sister rock gently as she played, her fingers working through a song only she could hear, a song whose rhythm and words were hers and had no translation. Once in a while, sound escaped from her, a hum or partial lyric. But even as I listened closely, it was impossible to figure out what she was playing. Mom, an insomniac, leaned against the doorframe watching Kim, too.

I fell asleep listening to my sister's murmurs. The sun was up when I awoke. Kim was still seated at the keyboard. Her bed was untouched. She kissed me on the forehead and left the room.

When I told David I was pregnant and wanted to have an abortion, he said he'd support whatever decision I made. Then he went with me to my gynecologist's office for my initial appointment. The doctor, a thin and graying white woman, said that I needed to be a certain number of weeks along before I had "the procedure." She placed her hand on my shoulder as we looked at a calendar hanging on a wall. She flipped the page up to August and we set an appointment for the termination two weeks after my wedding.

She left the room and I sat down on the examination table staring at the calendar. A nurse, a middle-aged Black woman, entered and pulled up a chair.

"Are you sure you want to do this?" Her question reeked of a chastisement.

"Yes, I am," I said emphatically. I didn't want to feel shame, but I did. I refused to let her know it or second-guess myself even though she twisted her mouth. When she handed me my appointment card and several brochures, I snatched them and left.

I've always excelled at compartmentalizing, locking away portions of my life. Refusing to dwell. Therefore, even then, I continued on with my life—my work, wedding plans, and our search for our new home.

After spending our weekends looking at a bunch of houses, David and I narrowed our list to two. One was in Bronzeville. I'd refused at first to even look at it because Bronzeville was the last place I wanted to live. Mom had begun entertaining the idea of leaving Lawless because crime and gang violence in the housing project had escalated dramatically in recent years. And yet, buppies—Black urban professionals—such as ourselves were buying and rehabbing the area's brownstones and graystones, filling them with baby grand pianos and African art. Newspapers were calling the new homeowners "urban pioneers" because they were also installing elaborate security systems with the hope that one day the crime would subside and they wouldn't be needed. David and I looked at a three-story brownstone that was about 4,500 square feet and around the corner from the Griffin Funeral Home. It was in terrible disrepair and would need a complete overhaul. Still, as we stood in the library gazing up through the holes in a ceiling adorned with filagree, we could imagine building a life there.

In the end, we signed the contract on the other house, located in a small town called Monee, forty miles south of Chicago. David had wanted land and we found a brown-brick two-story sitting on two and a half acres. His parents rode out with us on a Saturday afternoon to see it. We exited the expressway and the Monee water tower resembled a looming light-blue golf tee in the distance. As we drove through the town, population 1,000, David pointed out the one stoplight, the post office, and the building that was the combination village hall and police station. The two-lane opened up to cornfields and red barns and properties with horse stables.

The owners of our soon-to-be home had invited us to stop by whenever we wanted. We pulled into the driveway and the four of us walked up to the front stoop. David rang the doorbell. No one answered.

"We met the people next door," he said, jerking his head toward a beige house with aluminum siding about fifty yards away. "They have an apiary in the back with huge honeybees."

We left the front stoop and walked around the side of the house along a deck with a small in-ground pool.

"Possums and raccoons live in these woods." I lifted my eyebrows in mock disbelief. "The homeowner says they steer clear if you douse the yard in *coyote pee*."

David smiled down at the grass. His parents laughed.

"I'm giving your son one year of this. Just one."

"If only you could pick this house up and put it in the city," Sarah said.

There was no formal backyard, just a lush patch of maple and ash trees and tall grass whose tips shimmered like gold. The four of us stood in the midst of it all, listening to birds sing, admiring the sunlight sifting through the leaves.

"This is why white people live longer," Jim said, looking off in the distance before his gaze shifted back to us. "Let the police know Black people are moving to town."

It wasn't that he had faith in the police. He just wanted our presence to be on record. "You're getting married," he said, looking at the back of the house, at an enclosed patio and the kitchen window. "You have this lovely new home. I'm proud of you both."

We were two weeks outside of the wedding when the phone rang in Mom's apartment.

"So, Dawn, you're becoming a Trice?" A hail of laughter filled the line.

"Debra!" I yelled. "I see somebody got her invitation!"

By then we were talking maybe twice a year. I rarely asked her when she was going to stop dancing or when she was returning to school.

"My original best friend is going to have my name!" she said. "Who'da thunk it?"

"So, you *thunk* you can come?" When she didn't answer immediately, I said, "I'd love to see you and you've got to meet David."

"I'm going to try, okay, Dawn?"

"You promise?"

"Cross my heart. You're buying a house?"

I'd scrawled a note in the margins of her invitation.

"We drove out the other night and there are no streetlights," I said. "I knew there weren't any sidewalks. But no streetlights? If I hadn't promised to live there, I'd renege. Though, I have to say, that night sky, those stars? Lordy!"

Before we hung up, I asked her, "Are you keeping yourself safe?"

"I'm fine. All of this is just to make money for nursing school, Dawn. I really am going. And I won't have to worry about student loans."

"Debra, come on, girl. You're smart and you can do more than this."

"I'm going for real this time. Cross my heart."

My wedding was going to be held at the First House of Prayer Church. Although Mom, Granny, and Aunt Doris still belonged to the church, I was no longer a member. After college, I didn't return. Mom explained to her friends that I had to work on Sundays. While that was true, it wasn't the whole truth. I still believed in God and considered myself a Christian. But I reasoned that the church was in me, and as long as I lived a good life I didn't have to go to a physical space. Typically, nonmembers weren't allowed to have ceremonies—weddings or funerals—at the First House of Prayer. But I asked Prophet for permission and he granted it. Mom didn't make any demands on where I married, but I knew if I was going to wed in a church, it had to be the one where I grew up.

My wedding planner had warned me that three months was not enough time to plan a wedding. But Mr. Isaiah was proud of himself on the night of the rehearsal dinner. When our families arrived at the church, Mr. Isaiah met us at the door.

I'd known him since I was a child because he was a minister at the church. Tall and willowy, Mr. Isaiah sometimes would get the Holy Ghost in the choir and flail about until he passed out. His partner—a short and muscular man several years older—would run from the congregation up into the choir stand to carry Mr. Isaiah to the back of the church so that the nurses could revive him.

The night before my wedding, I, the prodigal daughter, walked into the sanctuary and immediately felt at home: the canopy of incense smoke over the altar; the wood-paneled walls; the choir stand with the mural of white Jesus; the rows of empty chairs; that center aisle with the red carpeting.

Mr. Isaiah walked up to me. "You're ready to get married tomorrow?"

"I'm ready."

"Okay, you sit in the audience. It's bad luck for the bride to participate."

"Oh, I don't believe in that stuff."

"I do." He led me to a seat near the front of the church.

Aunt Doris volunteered to be my stand-in. I looked over my shoulder at her, huddled with Granny, Mom, and Sarah by the church's main door. I was certain Mom was telling them that Dad wouldn't be attending the wedding. "I'm sorry but I ain't coming" were his exact words. He was upset because he had wanted his name on the invitations with Mom's and she refused, partly because of her lingering resentment that he'd never paid child support for Kim and me. My allegiance was with her, and his refusal to attend my wedding was my punishment.

The rehearsal started and Mr. Isaiah instructed Aunt Doris's second-oldest son to escort Mom, Granny, and Sarah to their seats. Then David and his two brothers walked up to the altar. Mr. Isaiah positioned them so that they stood on an angle with their hands folded in front of them. Mr. Isaiah must have been about six feet tall, but David and his brothers stood four to six inches over him.

Mr. Isaiah jogged down the aisle to the back of the church. Lila was to march first, then Kim, then the little flower girl, and then Aunt Doris, the bride. Because Kim hadn't been to church in a while, Mr. Isaiah hugged her tightly. When Kim and I were young, Mr. Isaiah would see Kim and me in the back of the church and say, "Sister Kim, do you mind if I brush your hair? It's so pretty." To my astonishment, my sister would stand quietly as he pulled a hairbrush from his briefcase and, in the gentlest way, slid his hand against her flyaways as he pressed them into submission. She never fought him the way she fought everyone else.

Kim's hair was dyed auburn and pulled back in a ponytail that night. Mr. Isaiah spun her around to see it and nodded his approval. He signaled for the pianist to start. The pianist was the church's new backup musician. Mom had never heard him play, but we were happy to get him because he was cheap. When he began to rock on the bench and thump out "On the Wings of Love," we understood why. The sanctuary filled with an off-key tinny sound that pierced our eardrums and made nearly everyone wince. David and I looked at each other across the room and nearly burst into laughter. Mom turned to look at me and mouthed "What the . . . ?"

Of everyone who walked down that aisle, I watched my sister the closest. Kim walked while chewing her tongue. Holding her pretend bouquet, she looked straight ahead at the altar and stepped steadily and methodically as though she were crossing a canyon on a tightrope.

She reached the altar, followed by the flower girl. And then the pianist began to stumble through "Here Comes the Bride," which was even more awful than the processional. Uncle Henry joined Aunt Doris, looping his arm through hers.

"I'll be all warmed up by tomorrow," the pianist offered.

No one in that church entertained any delusions that was possible.

The next morning Kim came to Mom's apartment to do my makeup—in between me throwing up—and then helped me into my white mermaid gown. It wasn't until I piled my hair atop my head and pinned on my veil that I finally started to feel like myself.

Just after 1 p.m., the temperature climbed near 100 degrees and I was standing at the end of the aisle, getting ready to walk down it. Massive floor fans stirred the heat and the white liner covering the red carpeting leading to the altar. Mr. Isaiah kept fighting with it, smoothing it over.

In the pianist's hands, the wedding march sounded like a funeral dirge. Still, the audience stood as I began to walk, looking left and right, smiling at so many familiar faces. The handful of people who knew why I was walking alone probably thought I was looking for Dad, holding out one last hope he would attend. But I'd grown accustomed to him being him. My gaze, however, swept across the hot, gleaming faces, searching for Debra. The photographer snapped his fingers for me to look at him, but I smiled at Thomas instead. Standing near the altar, the videographer waved at me, trying to get me to focus straight ahead. When I didn't see Debra, I wasn't surprised. Still, that didn't stop me from looking for her at the reception. My new in-laws got a city permit to cordon off the street in front of their house and they set up decorated tables and hired a DJ. But Debra didn't come.

The next time David, Kim, and I were together, I was sitting between them in the doctor's office. We were flipping through a white album of wedding proofs, laughing at one horrible photo after another. The pictures reflected the photographer's price. In each photo, our faces were oily. The heat had puffed my hair up and the veil lay askew. It brought to mind those glum Depression-era portraits. No one would ever have known we were so happy.

We were midway through the album when the nurse came from behind a door. "Dawn?" I jumped when she said my name.

"You want me to come with you?" David asked, standing and hugging me.

"No, I've got this." There was a catch in my voice. I hoped they didn't notice.

I gave Kim my purse and wagged my finger at the album. "You guys sit here and see if you can find something worth salvaging."

The nurse led me down a short hall to an examining room. She left as I changed into a flimsy gown.

The doctor entered the room and instructed me to place my feet in the stirrups. What happened next didn't take long. But when he looked up at me from between my legs to tell me it was over I began to sob. Not uncontrollably but in that powerless way when the tears just escape and run with abandon.

"Should I get someone?" His voice had no inflection, no derision, and that made me cry harder.

I shook my head. He reached behind himself to a counter and handed me a tissue speckled with the blood from his gloves.

I dried my eyes before I left the room and wore a smile as camouflage. But David and Kim, I'm sure, could tell I'd been crying. He draped his arm around my shoulder. Kim took my hand and held it as we walked to the car. We never talked about that day again. For me, it was my second chance and I affixed it firmly in my rear view. I allowed all of it, like dust trails, to just fade away.

A couple of weeks later, David and I moved into our new house. The living room had a stone fireplace that stretched from the floor to the cathedral ceiling and was accented by windows. The fireplace was the focal point of the house and even the movers commented on how nice it was.

On the first night, we slept in the living room on David's futon amid unopened boxes. We had no furniture to put there or in the dining room. We planned to furnish as we could pay for pieces outright rather than use credit.

When David fell asleep, I stared up at the moonlit fireplace. I'd never lived in a place so dark at night and disconcertingly quiet. I silently reaffirmed my commitment to living there one year. Afterward, I was heading back to the city.

The next day we made our first trip to the Farm & Fleet to buy coyote pee so that we'd have it in time for the spring. We drove to Montgomery Ward to price riding lawn mowers. Later that evening, I stood on the deck watching the sun sink behind the trees and David used a net on a long pole to fish wayward leaves out of the pool. We had no neighbors on that side of the house, just woods. So, when he finished, we skinny-dipped under an umbrella of stars. Treading water, I listened to eager crickets throw their voices and tuck themselves in trees spangled with fireflies. This was heaven.

When I think about why I pushed my sister and felt a stake in Debra's future, it's because I wanted them to have their own piece of heaven. I'd never felt like I'd totally *arrived*. Or that what I had couldn't quickly disappear like a mirage. But that moment filled me with a sense of accomplishment. I wanted Debra and Kim to experience that. They didn't have to do things the way I did them or want what I wanted. The truth is, David and I hadn't aspired to live so far from the city or in a predominately white community. But he'd wanted land, and this was where we'd found it, along with neighbors who would become dear friends. No, Debra and Kim didn't have to dream my dreams.

I just wanted them to have—and make—better choices.

chapter nineteen

The Steps

· · ·

As soon as I opened the door to the VFW hall's recreation center, Kim and I smelled cigarette smoke and bad cologne. A young white woman, not much older than us, sat behind a wooden desk.

"Here for the meeting?" she asked through chocolatey teeth. On the counter in front of her was a jar marked "Merry Xmas" containing red and green Hershey's Kisses. Behind her, a framed photograph of President Ronald Reagan hung on the wall.

"Yes," I said.

The young woman stood and handed us a sign-in sheet and two name tags.

"First names only."

I wrote my name on one and Kim's on the other. I handed Kim her name tag and she laughed. "I think I can write my own name."

"Oh, sorry."

The woman licked her fingers and pulled two sheets of paper from a collated stack on her desk and handed them to us. In a large font were the words "The Twelve Steps." Underneath were twelve bulleted points explaining the principles for overcoming addiction.

The woman pointed down the hall. "Second door on the right."

We started to walk away but I turned and saw that she was staring at us. "Enjoy the remains of your evening."

"Remains?" Kim mouthed. Snickering, she said, "Enjoy the *remains*?"

At Thanksgiving dinner, a couple of weeks before, Mom had pulled me to the side to tell me that she worried Kim was drinking too much. Mom had been concerned for a while but noticed her "throwing them back" at my wedding reception after David and I left. I told her that Kim drank like most twentysomethings our age, but Mom looked scared. In college, I'd become close friends with a white architecture student who, as an undergraduate, had been an alcoholic. I called him, and he told me to look in the Yellow Pages for an Alcoholics Anonymous meeting and take her. I found one a few miles from Normal. Then I called my sister.

"Your mother thinks you may have a drinking problem," I'd said to her. "Please just humor me and go to an AA meeting. I found one, tomorrow at 7 p.m. It could be helpful."

"You think so, huh?" She chuckled. "Okay, I'll go."

I was surprised she had agreed so quickly.

We entered the room from the back, near two rectangular tables with slightly warped tops. One was set with liters of orange, red, and grape soda and paper cups; the other, a small stack of Bibles and pamphlets, a few boxes of donuts, and paper napkins. Cigarette smoke shrouded the room.

About ten white men, in their sixties with gray hair and sizable guts, were seated on metal folding chairs arranged in a circle.

Everyone in that room was painfully aware of Chicago's segregated neighborhoods: streets you didn't cross, whole city blocks that could easily have been picked up and plopped down into some Mississippi backwater.

"You're welcome here," a man said as we stood in the doorway, deciding whether to enter. He got up and unfolded a couple of chairs that were propped against a wall next to the American and City of Chicago flags, next to removable and laminated placards that had been taped to the wall for the meeting. Written on one: "The express elevator to sobriety is broken. Please use the Steps."

The man placed the chairs in the circle.

"See Jerry over there." He pointed. "He's been known to take off his prosthetic arm to make room in the circle, in case we have to squeeze in tight."

The men laughed as Jerry hoisted a metal arm and waved.

Still uneasy, I reached for Kim's hand and whispered, "We should probably go."

"Come take a load off," another man said. He had a bad upper plate. I knew this because Mom always discreetly commented on people with ill-fitting dentures.

"No, let's stay," Kim said, skirting my hand.

We joined the circle.

The man who got the chairs turned to us. "I had a Colored bunk-mate in Korea. We treated each other like brothers." He placed his hand over his heart. "I'm Tate."

I hated the word "Colored." It made me think of Jim Crow and subjugation. But our own grandmother still used it—and the word "Negro"—to describe Black people. It didn't matter that Kim and I explained that "Black" and the new term "African American," still in its infancy, were preferred.

"Don't know a thing about no Africa," she'd huffed.

The men quieted after we sat down, so much that I could hear the ceiling fan beating lopsided overhead as it stirred the smell of smoke and insect spray.

After the introductions—first names only—and prayers and other formalities, Tate leaned forward, his elbows on his knees, and rubbed his hands together. He and several of the men spoke about their progress since the last meeting. Newcomers talked about what they had lost or stood to lose.

When Kim pulled out a cigarette, Tate handed her a metal ash-tray.

"Dawn," he said, eyeing my name tag, "why are you here this evening?"

I didn't know what to say. I sat up straight, fidgeting a bit. I didn't want to light into Kim. I was happy that she agreed to come along and I enjoyed being in her company.

After a few uncomfortable seconds, my sister said, "She's here because of me. I'm the screwup."

"You're not a screwup." I wasn't giving these white men anything beyond our presence. I figured that despite their niceties, deep down they still saw us as stereotypes—young Black women who worked low-wage jobs and were uneducated.

"Maybe she is a screwup," Tate said. "That doesn't mean she has to stay that way." He cut his eyes to Kim. "That doesn't mean you can't change."

Kim looked at me and then at Tate. "My sister is smart and has done really well." She grinned slyly. "But I'm not her."

"Nobody's asked you to be." I tried not to sound snippy.

"That's fine," Tate said to me. He could tell Kim hit a nerve. He turned to her: "You want to talk about when you started drinking?"

Kim looked up at the ceiling. "I used to steal my stepfather's liquor or our uncle Henry's. Andrew drank gin. Uncle Henry wasn't too particular."

Damn. I had no idea. I leaned forward to catch my sister's eye, but she intentionally avoided looking at me.

During one family get-together not long after Andrew moved in, he had Tanqueray and bottles of wine on the flat top of the stereo console. I secretly combined Coke with Tanqueray and felt grown up as I sipped my cocktail. I allowed Kim to sip from my cup. Soon I was at peace with the world. Later, after everyone left, I was at war. Lying in bed with my head spinning, I somehow found my way to the bathroom and spent much of the night with my head in the toilet, hurling quietly. I didn't want to wake Mom. Kim, however, slept through the night.

"Tell us why you came today," Tate said.

I answered, "She's here because I asked her to come with me."

"So that tells me why you're here," Tate said to me. "I'm asking Kim. Do you drink to excess? You have a problem?"

"I drink," Kim said, looking at me. "I drink socially. No, I don't have a problem."

"Okay." He smiled. "I used to drink socially. But I also drank alone pretty good."

"We have relatives," I said. "Our stepfather and uncle, as Kim just mentioned, are, for the most part, functional alcoholics. She's not like them."

"I'm here to tell you," said Jerry, "there's more than one way to be an alcoholic."

"I've gotten myself into trouble over the last few years," Kim said. "I gave our mother a hard time."

"Hell," I corrected.

"Hell, okay. I was ten the first time I ditched school. I had a friend who lived across the street from us in the housing project and her bedroom window faced our building and parking lot. I would go over there in the morning and wait for our mother to pull out of her space. Sometimes I'd sneak back into the apartment and watch soap operas all day."

Kim turned toward me to gauge my reaction. Now I evaded her gaze.

"Some days I'd just slam the front door when Mom was in the bathroom and then run back into our bedroom and I'd hide under my bed. I'd only come out after I heard her double-lock the door."

If anyone else had told me this, I would have called her a liar. I wondered what else I didn't know. Or couldn't have known. Or chose not to know about my sister.

We stayed until 10 p.m., nearly three hours. My body felt wrung out. I hadn't anticipated that she would reveal so much. But she didn't talk about Brandon. Not one word. When the evening ended, the men shook our hands and invited us to return.

Pulling out of the parking lot, I seized the moment to pry further.

"So, tell me why you spent so much time at that pool hall on 43rd Street."

She smiled. "It was fun. And they saw me as being me."

"And not me?"

"Nobody knew you, big sister. They just knew me. One guy told me that I didn't act like most women he knew. I wasn't loud and I didn't curse. He liked my jokes. He said I was different. And I liked being different."

We had arrived at Normal. She was about to get out of the car when I grabbed her arm. "Wait. You promise me you're okay?"

"I'm fine. I promise. But I'll go back with you next week." She patted my hand. "If you think it will make *Mom* happy."

My sister jogged up the porch steps. She unlocked the first door and waved at me before entering the second. I sat in the car, staring at the front door. I forced myself to believe that I wasn't worried about her. She had done some stupid and reckless things—more than I'd realized—but she was resilient and a fighter. She had grit. Whatever she was going through, she was going to beat it.

I thought about a Saturday afternoon when we were girls, racing down the stairwell in Lawless. I was ahead of her and she yelled at me.

"Don, what floor are you on?"

"Eight."

My sister was little but full of fuel, running hard. I could hear the sheer ferocity of her sandals slapping the concrete. "I'm on nine," she relayed without me asking.

I didn't have time to ask her. I was too busy concentrating. There was a rhythm to running, to jumping and not slamming into a wall. I'd found it and I was speeding up.

"What floor now, Don?" she yelled, nearly winded. I knew her cheeks were rosy.

"I'm on five." I could hear her footfalls ricocheting off the walls. My sister conceded nothing.

"What floor now, Don?"

"I'm on two."

And when I arrived at the shiny black lobby door, I held it open for her as her feet continued pounding concrete.

I could hear her determination to catch up. I could feel her fight.

chapter twenty

Leaving Lawless

. . .

K im was right about Mom never moving into Normal. Instead, when she was ready to leave Lawless, she set her sights on a building that Jim and Sarah recently purchased —a nine-flat, with spacious apartments, farther south of Bronzeville and not far from the lakefront. David's parents sold their house and moved into one of the units, and his two older brothers lived there as well.

Kim and I spent a Saturday helping Mom pack up the apartment. Standing in our old bedroom, we marveled at how such a claustrophobic space could hold more than two decades of stuff. Over the years, I had rearranged the room, often trying to optimize space. But now, with the twin beds gone, along with the nightstand and the larger of the two dressers, the room looked tiny, incapable of accommodating our past. I pawed through a small cedar chest that Uncle Al had built and found an album that included Kim's and my science fair ribbons, report cards, and elementary school class pictures. I homed in on my third-grade photo. In it, Debra sits on the very first row on the far right. Her head is slightly cocked to the side and her smile is unnaturally restrained. I'm on the top row, the only girl with the taller boys, standing near Mrs. Love. In the back of the album—slipped in because there was no real place for them—were two obituary programs from Candy Love's funeral. I only noticed them when they slid out.

Kim was removing clothes from her dresser and I was cleaning out the closet when I found a plastic pumpkin of fossilized Halloween candy bars that she had stockpiled and a couple of old letters from school that she'd hidden when our mattresses were no longer safe havens. I cleared my throat to get her attention and then waved the envelopes at her. We both laughed.

"That was a lifetime ago, sister," she said, folding clothes and placing them into two piles—one for keeping and the other for giving away. The giveaway pile was larger.

I was about to take a garbage bag of trash to the incinerator room when I noticed Kim standing motionless, staring into the last drawer, her face both solemn and searching.

"Are you okay?"

"I'm fine," she said, sounding far away.

As soon as she spoke, it hit me. The little aspirator. I walked over to her.

My sister unwrapped the scarf and held the blue plastic tube in the air. I placed my arm around her waist and lay my head on her shoulder. "What can I do for you?"

"How do you keep moving forward?" she asked, as if the question needled her. "You never, ever look back."

I turned to face her, and her eyes held a deep earnestness. My sister was the one person in the world I wanted to help, but she rarely asked for it. In fact, she rarely asked anything of me. And now, for the second time in this room, she was asking me a question whose answer I did not know. Years ago, I couldn't tell her what happened to Brandon's remains and now I didn't have a concrete answer for how I moved on. Although she didn't say the word, I knew she was referring to my abortion.

"Please," she pressed. "It's so effortless for you. Tell me how you do it."

"It's not easy," I said. "I suppose I just focus on the other stuff I'm trying to do."

"Brandon would have been four this past February." She swallowed hard, as though saying his name was an almost impossible feat.

She hadn't said it in so long that I didn't want to speak for fear of silencing her.

"I would have gotten him a birthday cake with four candles and thrown him a party." She stared at the aspirator. "I wish you could teach me how to forget."

I looked outside at the next tower, a wall of windows.

"I can't teach you how to forget. But maybe we can find a way to move on. How about I finish up in here?"

"I'll be okay." She jutted her chin, managing a tepid smile. I placed my forehead on hers.

"You can make your mouth say anything," I said, stealing a line from Mom.

"Don't worry, and I know you will. I'm just caught up in leaving this silly old place."

When our bedroom was finally empty, Kim and I walked into the living room. We stood in front of the window, looking at the lake and the housing project. It was late spring, but the project had the same desolate look all year round no matter how the sun shone on it. There were never any colorful spring flowers. No rainbows dancing around summer lawn sprinklers. No pumpkins or gourds or Christmas lights or trees.

Behind us, Mom was in the kitchen packing the last box. I used to wonder why she looked out the window so much. Over two decades, we each had a front-row seat as the housing project unraveled before us.

As the movers took the last boxes, Mom joined us at the window, leaning against it one last time. "The city would never have allowed this to happen in a white neighborhood," she said, her voice echoing around the living room.

The guys were not like the young toughs of her childhood. These were gangbangers and drug dealers who had guns and sold reefer and this new drug called crack. They were occupiers, along with rogue police officers, who took over vacant apartments and transformed many of the mailboxes into repositories for drugs. Residents had to get post office boxes because the mail carriers no longer came through. Residents had self-imposed curfews. As the years passed, it had become more difficult to remember or even conceive that there was a time before the loss, the ruins, and every broken thing the mind conjures about *public housing*. It was hard to believe that there was a period during Mom's childhood in the Ida B. Wells Homes when the flowers and grass were lush and the dirt had purpose; the ground was not at all hard and fallow; and the crumbling brown buildings didn't look snaggletoothed on account of missing bricks.

Once, the mortar had held.

I placed my hand on my mother's shoulder. "Will you miss living here?"

"No." She brushed my hand away. "When it's time to move on, you simply do." Standing, she shook the strain from her back. "Come on, now. Let's not ass-drag."

K im rode with me as we followed Mom to her new place. Then I drove Kim home. She cocked her head before she got out of the car.

"Hey, I have to write an essay on *The Odyssey* and how its figurative language demonstrates the book's themes. You mind looking at it for me next weekend?"

"Not at all," I said, trying to remain low-key about it. Inwardly, though, I was excited that she was asking for help. Despite her breakdown seeing the aspirator, I saw this as a sign she was going to be okay. She was still healing, I told myself.

With her full-time job at the nursing home, it was taking a bit longer for her to finish her associate's degree. Still, she'd set her mind to graduating and it seemed within her grasp. When I arrived the next Saturday, I followed her into the dining room. On a card table sat her secondhand typewriter, an ashtray overflowing with cigarette butts, and a cup of black coffee. I bent over to look at what she'd written.

"It's not ready yet," she said, steering me away from the page. She wiped her hands on her blue jean cutoffs and cracked her knuckles.

"Okay, okay." I stepped away.

Dust coated the built-in china cabinet. In the living room, just off the dining room, the furniture Mom had once covered in plastic or white sheets was now stained and falling apart.

I drifted into the kitchen toward a small stack of papers on the table.

"Don't touch my shit!" Kim yelled, laughing, from the living room.

I put my hands up and stepped away.

"I'm just kidding," she said over her typing. "They're just reports."

She had to write short narratives whenever something eventful happened during her shift at the nursing home: *Two residents got into a scuffle so Jack and I separated them and gave them a cooling-down period. . . . Greta adamantly refused her medicines this morning. They will need to be administered this afternoon. . . . Jodie was inconsolable and running a fever. I held her hand and rubbed it and had her sit in the rocking chair for a while.* The vignettes gave me insight into the type of work she was doing and, more than that, how compassionately she was handling it.

The shades were drawn in the back of the apartment and light from her television strobed from her bedroom. She'd told me that the reason she chose the overnight shift at the nursing home was because she had trouble sleeping. During her nights off, we'd sometimes talk into the wee hours and I'd hear the television in the background. Even with that, sometimes she couldn't fall asleep until daybreak.

"I'm almost done!" Kim yelled.

I peeked out of the bedroom and looked down the hall. Kim was sitting at the card table, reading while bouncing her right leg absent-mindedly like Mom.

I walked over to her and she handed me five pages. I smiled the whole time while reading them. I had few editorial marks because of her well-conceived arguments. She finished the paper and by the time I left, it was nearly midnight.

I sat in the car for a few minutes. The shades were drawn, and I watched my sister's silhouette crossing the living room, flicking on all the lights in the apartment. It wasn't the first time I watched her do this. Mom complained about the high electric bills. Kim's solution was to allow friends—some of them ne'er-do-wells—to stay with her. It occurred to me that she wasn't just an insomniac.

I was beginning to believe maybe my sister was afraid of the dark.

chapter twenty-one

Pasties

. . .

Debra spoke in euphemisms. "Dancing" was her word for strip-ping. The men—and women—who came to watch and do more than watch were "dates." Work was a "party." I'd given up wondering when she would quit dancing and I couldn't remember when I'd last asked her about returning to school. Almost every time we connected she made a new promise:

On Monday, I'm taking a test to qualify for a new job.

On Monday, I'm enrolling in nursing school.

On Monday, I'm starting classes.

The truth was that her life had devolved into one eternal week-end. It became easier to chase the past, the only place where we found common ground.

I told her that Mom had left Lawless and she said, "Pretty soon, nobody I know will live there. Did you remember to look under the carpet in the hallway to see if we left any notes? What if someone finds them?"

"I forgot about our notes." I laughed.

"We kept Miss Polaroid there for a while. She got me into so much trouble."

"She got us both into trouble." Feeling a swell of nostalgia, I said, "How about I finally take you up on your offer to come to Indianap-olis?"

"You want to see little ol' me? It's about time!"

We set a date for mid-August when I'd be on vacation. As soon as I hung up, I called Kim to invite her to come, too. We'd never taken a day trip, just the two of us. The thought of us being on the open road together conjured all kinds of warm and fuzzies. It would be a good opportunity for us to reconnect.

I picked her up on a windy Saturday morning in my new Chevy Geo Tracker. I allowed my sister to get comfortable before I handed her the map.

By the time we merged onto Interstate 65, the wind was so strong that it took everything I had just to keep my little SUV in my lane. For a moment, I thought it might be too dangerous to make the two-and-a-half-hour trip. But I had promised Debra. And I had promised Kim.

"Your brother-in-law stocked the cooler with sandwiches and pop," I said, pointing to the back seat.

After a few minutes on I-65, either the wind died down or I'd gotten used to my death grip on the steering wheel. Semis that had pulled off to the shoulder were reentering the right lane. I had the air conditioning on, and Kim asked me, "Can I roll the window down for a quick second?"

"Absolutely," I said, tightening my grip on the wheel.

The way she breathed in the air—as though it was the first deep breath she'd taken in ages—made me want to ask her if she was okay. But I tended to do that a lot and I told myself to just be a friend today. Not a surrogate mother. Not a big sister.

"Remember how happy we would be the night before we left for the Gospel Tour?" she asked, rolling up the window. "We could hardly sleep."

Every July, our church traveled to a different city across the country and sometimes Canada. That's how Kim and I got to see Washington, DC, New York, Boston, Miami, Memphis, Denver, Las Vegas, Honolulu, Toronto, and so many other cities. Granny and Aunt Doris took us on the trips because Mom preferred a rare week of peace.

"You remember we would get up so early?" I laughed. "It was the only time Mom didn't have to hurry us. We got dressed so fast. It would still be dark out and the project would be quiet."

"Mom would pick up Granny and Aunt Doris and a block before the church, we'd see that long line of chartered Greyhound buses, exhaust fumes billowing."

"We'd watch Mom from the window walking back to the car. She was happy to get rid of our Black asses. She'd be practically dancing! She was like, 'Partay! A whole week without you Negroes. . . .'"

And in unison we said, "'. . . tugging on my very existence.'"

Kim threw her head back and her long neck pulsed with laughter. I surreptitiously inhaled, searching for the smell of alcohol. I was pleased that I didn't find it. We hadn't returned to an AA meeting and what for? *She didn't need it.*

"If we were lucky," Kim said, "we'd be on a bus with somebody who could not just sing but *sang*! Amen?"

"Amen," I said. "And somebody who could *burn*."

"The smell of that fried chicken and cornbread would be talking to you, baby."

"You hear me? Speaking in tongues!" I sat up straighter. "How about something from Brother Joe, Sister Kim?"

Brother Joe was a baritone who could tear up a Negro spiritual. It must be said that neither my sister nor I got the singing gene from our parents. But in that moment, Kim found a rhythm by stomping her foot and slapping her thigh. Then she opened with a deep and moody alto:

You know I promised the Lord that I would

I joined in with:

(Hold out, hold out, hold out)
You know I promised the Lord that I would
(Hold out, until He meets me in Galilee)

The words lingered after the song stopped and the moment reminded me what I loved about our childhood church, being swept up in the comfort of song and the spirit.

"Why did you let Mr. Isaiah do your hair when you hated anyone else to touch it?"

"He asked me. Nobody else asked me. They just took it for granted that they could do whatever they wanted."

"It was that simple?" I laughed.

"It was." She reached behind her. "I'll take one of those sandwiches now."

Not long after she ate, her head bobbed, and she struggled to keep her eyes open. She pulled her blue jean jacket from her tote between her legs and folded it behind her head. After a few minutes of trying to keep talking, she said, "My sleep has really come down on me." It was something Mom always said. She faced the afternoon sun and dropped off. Several times, she stirred a bit and I wanted to pat her back. My eyes kept darting between her and the road. I'd watched her sleep for much of her life, trying to understand her, to know her without the artifice of a smile or glib comeback and I remained uncertain about how much I really knew.

Kim was still out when I pulled up in front of the Trice family's duplex.

Seeing the Tracker, Mrs. Trice exited her side door of the duplex with her purse and car keys in her hand. Her hair was short and tapered now and she was still lovely. She pulled each of us toward her for an embrace.

"I'm sorry I have to leave," she said. "I have a part-time department store job."

"I'm so sorry we're late." I'd forgotten that Indianapolis was on Eastern time and we were arriving later than I thought.

"Debra had to run a quick errand," Mrs. Trice said as she walked to her car on the side of the house. Before she could open the car door, Debra ran up behind Kim and me and hugged us both at the same time.

"Kim, you're so pretty!" Debra said. "Look at you all grown up!" Debra hadn't seen Kim since she'd last seen me—that time when Debra drove up with her girlfriends. "And, Dawn, look at you! Look at your big ol' French braid!"

Debra sounded like her normal effervescent self. But it was impossible to ignore—and painful to see—how gaunt she was. She'd always had dark circles around her eyes, like her father's, but now they were even darker.

She led us into the living room and walked over to the coffee table.

"Dawn, you remember these pretty pins?"

Kim and I sat on the sofa. Debra sat on the floor on the other side of the table.

I looked down at a gold starfish, a cat pulling a Christmas tree, and another cat pawing at a mouse dangling from a chain. I could feel my face heating up from embarrassment. I'd given them to her as birthday and Christmas gifts. They were not the type of presents most kids offered.

"Those must have come from Granny," Kim chuckled. "She had a closet full of trinkets and Mom raided it when we had to give someone a gift."

"Totally inappropriate gifts for kids," I said. "I went to a girl's birthday party and she opened my gift, frowned, and asked, 'Who gave me this?' I quietly cringed."

Debra scooped up the trinkets. "They were the best gifts ever." Changing the subject, she said, "You remember how we used to go into the laundry room and look under the machines for money? If we got a good day, we'd find a whole dollar."

"Then we'd either walk to the candy car or to Woolworths," I said.

"Indy doesn't have candy cars. If they did, they probably would sell corn."

For about three hours, we continued this way, winding back the clock, relying on the past to gloss over the present. Then Debra looked down at her watch. "It turns out I have to work tonight," she said, making a sad face. "A last-minute thing. But you guys can come with me and see the show."

Kim and I looked at each other. This wasn't the plan, but that was Debra, spontaneous, impulsive.

Debra led us upstairs to her bedroom, where posters of our 1970s teen heartthrobs like Foster Sylvers and Michael Jackson adorned the walls. Skimpy outfits, G-strings, and pasties lay strewn across the bed along with newspapers that she read avidly. Kim pushed a few items aside to sit down. Debra took a shower and returned to the room with a towel wrapped around her body. When she took it off, her breasts were perky and nearly perfectly round, but I could see the bony relief of her rib cage. She flitted naked around the room and as she rifled through the outfits, deciding which one to wear, Kim picked up a pastie lying on the bedspread.

"How did you start?" Kim asked.

"Dancing?" Debra stepped into a G-string.

"Yeah." Kim held the pastie up to her chest.

I pressed my lips together and rolled my eyes at my sister. Debra must have seen me because she smiled as she took the pastie from Kim and placed it on the dresser. Her father's funeral program was tucked into the mirror.

"I started by accident." Debra dabbed concealer under her eyes. "At first I was a cocktail waitress at a topless bar. The clientele consisted mainly of white men in suits with lots of money. One night the DJ announced that the waitresses were allowed to take the stage, tops optional. Me, being the free-spirit, fun-loving person I am, I thought it would be fun to do something spontaneous. Once onstage, I started to get a little nervous but then I said, 'What the hell!' And off went the top!"

I watched Debra as she brushed on eye shadow and used powder to even out her once-flawless complexion. Soon, she was gorgeous again.

"When the two songs had ended, I left the stage with one hundred dollars in tips. The next day, I traded in my towel and tray for a G-string and heels."

"Kim is working at a nursing home and she's going to school." As soon as I said it, I realized it sounded like I was disparaging Debra. I wasn't meaning to. I was only trying to brag on Kim.

"Stop it," Kim said, looking directly at me.

"What? Your paper on *The Odyssey* was really good. Did you ever get your grade?"

"I got a C-plus," she said, clearly annoyed.

"It was better than a C." I couldn't help but look disappointed. "You can contest that grade. Talk to your professor—"

"I turned it in late, Dawn," she said. "He docked it a grade."

"Late? You were done early. You had time to spare."

"I know, but I just messed around and wanted to change things. I fucked up."

"I'm proud of you, too, Kim," Debra jumped in before I could respond, defusing the moment. "Why don't we just head out and have a great night?"

We got into my car and I drove to Indianapolis's west side. I'd never been to a topless bar or strip club before. I'd seen them in the movies. In this club, I took in the bar and runway-type stage, the tables and chairs. Debra led us to a back area, a makeshift dressing room with walls of mirrors and makeup tables and women.

Kim and I stood near the doorway, getting a contact high from the lingering smell of weed. Some of the women were already topless. A few were dressed in short robes.

"Hey, y'all!" The women's attention trained on Debra. "These are my friends from Chicago."

"What up, Chardae's friends!" one woman said while putting on lipstick.

"Chardae?" I whispered to Debra.

"My stage name." She winked.

Because the room was already smoke-filled, Kim, for the first time since the trip began, pulled out a cigarette. Debra had told me that the dancers fell into several categories: drug abusers, prostitutes, college students, underaged runaways, and moneymakers, women who danced because it was fun and easy money. She placed herself in the last category, but I was afraid that her thin frame suggested she was also an addict.

Across the room, I could see our reflection in the mirror. Kim finished her cigarette and sidled close to me in a silent apology. She bumped her shoulder against mine. I smiled and returned the bump.

"Let me get you guys some seats," Debra said, taking a pull off a joint.

"We can't stay," I said. "I want to get back to Chicago before midnight."

"Of course, I get it," Debra said, hugging me and then Kim.

The truth was that I didn't want to see her dance. She had so much more potential than that. I used to hate it when I was editing a *Tribune* story about something bad that had happened in a posh neighborhood and residents were quoted saying, "This wasn't supposed to happen here." I always felt like, *Where is it* supposed *to happen?* But Debra wasn't supposed to be *here*. Mrs. Trice knew what her daughter was doing for a living, but I can't imagine she had ever come to a show. It would have been too hard to watch her in the presence of so many people who did not know she was smart, kind, and funny. Kim and I left as the show began.

About six months later, Debra called.

"I'm done with dancing, Dawn. I did my farewell tour. I went from club to club and had the DJ tell the audience, 'Say goodbye to Chardae, this is her final dance.'"

"I'm so, so, so happy. What made you quit?"

"It's time to be productive. I was working five to six days a week, doing coke to stay awake and drinking too much. Daddy was an alcoholic and that worried me."

"I didn't know that," I said.

Debra told me that she was officially taking classes at a vocational school to become a certified nursing assistant. She wasn't about to apply or enroll "on Monday." She was already there. It was the first time since Debra returned from the air force that she was executing a plan.

I hung up happy that she'd called. She had turned a corner and was finding her way. It was only a matter of time before Kim won admittance into a four-year college, earned her bachelor's degree, and started a career. For both of them, I allowed myself to imagine a future so promising that the past would be remembered only as a series of bumps they had to navigate to get there.

chapter twenty-two

"Prophet Told Us a Storm Was Coming"

. . .

When Kim and I were kids, we endured the First House of Prayer's endless church services by waiting for the Holy Ghost, or Holy Goat as my sister called it. At a point during the service, the music or preaching would crescendo, and the spirit would take command of parishioners' bodies. Aunt Doris got happy nearly every Sunday. She'd bolt out of the choir down the center aisle of the church, patting her body as though tamping out flames. "Just have your way, Lord!" she'd scream. Granny didn't get happy often. But when she did, we knew because she'd be the only person still standing, and in a trance, clapping wildly when everyone else had returned to their seats. Mom rarely, rarely caught the Holy Ghost. But the one time I remember vividly, she tore up the choir, flailing her body across chairs and people. Afterward, the choir looked like a hurricane had ripped through it. Terrified, Kim stood and started crying. But Prophet hurried down the aisle and took her hand.

"It's only the spirit, child," he assured her. "It will all be over soon."

I was thinking about the Holy Ghost, the Comforter, while looking out my living room window on a Saturday morning in early May 1993. My sister was in need of one. Mom had just called to say she wanted to take Kim for a ride, so they were driving out to see me. It was a long drive and they didn't just pop by. Over the last year, Kim had been struggling. She'd left the nursing home, saying it was too demanding because she needed more time for school. David had gotten her a job working the overnight shift for a friend who owned a Shell gas station. Six months later, she got fired for falling asleep at the cash register. She told David it had only happened once on a night when she was dog-tired. But David's friend confided that it had happened far more than once. Kim's boss at the nursing home welcomed Kim with open arms after she'd asked for her old job back. She had been known for being dependable and caring. But when she started calling in sick too much, the boss had to let my sister go.

When Mom and Kim arrived at my house that morning, Kim's face looked puffy. Her lips were red and swollen in a way I'd never seen before. She wore black pants and a Michael Jordan jersey and over it a ratty overcoat I didn't recognize. It reminded me of a mangy animal, something a homeless woman might have rescued from the trash.

"I've got to pee," she said. She hugged me and the smell of alcohol engulfed her.

"Do you mind taking off your shoes?"

Mom slipped hers off immediately and walked to the kitchen.

"Why do I have to take off my shoes?" Kim said, attempting to exert what little control she had left.

"My neighbors' geese have been wandering into our yard, shitting everywhere."

Kim looked at the bottom of her shoes. "I'm all good," she said dismissively.

"I'm just trying not to have goose shit tracked in my house. Whether you can see it or not. That's all."

"God forbid anybody make a mess in your space."

She stormed out to Mom's car, got in, and turned the ignition. I thought she was about to leave, but she just sat there, pouting. I let her stew for a while and then I walked out and sat in the back seat behind her. We said nothing for a few seconds and then I tapped her shoulder, pointing to the geese imprisoned by a chicken-wire fence in my neighbors' yard. One flapped its wings as though mounting an escape.

"Why doesn't she just fly the hell away?" Kim muttered, looking at me in the rearview.

"She could have when she was younger. Now she's too heavy to fly."

My sister kept staring at the flock, her expression vacillating between annoyance and sympathy.

I pointed to a section of grass not far from the geese. "That area there is our in-ground septic tank. There's a pump inside that shoots waste from the house out to a septic field. I heard about a woman whose husband was cheating in their house and he got caught because he was flushing his condoms down the toilet unaware that they get tangled in the pump. He had to explain that to his wife."

The furrows in my sister's forehead relaxed.

"Will you come back inside?" I placed my hand on her head, forcing a nod.

"Okay," she said, smiling weakly. "I have to pee really bad."

Inside the house, Kim stooped to untie her shoelaces. It broke my heart to see her hands trembling.

"Kim, you don't have to—"

"No," she said, looking up at me. "I want to be respectful."

She removed one shoe, but the other had a beast of a knot. Her face collapsed into the most terrified expression. "I can't do it!"

"Please go. I'm begging you. Please, just go pee. I don't care. I promise."

She was in the bathroom for a while and I knocked on the door. I opened it and she was washing her hands and looking in the mirror.

"I think I pissed myself a little." She looked as scared as I'd ever seen her.

"Don't worry, we'll fix it." I smiled to lighten the mood, but I'd never been more afraid in my life.

I took her upstairs to the bathroom and turned on the shower.

"I'll start a load of laundry with your pants and will leave you some sweats on the bed."

When she stripped down, her skin looked blotchy, like she hadn't showered in more than a few days. It reminded me of a little mottled boy in the third grade whom I thought had bad skin until I saw the nurse drag a cotton ball drenched in alcohol across his arm. She removed a thick stripe of dirt that smooshed the fibers.

Although my sister's body wasn't that dirty, it still disturbed me. I'd seen Kim naked all her life—I'd known her body like my own. The wisps of dark hair on her toes and fingers and the faint shadow down her spine. Now I felt like a voyeur staring at her, so I turned away. She was too fragile for me to ask her when she'd last washed or to comment about the smell of stale liquor overwhelming the room.

"When you finish, I want you to take a walk. The air will make you feel better."

She peeped out of the steam, nodding, acquiescing. "Okay, I'll do whatever you say."

Mom and I were seated at the kitchen table talking when we heard the front door close. We walked to the living room window. Mom looked at Kim as though willing a plane to take off.

"Your sister doesn't want you to know, but she had a bad accident the other night. She slammed her car into a tree."

"What? Where?"

"In Washington Park. Luckily, it happened around 2 a.m. and no one else was involved. But she totaled her car and it's a miracle she was able to walk away. The police weren't around. I called your father and he took care of the car."

Mom turned to the fireplace, studying the jagged stones and the way some jutted out like small cliffs. She stepped back to stare at the top, as if trying to figure out how to crest a mountain.

"I also hear she's become a fixture at the Fantasy," she said. The Fantasy was a lounge down the street from Normal. "They say she sometimes sits on a stool, drinking and staring up at the ceiling at the silver press-on stars."

The old me would have asked Mom who "they" were. The new me understood finally that didn't matter. I could no longer deny that Kim was an alcoholic. When my sister returned from her walk, the three of us sat around the kitchen table drinking tea and talking about nothing of consequence. Now, every time my sister smiled, I could see the mask.

Later that evening, after Mom and Kim left, I curled up next to
David in bed.

"Kim's in trouble. Her drinking is out of hand. She had a car
accident."

David sat up.

"She didn't hurt herself or anyone else, but I'm worried about
her."

"Let her come stay here with us for a while. She'd be away from
temptations," he said. "Without a car, she'd have to go to some fairly
extravagant lengths to find booze."

"I love my sister, but she doesn't come without drama."

"I'm not afraid of no drama. Tell your mother to come, too."

"Three Turner women under one roof? Whew, chile!"

"I ain't afraid of y'all."

David had an amazing ability to drop off to sleep as soon as he
closed his eyes. It was impressive how he could be talking one minute and then snoring before he finished his sentence. I couldn't sleep.
Guilt tugged at me. I felt awful because I had more reservations
about my sister staying with us than David. She would definitely
disrupt our lives, but that wouldn't matter if we could help her. We
weren't professionals. I wasn't sure we could, but we had to try.

I got up and went to David's home office across the hall. I sat at
his desk and picked up the telephone. It was after midnight, but I
knew Kim would be up.

"Hey, I want you to think about something." David had a pencil
and pad on his desk, and I started drawing concentric circles.

"What's up?"

"Your brother-in-law and I want you to stay with us for a while.
And, before you say no, just think about it, okay?"

I could hear male voices in the background laughing at something on the television. *Baby steps*, I told myself.

"I've thought about it. I'll come."

"Really?" The pencil slid out of my hand. "Yay!"

"But give me a couple of weeks."

"What's the matter with tomorrow or the next day?"

"I've got to get my affairs in order," she said, laughing.

She actually sounded much stronger than a few hours ago. Then something hit me: I wondered if she'd been drinking, if now she needed liquor to reconstitute herself, to bring the old Kim back to life.

"What damn affairs you got?" I laughed as I looked at David's appointment book.

"Girl, I got business. I gotta make sure everything is tight."

"Oh, please. How's Sunday, May 16?"

"Sounds good. Now get off my phone. Love you, girl."

"Love you back."

I walked into the guest bedroom next door, where Kim would stay and get herself together. Even though I hated cigarettes, I decided I would allow Kim to smoke in the room. But only if she opened the window. In a couple of weeks, the air would smell of lilacs from the bushes along the driveway. Spring was coming and, with it, the promise of a fresh start.

I had to work the Sunday that Kim would move in, so I planned for her to meet me later that night on the train. We could ride out to my place together. I'd board the 9:20 p.m. train downtown and she'd get on at one of the University of Chicago stops about fifteen minutes later. But Kim called me at work at about 2 p.m. to tell me that she wasn't feeling well and wouldn't be able to meet me. She had attended a going-away party for a neighbor the night before and believed she had eaten chicken salad or pork, something that hadn't agreed with her.

"I'm not hung over," she said. "Mom just stopped by after church and you can ask her. I'll come out tomorrow, okay?"

"You promise?"

"I promise."

I called David and told him that Kim would come the next day.

When I arrived home, it was about 10:30 p.m. and David and I went straight to bed. As usual, he fell fast asleep. It took me a while, but as soon as I dozed off, I was awakened by the answering machine across the hall in David's office. I thought I was dreaming. I hadn't even heard the phone ringing. The clock on the nightstand showed it was just after 11:30 p.m. I could hear Mom's voice, but when I tried to pick up the phone, it was too late. I got up to listen to the answering machine:

"Hey, baby. Just want you to know that your sister is having trouble breathing. She's on her way to St. Bernard's. You don't have to worry or come. I'll let you know as soon as I hear something."

Her voice was steady, and I tried to be calm as I hurried back to the bedroom to wake up David. I told him what happened and, despite Mom's instructions, we agreed to get dressed and drive into the city.

The hospital sat thirty miles away and the main road in our town was a notorious speed trap. But as soon as David reached the highway, he took advantage of the handful of cars out that night and drove like a madman.

"Please slow down," I said when the Tracker's speedometer hit 90 miles per hour. "Let's arrive in one piece."

If you've ever been to a hospital emergency room, you prepare yourself for a wait that feels interminable. People with chronic and untreated illnesses or those who just had the crap beaten out of them for whatever reason would be triaged first. I didn't think whatever was wrong with Kim was anywhere nearly as serious. I felt around the back seat, hoping to find a book to read as we waited.

We got off the expressway and David still drove above the speed limit, doing forty miles per hour instead of thirty. At red lights, he braked but then ran the light when he was sure the intersection was clear.

We were less than a mile away from the hospital when I decided that Kim and I would return to the Alcoholics Anonymous meeting at the VFW center. We'd only been to that one meeting, but the old men seemed sincere enough. I thought about the AA truisms: "The elevator is broken, use the Steps." "You're as sick as your secrets." Tonight would be our wake-up call. About a block from St. Bernard Hospital, I told myself that she would leave the hospital and come directly to our home. No delays. No excuses. David parked and we hurried through the emergency room entrance, where we saw Mom standing next to a woman in a black suit, clerical collar, and sensible soft-soled shoes.

Who is this woman? Why is she standing with Mom? Where is Kim?

We walked up to Mom and the chaplain turned to her and asked, "Is this everyone who's coming?"

"Yes," Mom said, looking at me and not the woman.

The chaplain smiled cordially. "Would you please follow me?"

As we walked, I suddenly felt as though I was hurtling down a shaft, clawing at its sides. I turned to Mom. "Where's Kim?"

"I just got here, too." Now her calm tone seemed forced.

"Ma'am," I said to the chaplain, "are you taking us to see my sister?"

"Just one minute," she said.

"But are we going to see her or not?" I stopped walking. I could feel a storm rising in my throat. Mom grabbed my hand and gently pulled me along as though I were a petulant child.

"C'mon, baby." Her voice had a rattle in it. "Let's just be patient."

The chaplain led Mom, David, and me to a cramped room with tube lights that hummed and walls that were the splotchy green of psychiatric wards in horror films. There were two folding chairs in front of a desk. Behind it, a chair unaccustomed to bending. The chaplain motioned for Mom and me to take a seat. We did and she stood between us. Soon, a doctor, a white man, entered the room. To this day he is vapor, faceless. The chaplain, an older Black woman, lowered one hand onto my shoulder and the other onto my mother's shoulder. I pulled away. *Why is she touching me?* I grew up with church women like her, the type who told you how she came to know Jesus, the type who had a heavy hand. She drew me to her, returning her hand to my shoulder.

This time, I didn't move.

The doctor looked at Mom. "Are you the mother of Kim Turner?" He began to flip through the thin chart, his prop to keep from having to look in my mother's eyes.

"I am," she said. Her back straightened. Her feet planted themselves solidly, squarely on the floor.

I suddenly felt the weight of the chaplain's hand. I lost myself in the grip of her touch. At that moment, I knew that there would be no need for another Alcoholics Anonymous meeting. No need to make plans to bring Kim out to my house. What the doctor said next was merely perfunctory. It was as though the sound had been turned down on him and all I could hear was blood swooshing in my ears as we were thrust into a vortex of pain. What he said was conveyed through a stranger's touch. I leaned over onto Mom and began to sob so hard I felt as though I was suffocating. As she held me, I could feel her shaking her head, but she did not cry.

Quietly, into my hair, she spoke, "Prophet told us a storm was coming."

The white doctor and the Black chaplain had no idea who Prophet was. They didn't know that every now and then he said something like "I want everybody to be careful next Tuesday" or "Check on your balances in the bank." But "A storm is coming" would have forced parishioners to brace and take heed. Mom had decided that this "storm" was her daughter's death, foreordained by Prophet.

Addressing the white doctor and the Black chaplain, Mom said, "This is my other daughter. She works for the *Chicago Tribune*." It was her way of letting them know that she had done something right. But she owed these strangers nothing. Not one word.

The doctor offered his condolences, a practiced morsel of sympathy, and left in a way that seemed efficient and clinical. After a few seconds, the chaplain asked us if we wanted to view Kim's body. Her soft-soled shoes passed in front of me and disappeared out of the room for a few minutes. When the chaplain returned, she led us through the waiting area. My feet moved but only because I willed them to do so. No one wanted to look at us. Not the nurses or the doctors on call. Nor the down-on-their-luck people in the waiting area. I sobbed and David held me up. Mom walked in front of us with the chaplain. The straps of her purse curled around her left fist, Mom had the countenance of someone walking toward a fight. She refused to cry.

The chaplain pushed a button and double doors swished open. We were in the examination area and a nurse stood akimbo by a bay, as though guarding it. She saw us and began to slowly peel back the curtain. I suddenly felt far away. Far, far away. I tasted bile. I stopped just close enough to see my sister's body lying on a gurney. I wasn't close enough to see her face. I couldn't look at her. I asked David to do it for me. What was on that gurney was an imposter, a stand-in

I didn't want to see. I could no longer lie next to her the way I did when she was newly alive. I couldn't get on my knees and look over her the way I did when we shared a bed. When David returned, I buried my head in his chest. I didn't ask him what she looked like. I didn't want to know. But years later, when I'm ready, he will tell me that her face was pale. Not the normal light-skinned pale, but a color that has no light. He will remember that her lips were a purplish blue and her mouth hung open. He will say that she did not look like she was sleeping.

Mom sat next to the gurney, stroking Kim's hand, talking to her as she removed her rings—costume jewelry that now was invaluable.

"Baby, you look so peaceful," she said. "You're at rest now."

David and I found a pay phone next to the waiting area. I called the taxi garage and was surprised that the voice that said "Jiffy" didn't belong to my father. The dispatcher reminded me that this was his night off.

"Do you have his home number?" I asked. It occurred to me that I always reached him at the garage. I didn't have another number for him. Besides, he was living in the city now, having divorced Betty. He had an eight-year-old daughter and a new wife, ten years older than me. Kim and I loved our half sister. When Kim was doing well, we had taken the little girl out on several occasions to lunch and to museums. She was the little sister Kim always wished she had.

"Just a minute, dear," the dispatcher said. He covered the mouthpiece and yelled into the garage, "Anybody got Mr. Turner's home number?"

I had no idea who was sitting around that television in the garage. And it was not at all surprising that although it was now after midnight, the old men were there.

The dispatcher returned to the phone to tell me that no one had Dad's home number. I thanked him and dialed directory assistance. The operator told me it was unpublished. I began explaining that my sister had just died, and saying the words felt self-mutilating. I handed David the phone.

"Miss, I understand you can't give out the number. We're at the hospital now. Can you call him and get him on the line?"

To our surprise, she did. David handed me the phone.

Dad picked up, his voice groggy. "Hello?"

"Hi, Dad. Can we come over? We have to tell you something."

"Okay" was all he said.

He gave me his address, but he didn't ask why. He knew nothing good was about to come from us visiting him after midnight.

When we arrived, my father looked scared—like he was staring down a deluge he couldn't outrun. He opened the vestibule door to let us in. He lived on the first floor of a two-flat building. He led us into his apartment. David and I followed. Mom walked behind us. He turned the light on in his living room and he could now see my face, my puffy red eyes. No one sat down.

"I'm so sorry," I said, bursting into tears once again. David held me.

"It's Kim?" he said.

Mom nodded. "She's gone."

Dad's eyes were vacant, and tears like I'd never seen before glazed his cheeks. His shoulders seemed like they should be shaking, but they were still. He covered his mouth with his hand. I'd never seen my father cry.

As we started for the door, Mom lifted her hand to touch his arm or pat his shoulder. But she did neither. I'd never known Mom to feel sympathy for her ex-husband. But she wouldn't have wished this type of pain on anyone. Certainly not him. She never thought that they would be so wholly tied together again by a feeling—and that feeling would be resounding despair.

We left Dad and drove to Aunt Doris's house. The house was dark when she answered the door.

"Mama told me that the ambulance had to come get Kim," Aunt Doris said. She turned on a lamp. When Mom sat down on a love seat, Aunt Doris sat next to her sister. David and I stood by the door. Mom placed her arm around her sister and held her. As Mom whispered the words, Aunt Doris gasped and burst into tears.

"What happened to her?" Her voice was leaden with grief.

"She'd been sick earlier in the day," Mom said. The seat cushion sighed as she sat up straight. "I called Mama and asked her to put

Kim on the phone. Mama buzzed her doorbell, which was her signal for Kim to come upstairs. I could hear Mama say, 'C'mon, Sugar. Your mother doesn't have all day.' Mama said she was walking up the stairs like she was climbing a mountain. She reached the top and Mama said Kim looked ashen.

"Kim took the phone and I asked her if I should drive her to the bus station."

"The bus station?" I interrupted.

"She was supposed to be coming to stay with us," David said.

"She had a bus ticket to Ohio," Mom said. "She was going to see a friend there. I asked her about her bags and whether she was packed. She didn't say anything. I heard Mama say, 'Child, your mother can't see you nod.' I heard Kim say she was going to lie down for a few minutes. She didn't say another word to me before she got off the phone. She just let go of the phone and walked back downstairs. Mama said to me, 'I guess she'll call you back.'"

Mom strummed the love seat's arm, as though she'd lost her train of thought.

"I said, 'Mama, go down there and see about her.' I held on for five minutes, ten, I don't remember. It seemed like forever. Mama came back to the phone. She was out of breath. She told me that my child was sitting on the sofa with her head slumped forward. I told her to call the ambulance and that I was on my way. I drove to the hospital and parked. As I walked to the emergency door, I passed an ambulance and this ol' dude, who was sitting on the steps, smoking. He looked at me and said, 'You here for the DOA?' I said to myself, 'Oh, shit. What did he just say?' She was dead before she got there." Mom's hands were folded in her lap and she looked at them as if stunned by their emptiness.

"I'm so sorry," Aunt Doris said, taking my mother's hands in hers.

"I am, too," Mom said. "She had a heart attack. That's what the doctor told us."

Then Aunt Doris pushed up and hurried over to me with an urgency I'd never seen from her. She held me tightly.

"Hold your head up, you hear?" she whispered forcefully. She cupped my face in her hands. "You've been an outstanding big sister."

Auntie meant well, but regret pressed against every inch of me. I could not have felt more like a failure.

By the time we'd told Granny and returned to the hospital to pick up Mom's car and followed her home, the sun was coming up. David and I sat in Mom's living room. She assured us that we didn't have to stay with her.

"I'll be fine. I think someone needs to stay with you." She looked at David. "Please make sure your wife gets some sleep."

On the expressway, David and I sat stuck in rush-hour traffic. It was Monday morning and commuters sat in their cars, applying makeup, sipping coffee, honking their horns. I wished I was in any car other than my own. I wondered how the world kept spinning. How was it possible that the morning had broken open and the sky had a gradient intensity that was strikingly bright, strikingly clear, so strikingly blue? Why the hell wasn't it crying?

Sitting there, I had another memory: the night Kim almost died. She was about three and I was six and we were on the sidewalk with Mom waiting for the No. 3 King Drive bus to take us home. Mom clutched Dad's dry cleaning in one hand and Kim's hand in the other. Several strangers gathered nearby, and we all watched cars zoom past until the light turned red. It was dusk and a breeze stirred from nowhere and rustled the plastic encasing my father's clothes. Mom snatched her hand from Kim's to save the dry cleaning, but before Mom could grab Kim's hand again, my sister broke away, sprinting into the street. A woman behind us screamed. Tires screeched as cars braked violently to avoid hitting her. A cab hopped the median. I looked up at my mother's face, contorted with fear and disbelief. It said, *Please, God, please, please don't take my child*. A couple of men dashed out into the traffic waving violently at the oncoming cars. But my little sister was oblivious to the danger and how close she was to death.

Kim was Duperman.

chapter twenty-three

A Sad, Sad Suit

* * *

In the four years since I'd gotten special permission to be married at the First House of Prayer Church, Prophet had doubled down on his rule regarding nonmembers not being allowed to have ceremonies in the sanctuary. Kim was no longer a member, so Mom's first call that Monday morning was to the funeral home down the street from the church.

Later that evening, Granny sat in Mom's living room with Mom and me, gently urging her daughter to reconsider and lobby to have Kim's services at the church. She reminded Mom that our family had a long history at the First House of Prayer and that Great-Granny Lessie had been held in such high regard that her casket was placed in front of the altar.

"I'm happy to do it for you," Granny said. "I know Prophet would make an exception."

"No," Mom said calmly. And that was that.

Two days later at choir rehearsal when Prophet announced Kim's death, he did so in his normal parlance, saying that "Kim has gone home to be with the Lord." Neither I nor my family attended, but choir members told Granny that parishioners groaned because my sister was only twenty-four years old. Prophet gave everyone the details of Kim's "homegoing celebration" and reminded them that the body was merely a container, a vessel and perishable, but the spirit lived on. He told them to give their loved ones their flowers while they could smell them. When my mother told me this, I thought that Kim had never, not once, been on the sick-and-shut-in list. Only now I knew that she should have been.

Two days later, on the afternoon before the funeral, I was with Mom in her kitchen when the telephone rang. As she listened to the caller, I knew immediately that it was someone from the funeral home because her expression changed from her trying to look cheery for me to her struggling to stop her face from going slack. When the call ended, she didn't remove the receiver from her ear. The cord of the wall phone stretched across the room to the stove, where she was standing. Her kitchen, this apartment, was twice the size of the one in Lawless.

"They say we can come see her now," Mom said as though she was speaking to no one in particular. I tried to hold back the tears. For the past several days, I felt as though an aquifer had burst inside me. I felt leaky all over.

I'm leaky, Don.

When the busy signal started, Mom walked over to the phone's cradle and pushed the hang-up button. She dialed Aunt Doris.

"Baby, I need you to do your sister a favor." Mom hated asking for favors, hated that there was something she couldn't do for herself. "Feel free to say no if you can't do it. I need you to go view Kim's body at the funeral home. Make sure she looks like my Kim."

I could not hear Aunt Doris's response, but she couldn't refuse Mom. Not in this moment. And yet I couldn't quite figure out why Mom assigned this task to her sister. Aunt Doris had a reputation for being a crier. During the week that I recovered from my tonsillectomy, she stayed with me and plucked tissues from the Kleenex box on my nightstand, dabbing her eyes as she watched contestants win money on *The Price Is Right* or *Match Game* or *The $10,000 Pyramid*. She cried during movies no one else found melancholy. Light flickering across her slick face, she'd blow her nose, oblivious to Granny and Mom glaring at her.

"I don't want none of that red lipstick they sometimes put on them either," Mom said. "Or that tacky-ass red fingernail polish."

She held the phone, listening, and then added, "No, we gave them Dawn's dress. It's burnt orange and the material wrinkles easily. Make sure it lays right." She placed the flat of her hand on her chest in a smoothing gesture. "And she should be wearing my scarf around her neck. You know the cream-colored silk one with the pretty flowers? And Mama's gold crucifix. Make sure it's straight. Nothing worse than a crooked cross."

Mom quietly nodded for what seemed like a long time. When she finally said the word "yes," it hitched itself to a long sigh. "I remember your pale blue handkerchief. Kim should absolutely have something from her aunt, too. She would have loved that. Thank you, baby."

Then Aunt Doris must have asked about her other niece, because Mom looked at me: "She's okay. She'll be alright."

T he next morning, we arrived early at the funeral home for the wake service. *We*, being Mom, Granny, Aunt Doris, David, and me.

For homegoing ceremonies not held at the church, Prophet dispatched ministers to funeral homes to care for bereaved parishioners. The ministers didn't officiate during the service, but they comforted the family in every other way. Mr. Isaiah loved Kim and specifically asked to support us. As soon as we entered the funeral home, he hugged each of us and took Mom's and Granny's trench coats.

The funeral home had five chapels and each was expected to be busy. The sanctuary that held my sister's services was one of the largest, capable of holding about four hundred people. Mr. Isaiah pulled his compact Bible from inside his suit jacket.

"Sister Kim looks beautiful," he said. It wasn't lost on him or us that this was something he'd said to my sister for much of her life. "If you're ready to view her body, I'm ready to escort you."

We walked to the chapel. Two doors opened up to a room filled with chairs, and all the way down the center aisle was an area with a small choir stand, an organ, and just enough breathing room for an off-white casket wreathed in flowers. During funerals, I'd seen Prophet open a casket and peel back a piece of cloth—sometimes it was quilt-like and other times it was diaphanous like a veil—revealing the deceased's face. From a distance, I could see my sister vaguely. Just her profile. I was twenty-eight years old and had never lost anyone so close to me. I couldn't bear to see Kim's body in the hospital. And I'd been warring with myself over whether I wanted to view her in a casket. Now I was sure that I didn't. As Mr. Isaiah began the procession, he read the 14th Chapter of John:

"Let not your heart be troubled. Ye believe in God, believe also in me."

Mom, Granny, and Aunt Doris followed him. Mom took Granny's hand as though she were comforting her mother, but really it was the reverse. Aunt Doris followed behind Mom but stopped and turned. She reached out her hand for me, and David said, "I've got her."

Aunt Doris nodded.

But I couldn't cross the threshold. I couldn't move.

Mr. Isaiah continued: "In my Father's house are many mansions and if it were not so I would have told you. I go to prepare a place for you and where I go there ye may be also . . ."

When Mom, Granny, and Aunt Doris reached the casket, the three of them stood there with Mom in the middle, holding one another around the waist. A triumvirate of power and steadfastness, a formidable line of defense against anything and anyone. On the night we told Granny that Kim had died, Mom had her sit down at her dining room table and Mom put her arm around her mother before she uttered the words. It was the first time I'd seen Mom touch Granny in that way. Granny's shoulders slumped and her body retreated into a concave. But now she stood starched upright, her daughter secure in her grip. Not one of them shuddered or quaked or keened. At least, not that I could tell. They stood there. They stood there. They stood right there with their arms laced around one another's backs the way exposed tree roots crisscross one another directed by the elements and time. They stood there. Until, together, they turned away.

Once again, I could see my sister's body and the orange dress that I wanted to imagine I'd only let her borrow. I blinked back tears as I backed away from the door:

I can't stand to see you leave me. Just go.

I returned to the open area of the funeral home. Dad had arrived and was talking to Uncle Henry, Uncle Al, Jim, and Sarah. So many people had come out that the chapel overflowed even before the funeral started. I began greeting my friends and colleagues, professional types who came to support me and a ragtag group of people, many who lived near Normal. Some were gangbangers and drug dealers whom Kim and I had known since they were little boys. Despite their current lifestyles, they still carried Granny's groceries if they saw her walking down the street. I had not seen them in years, but that day we reunited for Kim.

Mr. Isaiah walked up as I was speaking to a colleague and stood off to the side. When she left, I waved him over.

"Are you sure you don't want to see her one last time?"

"That's not her."

"I won't leave your side, if you want to go," he said. He took my hand in his. "She's the prettiest corpse I've ever seen in my life. Looks just like she's sleeping."

"I watched her sleep all of her life. She's not sleeping."

"I did her hair," he said. "These funeral people don't know the first thing about hairstyling. I brought it forward, so it dips in front of her forehead. You know how she felt about her forehead." He patted my hand. "I did it just how she would have liked it."

"What would we do without you?"

For a fleeting moment, I allowed myself to look for Debra, scanning the people waiting to enter the chapel. Debra wasn't home when I called her and I'd told Mrs. Trice about Kim's passing. When Debra called me back, she'd spoken with David and she and I had not connected. I didn't know whether she was coming. I didn't know how her life was faring. In that moment, I could not muster the energy to care.

I continued to embrace everyone who approached me, many of them family members and church members I'd not seen in years. I made it my mission to be charming and witty like the hostess at a going-away party. And, for a few minutes, the delusion held. And then I saw Ted enter the funeral home. Ted was a panhandler and addict Kim knew and bought soup for from time to time. He was probably in his midthirties but he looked twenty years older, perpetually down on his luck, "ass-out" as Mom would have said. His signature line was "Hey, mister, you got two quarters?"

The first time I met Ted, I was newly married, and Kim and I were walking down 35th Street. He said, "There she is, my Kim-Kim. Remember when you were in high school and we sat out that afternoon and put together that puzzle? Just you and me."

"There you go again, Ted." She smiled and wagged her finger at him. "Always trying to shake the damn past for loose coins."

Kim told me that she had seen him riding a bicycle standing up. As he rode closer to her, she realized that the bike had no seat. Some poor delivery guy thought he could deter theft by removing the seat and locking his bike. He didn't know Ted. Adaptable as all get-out. Ted picked locks as fast as anyone could use a key. What did he care about a seat? He sat all day. And then there was that winter, on an arctic-cold day, when Kim saw Ted on the late-night local news being interviewed in a homeless shelter. The story was about how homeless Chicagoans fared during the cold snap.

"He's got a home, a good one," Kim had said. "He just doesn't want to follow anybody's rules."

Now Ted was shuffling toward me. He had the stooped posture of someone who begged for a living, someone accustomed to being supplicant. He rarely looked anyone in the eye. That's what happens after years of panhandling. The body assumes the position whether it's warranted or not. Ted was dressed in a suit that was so large it swarmed around his thin frame. He wore white tennis shoes flecked with mud. Hurrying toward the chapel, he nearly passed me.

"Hey, Ted."

He swerved. "Hey, Teach!"

I hugged him and he felt like loose bones under fabric.

"Do I look okay? I wanted to be presentable for Kim-Kim."

"You look perfect," I said, smiling at him.

As he walked away, swimming in his suit, I came undone. Maybe it was that sad, sad suit that suggested the lengths to which he'd gone to be there. He'd cared enough for my sister to sober up just enough to say goodbye. His effort, valiant in its own right, overwhelmed my defenses. I had cried every day since Kim died and it was foolish of me to believe I'd hold it together on the day of her funeral. David, who had been standing a few feet away despite my insistence that I was fine, took me into his arms. Dad appeared, and when he couldn't figure out exactly what to do, he stood off to the side. That was my father: present, but only by degrees; nearby, but only when absolutely necessary.

Word of my breakdown reached Mom and she hurried out to check on me.

"We will get through this," she said, taking my hand and sweeping me off to the side. As a distraction, she said, "I think I saw Ronnie in there."

Of all the people milling about, I wondered why Mom mentioned Mrs. Ronnie Matthews. In kindergarten, Kim had become close with Mrs. Matthews's son, Lance, and that meant Mom had to spend time with Mrs. Matthews, who was ebullient and talked incessantly. One day Mom told her, "Your mouth sho' don't know a Sunday, do it?" It was a line she'd gotten from Dovie, the Caribbean maid from the motel years before.

Midway through the school year, Mom was volunteering in Kim's kindergarten classroom and peeped inside a folder that had been left on a counter. She learned that Lance had been born intersex and Mrs. Matthews and her husband had to choose whether their child lived as a boy or a girl. Mom never understood how Mrs. Matthews could be so cheery all the time. What if she and her husband had guessed wrong?

"She has really grayed, bless her heart," Mom said now. "But she looks just the same. I saw Lance a few years ago on that 'L' platform."

"I remember," I said, sniffling. "You wanted to fix him up with Kim."

"He was so handsome and broad-shouldered and so tall. He sure turned out to be a fine, fine-looking young man." Mom pulled a piece of tissue from her dress pocket, wiping my face. "I guess Ronnie knew who her child was from the very beginning and exactly what he needed."

"And you knew yours, Mom," I said. Now I was the one squeezing her hand and patting her back. "You knew her and you did the absolute best that you could do."

Mom smiled at me and heaved a great breath, inside of which was a faint gasping sound, a holding back, a hesitation. In the days since Kim died, I hadn't seen my mother cry once. Not when we were in the hospital emergency room and not as we drove around that night delivering the news. Not when the police interviewed her and several neighbors about Kim's death and would later determine there was no foul play. Not when we entered Kim's apartment and her bedroom and saw the clothes scattered around her bed and the open suitcase she left without. Not even when we learned from a kind nurse, who wasn't supposed to say anything official yet, that there had been no evidence of drugs in Kim's body. I hadn't thought there would be. But that wasn't surprising because I'd long been in denial about my sister's drinking. That would end years and years later when I'd finally read her death certificate, which listed her cause of death as "chronic alcoholism."

Mom looked toward her gray-haired friend and placed her arm around my waist.

David, standing nearby, joined us and we walked into the chapel. The casket was closed. We walked down the aisle and took our seats in the front row. Long ago, after Candy Love's funeral, Mom had told me that a parent could survive the profound tragedy of losing a child, even though it was the hardest thing that any parent would face. She was right. Mom would be one of the survivors.

Her daughter, baby Brandon's mother, would not be.

In the months that followed, Mom and I spoke sparingly about Kim. She told me that she had no idea how long her daughter's eyelashes were and how Kim looked more like herself in the casket than she had recently in life. Other than that, Kim's absence was an expanse often too difficult for us to accommodate. But I recall one instance the following winter during the first below-zero temperatures of the season. My mother—a believer in God, in Heaven, in the great beyond—surprised me when she looked down at the snow-covered, frozen ground and said, "I wonder if my baby is cold down there."

part three

chapter twenty-four

"Dawn, Can You Take My Call?"

. . .

I lay in bed massaging my mountainous belly. David had helped me strategically surround my body with pillows, wedging one against the left side of my torso, another between my legs, and the last under my right arm. The kitchen was below our bedroom and a cacophony of sound floated up as he pulled pots and pans from the cabinets. It was Christmas Eve, a Saturday morning, and despite my December 31 due date, I was determined to still cook turkey and dressing, a spiced ham, broccoli casserole, macaroni and cheese, and yams for Christmas dinner. My brother-in-law had invited the family to his church the next morning because he was surprising his girlfriend by proposing. Afterward, the family was driving out to our house to eat. Because this was my second holiday season without Kim, my nesting dovetailed just fine with my determination to not dissolve into sadness. Mom thought I was insane but agreed to come out to help me.

The baby kicked and a hump poked its way across my T-shirt before disappearing.

Okay, Zachary.

David and I had decided to wait to learn the sex of the baby. But we had chosen names: Hannah for a girl, Zachary for a boy. As I rubbed the baby's foot—or what I thought was his foot—it struck me that I didn't remember what Kim's feet looked like. I remembered her hands, her arms and legs. The cherry-red birthmark at the back of her neck, under her hairline. The freckle in her palm. Her smell. But not her toes. I sat straight up in the bed. Over the last year and a half, I'd been having these sudden, upsetting observations about my sister. Mom found it disturbing that she couldn't dream about Kim despite keeping photos of her on the nightstand. I dreamed about Kim all the time. But there were no pictures of my sister's feet.

I placed my hand on my side. *Your aunt would have spoiled you rotten.*

When the doorbell rang, I heaved my body from the bed and into the shower. By the time I dressed and plodded down to the kitchen, Mom was chopping carrots, celery, and onions. She had washed the turkey and stuffed it with sage and other herbs, shredded the cheese for the macaroni, skinned the sweet potatoes and had them boiling.

I walked over and hugged her from behind.

"Child, get your big belly out of my back." She kissed my cheek. "You know this dinner makes no sense. You're about to pop."

"My doctor says I have a few more days."

"That doctor doesn't see what I see."

I'd left my book, *What to Expect When You're Expecting*, on the kitchen table. It was not there, and I looked around the kitchen and saw it on top of the refrigerator. If I'd asked Mom why she moved it, she would have said it was in her way. The truth was, she hated the book. Earlier in the summer, she had flipped through it and sniffed. "You can read all you want, but parenting is a crapshoot. Just do the best you can."

I loved my mother, but throughout my pregnancy I promised myself that I would parent differently. Although we had a strong relationship, it had its fissures, born of resentments. I never understood why she couldn't control Kim. I was angry at her for laying out expectations and not holding my sister accountable. I, on the other hand, would parent firmly. I would demand that every rule be followed, and I would follow up with consequences. I wasn't sure at what point we had lost Kim, but I was determined not to lose my child. I was so terrified about making mistakes that I often stood in front of the changing table in the nursery, miming putting a diaper on an imaginary baby because I'd never changed one.

When Mom and I finished cooking the Christmas dinner, we put up the food and she, David, and I ate leftovers. We then got ready for bed.

Because the guest room was now the nursery, David had put fresh linen on the sofa bed in my home office. I stopped by the room to say good night to Mom.

"My sleep has come down on me," she said as I stood in the doorway. "Don't go into labor without me."

"I'm not having a baby on Christmas Day," I said. "He'll be cheated out of gifts."

In my bedroom, I crawled under the covers and fell fast asleep. I awoke at four o'clock in the morning and poked David.

"I feel funny" was my highly medical assessment.

"Let's time those funny feelings." He grabbed his eyeglasses and wristwatch off the nightstand.

By eight o'clock, we were in the emergency room of the hospital where I was scheduled to deliver. The on-call resident determined that I was very early in the process and I should go back home.

As soon as Mom heard the garage door lifting, she met us downstairs.

"You were right," I said. "I'm in labor. I've been told to try to walk around as much as possible."

"You don't have to tell me," she gloated. "I know what I know."

December 25, 1994, was one of the warmest Christmases on record in Chicago, and the temperature rose to close to sixty degrees. Mom, David, and I had breakfast, and David, holding me by my arm, began to walk with me up and down the driveway. I turned and saw Mom, framed by the living room window, watching my every step. She called the family to cancel dinner.

The labor continued into the night with Mom and David by my side in the hospital's birthing room. Just after 10 p.m., the baby arrived. The doctor said, "It's a girl and she's got big feet and hands." Mom would later tell me that Hannah entered the world with one hand above her head as though she were waving at her public. David would later say that the moment was so surreal that, for a second, he couldn't figure out how the doctor knew she was a girl.

The nurse cleaned Hannah up and returned her to me in a Christmas stocking. She had light skin with a head full of dark hair and dark marble-like eyes. She looked just like her father. I rolled down the stocking to examine her ten toes and ten fingers. Then I snuggled her close to my heart and inhaled her, falling more in love than I'd thought possible.

Mom returned home and by the middle of the next week, she called to say that Aunt Doris and Granny were eager to see Hannah.

"I can't hold them back any longer. And there's one more thing: Your father wants to come, too. Is that okay?"

"It's fine."

The way I viewed my father had shifted over the last year and a half. He was indeed the man who had hurt my mother and had missed two of my graduations and my wedding. But he was also the man who had lost his child. That last part had chiseled away parts of the resentment I'd felt toward him for years. After Kim died, he'd begun calling me once a month to check in. And I called him. We never talked long or about anything substantive. The exception was when I called to tell him I was pregnant.

"I'm finally going to be a grandpa!" he had said. I could hear him smiling.

On the day he met his granddaughter, the house was filled with people, but he sat on the living room sofa in front of the fireplace, holding her, utterly enchanted. He cooed and said over and over, "You smiling at me? I think you're smiling at me."

Briefly directing his attention to me, he said, "Are you sure she's your child?"

Aunt Doris, sitting nearby, sucked her teeth. "That baby looks as much like her father as Dawn looked like you. Now, let me hold that sweet sugar."

Before Dad handed Hannah to Auntie, he said, "I think I can see Kim in her."

With that, Mom, who had been spying from a distance, eased over to look at Hannah, as though she needed to see what my father saw, from the exact angle. Mom tilted her head, searching for her daughter.

"It's her coloring, that's all." She walked away.

I took a three-month leave from the *Tribune*, and whenever Hannah slept, which never seemed enough, I holed up in my office and worked on a novel I'd been writing for years. Before Kim died, my literary agent had sent it out and it was rejected all over the place. But editors had written constructive rejection letters, and I'd been using their comments to help rewrite the book. Hannah held total dominion over my life and there was something about knowing she could awaken at any moment that sharpened the story and pushed the words out of me at a feverish pace.

Although I had been working on the story for a while, I didn't really know what it was about until after the *Chicago Tribune*'s 1993 "Killing Our Children" series. A staff project, the series examined in detail the causes and effects of children under fifteen who had been slain that year in the Chicago area. The project was in response to the record 928 murders that had occurred in 1992. Fifty-seven of the deaths involved children, many of them Black.

After the series ran, I decided that I wanted to write about a child who died, and then examine who or what was responsible. The man charged with her murder or the drug-ridden community where she lived? Then what about the residents in the well-to-do, gated community next door, where people wanted to keep out the "bad elements"? What about the generations of institutional forces, the segregation and redlining and disinvestment that had pressed down on the whole neighborhood?

Hannah was nearly three months old when I mailed ten completed chapters of the book to my agent, and she loved them. She asked me for a synopsis of the remaining twenty chapters. Within a week, *Only Twice I've Wished for Heaven* sold as part of a two-book contract to Crown/Random House. After Kim died, I never thought I'd have anything to look forward to. But now I had a baby daughter and a book deal.

Life was good. Life felt really good until Hannah was fourteen months old and our incredibly healthy child came down with a fever.

It was, we thought, an ordinary fever and David took her to her pediatrician on a Friday. She prescribed antibiotics for what she believed was a routine ear infection. By late Saturday night, Hannah's body radiated even more heat. After midnight that Sunday morning, David was so tired from having gone downstairs so many times for juice and water for Hannah that he missed a step and fell down the stairs. He sliced his foot open on the molding at the bottom of the staircase and had to drive himself to the emergency room. He hated having to leave us. I hated not being able to drive him. But I did call a girlfriend who lived near the hospital and asked her to meet him there.

At about 8 that morning, Mom called to see how we were doing. I tried to put up a good front. I told her that David had fallen down the stairs and had returned from the hospital with thirty stitches and powerful painkillers. About an hour later she was on my doorstep. She gave Hannah a sponge bath in rubbing alcohol to reduce her fever. But that didn't work. When Hannah became lethargic, her eyelids drooping, Mom got so scared that she suggested we take her back to the pediatrician who had Sunday hours. I wasn't so sure. But my mother was firm.

We entered the doctor's office and Mom found a seat and held Hannah. The waiting room was crammed with coughing and wheezing children. One kid had a yellowish-green gook oozing out of his eyes and nose. As I stood at the desk taking care of insurance matters, I looked around at the children, and my mother could read my concern and attempted to shield Hannah from the fog of germs.

I sat down. She was rocking Hannah, who by now was hardly moving.

"Let's come back tomorrow," I whispered. "I don't want her to get sick here."

Mom knew I was sleep-deprived.

"No, baby," she said, gently rocking. She didn't even look at me.

"But look at these kids," I pressed.

"I'll sit with her in the hall until she can be seen. But we have to wait."

When it was our turn, the doctor saw how lethargic Hannah was and lifted her eyelids. He recoiled a bit.

"What's the matter?" I asked.

"I don't like the way her pupils look," he said. I could tell he was trying to measure his tone so as not to alarm us. He told us to drive her to the emergency room of the nearby Christ Hospital, one of the best children's hospitals in the Chicago area. He said he would call ahead to tell the staff we were coming.

In the emergency room, a nurse met us as soon as we signed in. I assumed she took us to the front of the line because of the doctor's clout. Before I carried Hannah into the examining room, I asked Mom to call David on a pay phone to tell him where we were. I told her to tell him not to worry. We would be home soon. About an hour later, he was hobbling on crutches through the emergency room's sliding glass doors. His father had driven him. I kept asking the nurses when we could leave. It wasn't until an emergency-room doctor, an African American woman, came out to tell us that she'd paged the chief pediatric neurosurgeon to have him come in that I began to understand how serious Hannah's condition was. I told Mom to go home, that we would call her with more information.

Hannah was moved upstairs to the pediatric intensive care unit. It was about 10 p.m. when a grim-faced Asian doctor came out to get us. Introducing himself as Dr. Yoon Sun Hahn, he led us to a small room and asked us to sit down at a round table. I pulled out a pen and a small notebook. He said that Hannah had a brain infection. They could not determine the exact type because they couldn't do a spinal tap to test the spinal fluid. He explained that the procedure would cause her brain to herniate and that would kill her immediately. Where the infection started wasn't clear. Now it was moving through her brain like a wayward spark. Doctors were flooding Hannah's system with powerful antibiotics, praying something would work. They had placed her in an induced coma.

"Our primary concern right now is that the infection has caused your daughter's brain to swell," he said. "It is pressing against her skull. The skull"—he tapped on the wooden table—"is hard and resistant. The brain will have no place to expand into. If it continues to swell, she will die."

I don't remember what happened next. But David would tell me later that I kept taking notes until finally I said, "So when can we see her?"

Dr. Hahn had us put on gowns and masks before taking us to an isolation room inside the ICU. Arms and legs splayed, Hannah wore only a diaper as she lay on the bed. A complex web of wires and tubes extended from her little body to several machines that beeped or swished or gurgled. She was breathing with the aid of a respirator. David saw her and fell to his knees. I walked over to her and touched her face and arms. I twirled her hair around my fingers.

We went into the lounge area. It was empty and the lights had been dimmed. I placed my face on the floor and began to pray. Although David hadn't grown up in the church as I had, I asked him to pray, too. We walked over to a bank of pay phones lining the walls and called many of our relatives and friends to ask them to pray with us.

During the first two days in the hospital, a slew of specialists and surgeons worked on her case. Although they weren't sure whether Hannah would survive, they said we had gotten her to the hospital in time to give her a fighting chance. Early on, nurses barely made eye contact with us. They explained what they were doing and were professional, but they kept their distance. No one was more standoffish than Dr. Hahn. Nobody dared get close to a couple who were about to lose their toddler. When we weren't in the ICU with Hannah, we huddled in the lounge around a table overflowing with medical books from the hospital's library. We learned how to convert Celsius to Fahrenheit because that was how doctors measured Hannah's temperature. We wanted to understand words such as *meningitis* and *paresis*, *hydrocephalus* and *shunts*. We needed to know what the pulse oximeter measured. We read everything we could about the intracranial pressure monitor (ICP) Dr. Hahn inserted in Hannah's brain to track the swelling.

As the days passed, the infection responded to the antibiotics and Dr. Hahn began to wake Hannah up slowly. We couldn't yet fully know the damage the infection had wrought. What was immediately noticeable was that the right side of her body was much weaker than the left because the left side of her brain had suffered the brunt of the infection's assault. Her left eye was no longer in line with her right one. It remained locked in the outside corner, a beautiful deep brown marble that seemed to have a mind of its own.

A nurse wheeled Hannah's bed from the intensive care unit, where she'd spent ten days, to a step-down unit. David, Mom, and I took turns going home. One afternoon I returned to the hospital to find Hannah playing with Dr. Hahn's stethoscope and Dr. Hahn himself smiling while talking to David. It was the first time we'd seen him smile and a major sign, a glorious sign, that he believed Hannah was healing.

Before Hannah's illness, she had been walking for a couple of months. Now, when she stood, she looked like a little stroke victim, her body tilted and unsteady. She had to relearn how to take a first step. And when she did, her right leg dragged slightly. She also had a huge cowlick where her hair had been shaved for the ICP monitor. By Easter Sunday, Hannah had been in the hospital for more than a month and we were getting ready to take her home. David packed the stuffed animals that visitors had brought, photographs we'd taped to her bed, books we'd read to her. David was almost done when a man in a white bunny suit stopped by the room and handed Hannah an Easter basket. She picked through the fake grass for chocolates and when she smiled, it was crooked. For the first time, I realized that it, too, had been affected by her illness. My lip quivered, but I refused to cry. Although she looked like the walking wounded, she was alive and healing. Our baby, born on a Christmas Sunday, was leaving the hospital on Resurrection Sunday, and that was our greatest gift.

When I think about the number of doctors who told us how *lucky* we were to have gotten her to the hospital, when I think about how much I didn't want to parent like my mother, I am shaken to my core. I know what would have happened if I hadn't listened to Mom and hadn't waited to see the doctor. We would have taken Hannah back home and lowered her into her crib. Later that evening, one of us would have looked in on her and thought for a second that she was only sleeping. My mother—whose parenting skills I did not want to emulate, whose instincts I doubted—had saved my child.

David, Mom, and I—and sometimes Jim and Sarah—spent the next year helping Hannah heal. We watched that little girl fight to walk up and down the hallway during physical therapy sessions and manipulate balls and toy pyramids during occupational therapy. After a few months, the physical therapy erased much of the weakness on the right side of her body. She no longer walked with a limp. Her cognitive skills, which doctors had warned could have been greatly impaired, were humming right along. She was meeting all of her age-appropriate benchmarks.

I had taken a leave of absence from work right after her hospital stint, and when I returned, Mom stayed with us a few days a week to help us with Hannah. Mom normally took Hannah to preschool. One morning I joined them. Mom saw how tightly I held Hannah's hand when she wanted to run off and play with the other children on the swings or the jungle gym. Mom had been telling me, in a gentle way, that Hannah didn't have to wash her hands every time she ate a piece of candy and she could enjoy a Happy Meal every now and then, and I didn't always have to touch her, afraid I'd feel a fever.

That evening, as I was drying dishes, Mom walked up beside me.

"Hannah's going to have to fall down and scrape her knees and catch colds and bump her head."

Holding the last plate, I stopped to look out the window. It was dark and I could see only our reflections.

"You can't protect her from life," Mom said. "She's proven she's tough. I remember when the doctor said she might lose her limbs and her hearing. Last I checked, she's got beautiful legs. They're a little knock-kneed like her father's. And her hearing is fine. Though she's like you and doesn't listen enough. Baby, she's tougher than all of us combined. It wasn't your fault that she got sick. You can't protect her so much from dying that you stop her from living."

I stood over the sink and cried into the dishwater.

It didn't happen overnight—and Hannah's illness would always hover—but our lives found a degree of normalcy.

By early December 1999, David and I were preparing for Hannah's fifth birthday and my second novel was about to be published. I came home from work one evening, and Hannah and David were out. As I unbuttoned my blouse, I checked the answering machine in David's office. An automated voice announced: "This is a collect call from an inmate in the Marion County Jail." In the background, I heard a faraway voice yelling, trying to circumvent the recording, "Hey, Dawn, can you take my call?"

I recognized that voice: Debra. I stopped unbuttoning. She and I hadn't talked since I'd told her about Hannah's illness. She was never home when I called and I wound up chatting with Mrs. Trice, who told me Debra had begun waitressing for one restaurant chain after another. When I asked Mrs. Trice how Debra was doing, she always said, "Oh, she's okay, Dawn." It was that same exasperated, wishing-wanting tone I'd heard from Mom when I was away at the university and asking about Kim.

Somehow, I was not completely surprised that Debra was calling from the Marion County Jail. I figured she had been locked up for disorderly conduct or public intoxication. I figured she'd have to hit a wall, and maybe this was it. I dialed the facility and an operator told me that inmates couldn't receive telephone calls. I had to wait for Debra to try again. I immediately reached out to Mrs. Trice, but Darlene, who was visiting, picked up. She told me that she was just walking out the door and couldn't talk for long.

"Dawn, she's been locked up for sixteen months."

"Sixteen months?" My stomach seized. Mrs. Trice would never have allowed Debra to remain in jail that long for something minor. "What happened?"

"She killed someone," Darlene said.

I slowly sat in the chair. It occurred to me that I'd been seated when I was told Kim had died and Hannah might die. "What did you say?"

"She's charged with murdering a man she was doing drugs with. She's in jail awaiting trial. Look, I'm sorry but I've got to run. She calls here on weekends and we'll have her call you. Debra can give you the details."

Darlene and I had never been close. When we were young, she, like me, had been the older sister who hadn't wanted much to do with her younger sister or her friends. But in that moment, I knew what she was feeling. I'd felt it after Kim died: the frustration from having tried but failed to save our sister, the sheer disbelief about the way things turned out, the desire to say, *I'm sorry to tell you this, even though you can't possibly feel worse than me.*

I hung up and the word "murder" bored deeply into my brain.

My Lord, Debra, what have you done?

chapter twenty-five

Diamonds and Other Birthstones

· · ·

That Saturday, I spent most of the afternoon in my home office with the cordless at my fingertips, waiting for Debra to call. I tried to work, but I mostly stared off into space, studying Hannah's Christmas stocking on the fireplace mantel or the Douglas fir that stood by the window. Every year, we drove to an Indiana tree farm to buy a nine-foot-tall tree that had already been chopped down and then decorated it with every ornament in the Christmas box. Our tree was buxom and gaudy, definitely no shrinking violet.

Whenever the phone rang, I pressed the talk button and hurried the person off the line. A few times, Hannah skipped in. She saw me staring out the window and said, "Mommy, are you working?" I had told her that I could be writing even when my fingers weren't touching the keyboard.

"Yes," I said, pulling her to me and munching her cheeks.

"Okay." She skipped out of the room. Sometimes she simply sat outside my door. But her father was home and she ran to him.

Although David had never met Debra in person, they talked on the phone like old friends, calling each other cousins, talking about the news.

In the midafternoon, the phone rang, and when the automated

voice began, I yelled, "It's her!" and closed my door and sat down at my desk.

"Hey, friend," Debra said, sounding hesitant.

"It's so good to hear from you. Girl, what happened?"

"I'm in so much trouble, Dawn, I can't believe it."

We were thirty-four years old, but that was exactly what the pretty little girl with the perfect outfit would have said while sitting on the bench outside the principal's office in a plume of sighs.

"How are you, Dawn? How's Hannah?"

"We're fine and we can talk about us later. I need to know how you are."

"Dawn, I shot a man named Raymond Jones. I never wanted to run away from that. But it was an accident. I promise."

I scooted out of the chair and settled onto the floor, pressing my back against the wall as if bracing for impact. "Please, tell me what happened."

I listened, rapt, as Debra allowed her story to unfold.

I wanted to get clean and get off the streets so bad. But I couldn't do it. I remember seeing an officer writing a speeding ticket and I waited for him to finish. Then I ran over and begged him to lock me up. He said he couldn't arrest me for nothing. I was about to walk away, and it hit me: I had my crack pipe in my back pocket. I pulled it out and said, "You can arrest me for paraphernalia." And he did. That was a big mistake. I spent one night in jail, but the arrest became part of my record.

It was awful what I put my family through. I was at a friend's apartment watching the news one night and getting high when a story aired about an unidentified African American woman, thirty years old. Her body was found in a field and she'd been shot. Mama faithfully watched the news, so I called her. I said, "Mama, that's not me." She asked me where I was and I said, "I'm fine. I'll be home soon." Then I hung up.

I attempted suicide three times and when I couldn't do that either, I decided I was going to live empty. I made a deal with God. I told him, "If you want me to be a dope addict, I'm going to be the best one." I tried to see how much crack I could smoke before dropping dead.

That's who I'd become when I met Raymond. We smoked dope

together. We confided in one another. He told me he was thirty-eight years old and had a wife, a young daughter, and a son. I'd begun to trust him. People on the street knew me as Brenda and as a rule, I didn't mix my street life and home life. But on the night he died, I broke my rule. Raymond and I had been together for three days and on the third day it hit one hundred degrees outside. I took Raymond to my air-conditioned house. Mama was at work. We smoked dope in my bedroom for hours. When it was gone, I told Raymond I'd get some more but he needed to stay in my bedroom. I returned and he was standing on the landing outside Mama's bedroom, looking down at me. I thought he was stretching his legs. We finished the new batch and Raymond left. I fell asleep. Later that night, Mama came into my bedroom, mad as hell. She said three of her rings were missing. Two diamond rings and another that held Darlene's and my birthstones. I was sure Raymond had them and I was going to get them back. I waited for my mother to fall asleep and I got drunk. I had a shotgun that I'd found in a drug house and I took it with me because I was afraid of the stray dogs in Raymond's neighborhood.

I drove to his mother's house. I parked the car crazy, on an angle in the middle of the street. I walked up to the house with the gun and Raymond's brother, Alan, was on the porch. He asked me why I had the gun. I told him about the dogs, and he told me to park the car right and put the gun up. I moved the car. But I kept the gun with me. I don't know exactly when Raymond came outside. That's still a blur. But while we were talking, the gun fired. To this day I don't know how. I remember a three-inch spark. I was so out of it that when he fell, I continued to talk to him as if he were still standing. I refused to look down. I told him goodbye and got in the car. Deep down, I knew he'd been shot. But I wouldn't allow myself to believe it.

I hid out for eight days and then went home. I asked Darlene to make the call so that I could turn myself in. While I waited, I walked out into the backyard, pacing and smoking. A police officer rushed from behind a tree and pointed a gun at me. He said, "Freeze! Put your hands up!" For a split second, I had the urge to run. But I lifted my hands. He handcuffed me and walked me around to the front of the house. Police cars lined the street. Darlene ran out crying and grabbed me so hard we almost toppled over. She said, "I love you so much! Debra, when did we lose you?"

By the time Debra finished, I was leaning against the window, shivering even though I wasn't cold. Over and over, I told Debra how deeply sorry I was. I didn't know when I'd walked to the window. Ordinarily, this would have been the type of Saturday afternoon that I found most restful. Snow falling and clinging to the sides of the trees like a dusting of powdered sugar. Squirrels scuttling in and out of the underbrush. But what I saw outside stood in sharp contrast to what I'd just heard. Tears clouded my view.

Over the next two months, Debra and I talked on the phone more than we had in years. She chronicled her life in jail, which she described as "not that bad." She related how at night, the harsh fluorescent lights remained on and several of the nine women in her dormitory used sanitary napkins as sleeping masks to block the light. Because glue was off-limits, they used toothpaste to affix photos to letters. When Debra told me she slept on a top bunk, that made me think of Lawless and how she would run into her bedroom and hide under the bunk beds when she got in trouble. Mrs. Trice would pull the beds out from against the wall to get to Debra, but she skittered like a salamander across the floor along with the beds to elude her mother. I could always hear the scraping noise across my bedroom ceiling and knew she'd done something wrong.

Most mornings after breakfast, she joined the women in the day area playing cards and board games at the stainless-steel picnic tables and watching television. They braided and rebraided each other's hair to pass time.

Debra's months in the Marion County Jail had settled her and she was no longer in a complete free fall. Although she had envisioned women living in mayhem, the strict rules created a structure and order she'd craved years ago when she enlisted in the air force and years later when she roamed the streets. "My father said the military would think for me and I'd miss my freedom," she said during a phone call. "Ironic, huh?"

But there was no peace. A man had died because of her and his family was grieving. Because of her. At times, Debra found that unbearable. She knew she'd have to carry it for the rest of her life. What she had to do now, though, was apologize to Raymond's family and beg their forgiveness. She didn't want to write them until after the trial because she didn't want them to think she was trying to sway their opinion of her. I told her that I wished I could have helped her, and she wrote me a letter:

January 27, 2000

Hello Dawn,

Believe me when I say that I'm exactly where I'm supposed to be at this point in my life. I was dying out there, inside and out. I prayed for God to somehow take me away from all temptations and give me a chance to get myself together. I needed to learn all over again self-discipline, self-motivation, an appreciation for life, how to set my priorities right, how to complete a degree without drugs resurfacing to take it all away. I will make this work for me so don't worry, okay? I just have a huge hump to get over.

I can say that jail is not that bad. The reason I'm in jail is what makes it so bad. Many people can better themselves if they choose to do so. The jail offers a GED program, drug and alcohol counseling, and a course that teaches you how to function in the outside world. I've never met so many grown women without a high school education. Some can barely read and write. Some take full advantage of the opportunities while others wait to be released, only to return to jail on the same charges. We call them the "repeats." One female has been arrested eighty-seven times for public intoxication. Eighty-seven times! You would think the court would hit her with "the bitch" (habitual offender) and then force her to attend an alcohol abuse program. Another female, however, was hit with "the bitch"—for prostitution! It's bad because she has no luck selling her ass—she keeps getting caught! (One time she was released on a Friday and rearrested on a Sunday!)

All in all, jail is what you make of it. My experience has been a real eye-opening one. I've learned that my life wasn't so bad after all. All along, I had the tools for a prosperous existence but didn't acknowledge them nor put them to use. I'll call soon.

Luv you,
Deb

A month after Debra's letter arrived, her murder trial began.

chapter twenty-six

Perspectives

...

On the morning of Debra's trial, I was walking through the *Tribune*'s newsroom, but my body felt like I was standing on the grounds of a power plant. A hum of nerves pervaded my entire being even though I tried to maintain a semblance of calm.

Debra's trial was expected to last two days. It was held in downtown Indianapolis in the Marion Superior Court Criminal Division Four courtroom before Judge Mark Renner. Her attorneys planned to argue that Raymond Jones's death was an accident and that Debra should have been charged with reckless homicide. A conviction carried a prison sentence of one to six years. The prosecution team asserted that Debra had intentionally shot Raymond. If found guilty of murder, she would face a sentence ranging from forty-five to sixty-five years. All I could think about was that she'd have to do half that time. I couldn't even begin to wrap my head around it.

In the newsroom, I lingered outside the office belonging to the editor of the *Tribune*'s popular *Perspectives* section. He was finishing up a meeting. *Perspectives* appeared in the Sunday newspaper and highlighted opinions and analysis on topics of local, national, and international importance. I'd sent the editor a message, telling him about Debra's and my story, and that I wanted to write about her. He replied saying he liked the idea and we should meet to discuss it.

By then, I had been an editor for much of my career at the *Tribune* and had only recently started writing for the newspaper. My goal was to cover the city as if it were a remote land, a frontier. With every story, I wanted to detach myself from what I believed or heard to be true in order to broach topics with an open mind. In many ways, Chicago had always been an enigma to me. Its race problem. Its segregation. Its grossly unfair division of resources that allowed some parts of the city to flourish and be world-class and consigned other parts to a more third-world existence. I wanted to write about people rather than pathologies. I wanted to explain how their hopes and dreams and life prospects were shaped by disparities and inequities. I was drawn to resilient people who managed to do extraordinary things with nearly nothing, people who had changed their lives despite seemingly impossible odds.

When the editor finished his meeting, he waved me inside.

"I really like this idea about you and your friend," he said, gesturing for me to sit in a chair in front of his desk. "We often write about people charged with murder, though. What makes this story different?"

"If I tell you that my friend was on crack and shot a man, you immediately think you know her story, that it's some familiar tale about inner-city African Americans and the perils of poverty and drugs."

He fiddled with a piece of tape, transferring it between his forefinger and thumb.

"But Debra's parents, like mine, were working-class people with middle-class aspirations. They tried to create a life for her filled with opportunities. We became friends in the third grade, and she went one way and I went another. I feel *There but for the grace of God go I*."

"That could never have been you," he said.

White male privilege. Acting as if the right combination of rage, desperation, hopelessness, drugs couldn't land you in a place you never dreamed.

"Of course it could have been me. Life gives us no guarantees."

I looked out the window at the NBC Tower across the street.

"Maybe it's a cautionary tale, right now. But one day it will be a redemption story. My sister died seven years ago, and I wonder what I missed with her. What I saw and didn't want to see. What I knew and didn't want to know. I feel that way about Debra."

"Let's do it. But let's wait for a verdict. If she's found guilty, we can run your essay after she's sentenced."

If she's found guilty. I left his office feeling sick. Hearing him say those words so cavalierly only pushed to the surface every ounce of dread I was trying to tamp down.

Later that evening, I considered calling Mrs. Trice to ask how the first day of the trial went. But I didn't. The last thing she needed was me peppering her with questions. I spent the next day working and trying to keep busy, trying not to look at the clock or wonder about testimony, closing arguments, or whether jurors would or could be fair and unbiased.

When I got home, I called Mrs. Trice. As soon as she said, "Hi, Dawn," I could hear a crushing sadness in her voice. I knew the verdict before she told me.

"It didn't turn out the way we wanted," she said. "They found her guilty."

"Of reckless homicide or first-degree murder?" I asked, hoping for a miracle.

"Murder."

"I'm so sorry." I was barely able to speak. Debra would be in prison for *at least two decades*. "What happens next?"

"The judge set the sentencing for May," Mrs. Trice said. "Her attorneys say it's commonplace to file an appeal and they'll do that after the sentencing. I hate that a man had to die, and his family is suffering. I hate all of this. But I know where Debra is now. I'm not worried about a phone call or a knock at my door. Maybe she can get some help, finally."

The Saturday after the verdict, I stayed close to the phone. When it rang that afternoon, I was in the family room with Hannah and David. I had the cordless next to me, and when I answered it, I'd never been so happy to hear an automated voice in my life. I ran upstairs to my office.

After accepting the call, I said, "Debra, I heard. I'm so sorry."

"Yeah." She breathed deeply, still adjusting to the weight of the verdict. "I was hoping to be found guilty of the lesser charge."

"How are you holding up, friend?"

"I'm okay, I guess. After the verdict, I ran to my dorm and wrote

Raymond's family a four-page letter. I apologized so hard, Dawn, and asked for their forgiveness. I put my heart in that letter. I put my soul in it."

She told me that during the trial, Raymond's brother, Alan, had said he hated that he woke Raymond up to come outside to meet her.

"I told Alan that I wish I could take away his grief. I told his mother, Mrs. Margaret Jones, that although I'd been suicidal when I was arrested, I understood I needed to pay for my sins and that I would in no way try to run from them."

A couple of weeks later, Debra called to tell me she'd received an envelope from Margaret Jones. For a split second, Debra said, she didn't recognize the name and when she did, she nearly fainted. She ran to her dorm and crouched down by her bunk so that she could read in private. She wanted to be alone in case the letter was filled with animosity. She didn't want anyone to see her cry.

> *Dear Debra,*
>
> *I received your letter and you have my forgiveness. So, when you feel you cannot make it, look up and talk to God, Jehovah is his name. Don't think of not living. He will not give you more than you can bear. . . . Do not worry about the past because Raymond has paid his price. For the wages of sin is death. . . . I have a grandson there in jail but thank God he is alive. He could have been killed, too. I will pray for you and as you say, you want to do His will. . . . I let the family read your letter and they are glad that you know you did something wrong. Please don't do anything to hurt your mother's and sister's heart. They love you very much. Show them you are strong, not for yourself but for them. Take care. I will keep in touch.*
>
> *Mrs. Jones*

Debra told me that after she finished the letter, she cried, ashamed of the grief she'd inflicted on Mrs. Jones and the family but grateful for their grace. Debra wrote Mrs. Jones back, saying she planned to make something positive come from this tragedy.

I had to speak with Mrs. Jones for my *Perspectives* essay, and on the day of our phone interview I sat at my desk in the newsroom, staring at a photo of Hannah wearing her eyeglasses and her hair in two thick braids that hung over her Girl Scouts' Brownies vest. I wanted to know how Mrs. Jones could so easily open her heart to the woman responsible for her son's death. Maybe what confounded me even more was that she'd signed a second letter to Debra, "Love, Mrs. Jones."

Mrs. Jones's voice held the slow, comforting cadence from her Mississippi lineage. By 2000, she had lost three of her eleven adult children to alcohol- or drug-related incidents. On the night Raymond died, she sat in the street holding his body. It was so hot that blood had congealed on the asphalt around her and when it suddenly began to rain heavily, she watched the water swish the blood down a drain.

"I saw Debbie at the bond hearing," Mrs. Jones told me. "She looked like a child that needed help. I felt sorry for her. She looked like she was in another world. People may not know dope is a serious problem. There are two sides to everything. I loved my son, but he was no saint. He died the way he lived his life. Raymond is gone now. Ain't nothing nobody can do about that. When Debbie talked about hurting herself, I told her, 'Don't bring no more pain to your mama or sister. God won't give none of us no more than we can bear.'"

"You signed your second letter to Debra, 'Love, Mrs. Jones.' To use the word 'love' is also remarkable."

"Not really. I'm a Jehovah's Witness. We are taught that love and forgiveness go hand and hand. So, I meant it: Love, Mrs. Jones." She was quiet for a second. "Debbie had a picture that her attorney showed during the trial."

Later, when I asked Debra about the photo, she told me that it was taken in 1991 during a certificate ceremony held after Debra completed training to become a certified nurse's assistant. In the photo, she's wearing the traditional white nurse's cap and the freshwater pearl earrings Mrs. Trice had loaned Debra for the event. She looks pleased and proud and her eyes are blindingly bright.

"I saw that picture," Mrs. Jones said. "I thought, 'What a beautiful girl.' My son had a before, too. Before he lost his FedEx job for calling in sick too many times. Before he lost his family and moved back in with me. Two weeks before he died, he got baptized. His friend said he shot up out of that water speaking in tongues. Then he took himself into the prayer room, kneeling on the mourners' bench, where sinners go to repent. He stayed for almost an hour. My son told me he was changing his life."

I thanked Mrs. Jones for her time and gave her my deepest condolences. I began writing and stumbled through a few openings before finally landing on this one:

> *The main corridor in cell block C in the Marion County Jail leads to two doors. First a solid steel one, then another with bars. The second door slides open to a rectangular room, the day area, where women in orange jail-issued uniforms gather at stainless steel picnic tables. They play cards and board games. They write letters and talk on the telephone. They braid and rebraid each other's hair. . . . Until recently I couldn't have cared less about this Indianapolis facility. Now I care far more than I ever could have imagined. One woman who has spent the last 22 months in the Marion County Jail is Debra Trice, 34, a childhood friend of mine.*

In the rest of the piece, I outlined Debra's and my friendship, beginning in Mrs. Love's third-grade class, our divergent paths, and that hot July day in 1998 that ended one man's life and changed the lives of so many others. I finished the story and left an "X" for the number that would hold Debra's sentence. Then I closed the file and waited.

The sentencing hearing took place on Monday, May 8, 2000, in the same courtroom that held the trial. The quirk about Judge Renner's courtroom was that the defense table didn't face the judge as the prosecution's did but the jury box. After listening to everyone who wanted to speak, Judge Renner asked Debra to stand and she turned her body to face him. She wore an orange prison jumpsuit and her hair was braided in cornrows.

He said that although he believed Debra may have committed a reckless act, he had to adhere to the sentencing requirements of the murder verdict. He told her that over the last two years, drugs had factored into all of his murder cases.

"It is, no doubt, a tragedy to you and your family and it's clearly a tragedy that befell Mr. Jones and has befallen his wife, children, mother, and sister," he said. "You, however, are different from most of the people that appear in front of me on these types of cases. You had a supporting, loving family and that was evident today with their presence and that was evident throughout the trial, and why you chose the path you did, I can't say. I do believe that you are remorseful now. The Court chooses, after review of everything and serious consideration and thought, to impose a sentence of fifty years at the Department of Corrections."

A couple of weeks later, Debra left the Marion County Jail in chains and under armed guard for the Indiana Women's Prison, where she would begin serving her time.

chapter twenty-seven

A Plan for Transformation

• • •

I was standing by my mailbox cubby in the newsroom, reading mail one afternoon, when I sliced open a letter from a Wisconsin woman pitching an article about a resale shop in the Ida B. Wells housing project. Although I'd traveled to neighborhoods around the city covering stories, I hadn't been back to Bronzeville—let alone the section where I grew up—in a decade. There were too many memories, too many ghosts. Called Joseph's Coat, the store was run by a couple of nuns from Holy Angels Church. They had set up shop in a vacant Ida B. Wells row house and sold coats and other items for paltry sums to help residents. The nuns named their little enterprise for the biblical story of Joseph, whose father gave him a coat of many colors.

Joseph's Coat intrigued me. But more than that, the city, with the help of the federal government, had launched its $1.5 billion reboot of the Chicago Housing Authority. Called the "Plan for Transformation," it was designed to tear down the authority's high-rises and refurbish the salvageable row houses. The idea was that public units scattered throughout the city and intermingled with mixed-income housing were preferable to warehousing people in towers of despair.

I agreed to check out the resale shop, and as I drove to the housing project to meet with Sister Sara, I thought about how generations of residents had grown up watching the nuns in their intimidating black habits, walking through the community. Most of the row houses surrounding Joseph's Coat were vacant and boarded up. The shop, like the few inhabited units down the row, had black bars on every window, the only sign of occupancy. I opened the door and a bell chimed, giving off the same high-pitched tinkle as in a quaint boutique. But inside, the lime-green walls buckled, and the ceiling drooped. Despite this, carefully folded clothes were stacked tidily on tables and wool and down coats were sardined onto a couple of racks.

"You must be Dawn," Sister Sara said, coming from the kitchen in the back. A petite, middle-aged white woman, she wore a veil and a pair of jeans with a white T-shirt.

"I am. Thank you for making time for me."

"On the phone, you said you grew up in the neighborhood?"

"Right across the street in Lawless."

She ascended a stepladder to arrange bags of oatmeal and grits on a high-up shelf. "I have to get it out of the reach of the vermin," she said. "Lawless is across the street but a far different place."

"Different in that it was well-maintained and didn't have the stigma of public housing," I said. "But Lawless's residents struggled, too. My family was on welfare from time to time. Same struggle, different packaging until crack became a game changer. Our fence didn't separate *us* from *them*, but mostly created a moat of resentment."

I paused. I knew I'd gotten off on a tangent. "Why is Joseph's Coat important to you?"

"We have a lot of addicts in this neighborhood and they need clothes and food and access to a phone and bus cards."

"Do you worry about the crime that can accompany addiction?"

"My family worries about it. I tell them my veil is my armor."

As the afternoon progressed, residents flowed in and out, most of them women.

A painfully slight woman who said she was six months pregnant with her fourth child told me she was sleeping on the floor in a vacant apartment. Sister Sara worried that the woman's weight loss was due to drug use.

Another woman nearly twice my age kept calling me "Miss Dawn" even though I told her it wasn't necessary.

A teenaged girl asked me if I had children. When I told her I had one daughter, she said, "That's all?"

"She's enough." I smiled into my notebook.

"I bet you're married, too."

I nodded. "I am."

"Must be nice."

She smiled but her tone was solemn, as though marriage was mythological, an urban legend. In that moment, I wondered what my life would have been like had David and I purchased that brownstone a few blocks away. Maybe we could have made more of a difference by living there.

I'd been in Joseph's Coat for most of the afternoon when I told Sister Sara I had to leave and that a *Tribune* photographer would call her to set up a photo shoot.

"Is it okay if I come back with follow-up questions?"

"Absolutely," she said. "I look forward to seeing you again."

I stepped outside and the park across the street was a patchwork of men and women, puffed up on crack or drink, lumbering across the dead grass and around the periphery of boarded-up buildings. Young men gathered on the benches.

Over my shoulder, the last of the four high-rises in the Clarence Darrow Homes, the project adjacent to Ida B. Wells, was coming down. Darrow was where those two boys dropped little Eric from the fourteenth-floor window in 1994. That horrific incident added to the many reasons why the city's housing projects needed to be transformed. And yet another part of the tale emerged a year later during the trial and stuck with me. Eric's eight-year-old brother, Derrick Lemon, had been in the apartment trying to stop the boys, but when he couldn't and his brother began to fall, Derrick broke out running down the stairs hoping to catch him. The idea of a child being dropped from a window was harrowing enough, but I couldn't help imagining that little boy—who was probably aware that there was no Tooth Fairy or Santa Claus—barrelling down fourteen flights, believing he could miraculously catch his brother.

As I stood there, I thought about my Doolittle friends who

had grown up here. Bruce, Eleanor, Wayne, Marcus, Anita, Erik, Angela, Glenn, and so many others. They worked in information technology, entertainment, law enforcement, and several were entrepreneurs. Growing up in the project was far from easy, but crack slammed shut a door that once was propped open enough for some kids to slip through.

And yet, Kim and Debra embodied the fact that there were no guarantees on either side of the fence.

Instead of returning to the *Tribune*, I drove a block west to Lawless and north to the opening. To my surprise, a little beige-brick building, an outpost, with gate arms on either side had been built. A security guard was peeping inside. I drove up beside him.

"What's this little building?" I asked.

"It used to be where we screened visitors," he said. "It just sits empty now. I'm making sure the kids don't play in it."

He said that after the outpost was shot at several times, no security guard would stand sentry there—even though it had bulletproof windows. And residents complained about the bottleneck from the long lines of cars. The idea was abandoned, which explained why the outpost sat empty with its gate arms lifted as if in surrender.

I returned to Bronzeville and Joseph's Coat later that summer with follow-up questions for Sister Sara. When I left her, I passed Lawless's southern border to King Drive and turned north. I saw a woman who looked like Debra's and my former teacher, Mrs. Love, walking to a car. When we were children, she'd told us that she lived in the neighborhood. I didn't know if Mrs. Love still lived there. I quickly circled back around, parked and hurried over to her.

"Mrs. Love?" I was eight years old again, giddy and suddenly hungry for approval.

"Yes, dear," she said, opening the door to a Buick Century. Everything about her exuded yoga: Her license plate ("YOGA"). Her posture. Her firm arms. She still looked like the teacher I revered, except for her fiery red hair.

"I'm Dawn Turner Trice." I pointed to my chest.

Her eyes narrowed as she studied my face.

"I was Dawn Turner when I was in your third-grade class in 1973." I wanted to say, *You helped me come out of my shell that year. I made a best friend.*

"Hello, Dawn. I'm so sorry. I'm eighty-four years old," she said coquettishly. "I've taught so many beautiful children over the years. I teach yoga now and I'm late for a class."

"May I take you to lunch sometime?" I sounded and felt like a groupie.

Mrs. Love graciously agreed, and we scheduled our lunch.

On the day I drove up, she was waiting for me and walked to the car in khaki capri pants and a pale-yellow knit sweater, with the same jaunty stride that I remembered. When she got in, I was hoping she'd had an epiphany and remembered me. But she hadn't. I would later write a commentary on our reunion for National Public Radio's *Morning Edition* show and say it didn't matter that she didn't remember me. I was too embarrassed to say it did.

At the restaurant we sat at a table near a window and she introduced me to her life beyond teaching. She believed in reincarnation. She held bachelor's and master's degrees from Northwestern. She felt at home in Greece and had studied cooking in Paris under Julia Child. "What do you do for a living?" she asked me.

I told her that I'd begun writing for the *Tribune*. Several of my elementary and high school teachers had seen my byline and contacted me at the newspaper to tell me how proud they were of me.

"It's one of the perks of writing in the town where you grew up," I said.

"You're a writer! That's marvelous!" Mrs. Love squeezed my hand, the adult equivalent of a gold star. "I take the *Sun-Times*, but I'm going to add the *Tribune*."

"I've also published two novels," I said, greedy for more gold. "I have a husband and a daughter, who's almost six."

"Sounds like you have a good life."

"It is." My gaze fell into my lap. "We almost lost our daughter when she was a toddler. But she's doing well. I just worry that in juggling a career I may not be giving her enough time and I might miss something."

She smiled. "When I was teaching, I knew mothers who sacrificed everything, and I told them to stop. It's not fair. Not for you or for your child. I say this as a mother who lost her only child. My daughter."

"I remember Miss Candy. She passed away the year I was in your class. I attended her funeral."

"How sweet of you." She reached across the table, folding my hands in hers.

"You say your daughter almost died," she said. "Focus on the *almost*. Take it from me, darling, a whole universe stands between losing and almost losing a child."

I drove Mrs. Love home and walked with her to her door. She told me how proud she was to have taught me. I remembered how she had guided my hand with hers to help me write after I returned from my tonsillectomy. I couldn't resist one more try.

"My tonsils were removed the year I was in your class," I said. "You threw me a going-away party."

To be polite, she searched my face one more time. But, once again, she came up empty-handed. Then it hit me.

"Does the name Debra Trice ring a bell? She was my classmate and best friend."

Mrs. Love's eyes widened. "Yes," she said, smiling broadly. "She was the pretty little girl with the light-brown eyes."

I smiled, too, even though I, a thirty-five-year-old woman, was hurt that Mrs. Love hadn't remembered me but couldn't forget the girl known for misbehaving.

"She had so much spunk, that one. I've wondered about her. How's she doing?"

"She's—" I paused. Mrs. Love recalled her former pupil before her fall. It didn't make sense to tamper with the past. "She's fine." I touched her arm. "I'll be sure to tell Debra you said 'Hello.'"

chapter twenty-eight

The Rock

. . .

D ebra sat in the open day area of her dorm amid maroon walls, green metal gates, and gray-blue doors, a color that reminded her of her neighbor's Adirondack chairs back home. She sipped her morning coffee as she read the April 10, 2001, issue of the *Indianapolis Star*. By then, she had been transferred to the Rockville Correctional Facility, "the Rock." After almost three years behind bars, she'd grown accustomed to the sound of heavy steel doors clanging shut around her and bells, alarms, and guards dictating her daily routine. This time of the morning, before she left for work in the prison's eyeglass shop, was hers. She appreciated the smidgen of calm and solitude. It was a throwback to a routine before crack claimed her mornings and laid waste to her day. She looked up from her newspaper as a group of women, dressed in their khaki pants and forest-green T-shirts, quietly filed into the building. As they approached her, several waved and gave her the thumbs-up sign. Because the women weren't supposed to speak, a couple mouthed "Congratulations."

Shrugging, she turned to make sure the corrections officer perched at a nearby station wasn't looking. She then mouthed, "For what?"

Finally, disregarding the guard, one of the women whispered plainly, "Bitch, you won your appeal. It's right in your newspaper."

The public defender who had represented Debra hadn't said a

word. Stunned, she flipped through the pages, scouring each one, until she saw the headline, APPEALS COURT REVERSES WOMAN'S MURDER CONVICTION.

The brief article said that in a two-to-one ruling, the Indiana Court of Appeals had "found that Trice's decision to remain silent after being read her Miranda rights was used against her at trial—violating her constitutional right to due process. The case now returns to the trial court."

Debra ripped out the page and, because inmates weren't allowed to run across the prison yard, she walked briskly, her mind racing, mapping out a different future. At work she secretly passed around the page to coworkers, as if it were a tightly folded schoolgirl's note. The old-timers warned her to temper her excitement. They said inmates who won their appeals tended to lose at the Indiana Supreme Court. Still, Debra felt hopeful, a feeling that she hadn't aroused in years. She spent the day as she often did, shining and measuring the lenses of donated children's eyeglasses, preparing them to be shipped to impoverished kids around the world.

Later that evening, when she called me, she could hardly contain herself. "Reckless homicide carries a one-to-seven-year sentence. I've already served almost three years. Even if I were resentenced to the maximum, whenever a decision comes, I will have already done that."

"Debra, this is the best news I've had all day!"

It was the best news. But I was also worried. Mrs. Trice had said the only good thing about this terrible ordeal was that Debra finally could get clean. I wondered if she could leave prison and stay sober. Was she ready? We'd had a conversation when she told me that she would still smoke marijuana when she got out. And that hadn't sounded like she was ready.

The following spring, a year after the appeals court reversed Debra's conviction, her public defender called to let her know that the Indiana Supreme Court had sided with the trial court.

"I'm disappointed but not surprised," she said. "My lawyer said I can file for post-conviction relief to try to get my sentence reduced. It's a long shot, but I'm still going to try. Listen, I've got other news! You're ready for this?"

Debra always seemed to have some bit of optimism squirreled away, something to blunt the sting of disappointment.

"I hear the drumroll," I said cheerfully.

"I've enrolled in the prison's college program, Oakland City University. They have professors who come here, and we take the same courses students on campus take to get an associate's or bachelor's degree. The only difference is that we don't have the full array of disciplines."

Over the years, we'd had countless conversations about her earning a bachelor's degree. But her addiction always stubbornly reemerged. This was the first time we could see what she could really do.

"Girl, I'm rooting for you. I'm so happy. And you know what? I want to come visit you. It's been way too long."

"You're coming to see your little jailbird friend!"

It occurred to me that the last time we'd been together was when Kim and I took our road trip to Indy twelve years before. Since then, Kim had died and Hannah had gotten sick and undergone years of recovery. The country had commemorated the first anniversary of the 9/11 terror attacks, and fear and uncertainty were still palpable. Time had passed like a fast-moving current. Debra and I both had gotten caught up in a swirl of everyday demands, relying heavily on phone calls and a flurry of letters.

The ride to Rockville, Indiana, was three hours long. My notebook and a pen lay on the passenger seat. I wouldn't be allowed to take them into the prison, but I wanted to recount the details of the visit as soon as I left. I had begun writing a column the year before and I planned to write about the visit. I had asked Debra to tell me about the women with whom she was incarcerated. The horrors that some of them were capable of made even me, a veteran journalist, wince. Debra told me what she'd heard from the grapevine and from some of the offenders themselves. One woman set fire to her own home with her three young children inside. A group of teenagers lured a girl to a cornfield and burned her alive because they envied her. A woman chopped up her husband and fed him to her hogs. She got caught because the police searched her pigsty and discovered his finger. Another stabbed her father and eleven-year-old son to death with no provocation, other than being high on crack.

"Can you imagine coming out of a drugged stupor," Debra had said, "and finding that you had killed your own dad and son, for no reason?"

I didn't want to imagine it.

Rockville, Indiana, home to the Rockville Correctional Facility, sits sixty miles west of Indianapolis, and in a county known for its old-timey covered bridges that draw tourists from around the world. Carved out of a cornfield, the prison itself had once been an air force radar station with a globe-shaped observatory.

I pulled into the prison's parking lot and ran my hand across the wrinkles in my lavender T-shirt, smoothing them out. It had not weathered the ride as well as my blue jeans. I had never been to a prison before, not even to cover a story. And if I had, this still would have felt different. Debra was my friend. I wondered if she was really as upbeat as she always was over the phone—if her thunderous laugh was real. I wondered what she looked like. The last time I saw her, she was thin, wasted away, even though makeup helped bring her old self back into view.

Inside, I passed through security and walked into the visitor's lounge. I was surprised by how bright and airy and immaculate it was. And part of that was owing to the room's floor-length windows that looked out onto a courtyard where visitors, weather permitting, could spend time amid greenery along with a fence with double rows of razor wire. A clock hung above a bank of vending machines. It showed 10:25 when I sat at a cube-like table to wait for Debra to walk from her housing unit across the yard. I focused on the blue door where the prisoners entered the lounge, smiling expectantly. The room held about one hundred people so far, half the occupancy limit, and the majority of the women and their families were white. I looked around, trying not to stare.

On visiting day, the women's crimes receded. Women cuddled babies or played board games with older kids. Well-coifed and effervescent, the prisoners at times were almost indistinguishable, except for the uniforms, from their visitors. In a corner by a window, an inmate snapped photographs of her smiling peers and their families. The photographs served as a fringe benefit to the visits. A few feet to my right, another inmate simultaneously bear-hugged two older women and a child. Tears flowed. Imagine a family in an airport terminal. To my left, a man and an inmate sat at a table, holding hands and leaning forward in conversation. See two lovers in a Starbucks sipping lattes.

Debra entered the room and I saw her immediately. She scanned the crowd looking for me. At thirty-six years old she was just as striking as when she was a child. I was relieved to see she looked healthier than the last time I saw her. Her hair shone in a neat bob style with bangs. Her khakis sported razor creases. Despite the abysmal prison food she'd told me about, she'd regained her weight. I stood and waved. She hurried to me and we snatched each other up so fiercely that we nearly tumbled over.

"Debra, you look fantastic!" I inhaled the smell of her hot-curled hair.

"Aww, Dawn, look at you!" She pushed me away and pulled me back to her.

We sat, both of us nervous and oddly jittery. Two friends who were also strangers; grown women who doubled as little girls.

"How do you feel?" I asked her, searching for something to say.

"Girl, I'm fine."

"And your mom and Darlene? How are they?"

"They're fine and so is my little niece," she said. "Mama doesn't let me want for anything. I've got a television, a radio, money for these ugly-ass clothes and my commissary items. Most of the girls in here don't have any support."

A blonde woman passed us en route to her family.

Debra sat up rigidly. "She's a meth-head and still gets high."

"Here in prison?"

"Girl, yes," she said. "Some inmates score cocaine, Ecstasy, and OxyContin. And even the twenty-four-hour time-released Benadryl can give an addict a decent high."

"Do you—"

"No way. If you get busted, you get a Class A or Class B and it makes it harder for you to go to school. It goes on your record and you could lose your job and visitation privileges. You might get assigned to a different dorm and be forced to bunk with a heifer who won't wash her ass. And whoever brought you the drugs could be arrested and charged. It's not worth it."

It thrilled me to learn that she was using her prison time to heal.

As Debra talked, she tugged on her crucifix, and that made me think of the door keys we used to keep on yarn ribbons around our necks. There were moments when it was easy to forget we were in prison. That was until the guards conducted a roll call and the women lined up to be counted. Each time a prisoner exited the bathroom, a guard frisked her. When Debra and I got up to get snacks from the vending machines, I attempted to hand her quarters. She looked over her shoulder at a guard.

"Girl, I can't touch that. You have to buy it for me."

I bought her a Snickers bar and we sat back down. Debra looked at the inmate who'd been taking photos of families since I arrived.

"Do you remember that picture of Kim that I found a couple of days after you guys left me?" Debra said.

"I don't remember."

"That time you guys came to visit me, after you left, I found a photo of Kim on my bedroom floor. Remember I asked you if you had brought pictures?"

I must have looked puzzled.

"I think you asked me to mail it to you and I don't think I did. I hope I didn't because that means I still have it. I never throw pictures away." Debra's face turned serious. "You must miss her a lot."

"I do. I used to pretend that she wasn't dead but in a witness protection program, and every now and then, when I was downtown at the *Tribune*, I imagined her skulking around some corner, watching me."

"Like when she used to follow us. She'd hang back and when we turned around, she'd try to hide."

Being with Debra made me feel Kim's absence in a way I hadn't in years. I suddenly felt a penetrating ache of loss and grief. I needed to change the subject.

"When was the last time you heard from Mrs. Jones?"

"She sent me a letter just last month. She always tells me, 'You're in my prayers.' And she sends me Jehovah's Witness literature with words of encouragement written in the margins." Debra shook her head while munching the candy. "Mrs. Jones said she would come see me, so I put her on my list. She said that she hopes I don't have to serve all that time they gave me."

"Good Lord," I said. "She must be a saint."

Debra nodded. "She's why I started college."

We talked for a bit more and I watched the rotation of women and their families entering and exiting the visiting center. Our time was winding down.

"Right after your conviction, you believed that jail was exactly where you needed to be. You still feel that way?"

"I can handle myself now, Dawn. I can make it on the outside. All I need is a tiny glimpse of daylight and I won't ever look back."

I looked at the clock. "I don't want to leave you!"

"Me, too, Dawn. You remember how I would hide in your closet when Mama came down to get me?"

"Or you'd leave something so you could come back to get it. I remember."

She looked over at the photographer.

"Despite all the time we spent together as kids, we don't have one picture together."

"We have our class photos."

"They don't count. We need one with just the two of us."

We walked over to the photographer, who was standing by the window. My hair was pulled back in a braid and Debra brought it forward over my left shoulder. I laughed. On tiptoes, she stretched her five-foot-three-inch frame as far as she could and placed her arm around my shoulder. I had nearly seven inches on her, so I leaned over to close the distance.

"Cheeeese!" we sang into the flash.

chapter twenty-nine

Dispatches to Our Fathers

. . .

I was researching a column in the special collections section of a South Side library, picking through an archival box, when my cell phone vibrated. When Mom called me during work hours, she always started with "Are you busy?"

"I'm just working, Mom," I whispered. "Everything okay?"

"Clara, the morning dispatcher, just called," she said. "Your father's fine but he's had a heart attack. He's in the hospital."

I held the phone to my ear. I was surprised by how Mom's tone lacked the normal vinegar reserved only for her ex-husband. How she'd harnessed an enormous amount of restraint by not adding, "Who knew he had a heart?"

However surprised I was by her, I was shocked by how much the news rattled me. A half hour later, I was standing in the doorway of my father's two-bed hospital room. One bed was empty, and Dad was asleep in the one closest to the door. He lay atop the covers, flat on his back in his hospital gown with his fingers knitted over his chest and his legs crossed at the ankles. I could see his birthmark—that white lightning bolt that streaked the length of his leg. I hadn't seen it in ages. Next to his bed on the side table were a transistor radio with the earpiece, a shaving kit, hospital socks, and his comb lined up neatly. Over the last decade, he had worn his hair relaxed and dyed bottle-black. He'd asked his stylist to dab some color onto his mustache, too.

"He might wear down," Mom had said. "But God forbid he show some rust."

I walked into the room and stood over my father. I was so sure Dad was asleep that when he took a deep breath, it scared me, and I gasped. His eyes sprang open.

"What you doing here?" he said, blinking hard.

"I can ask you the same thing."

He felt around for his covers and pulled them over him. "I stopped taking my medicine because my doctor retired. He was ninety years old."

"And you think there are no more doctors?"

"Let me get you a chair," he said, straining to get up.

"No, that's alright. I've got to go back to work. I'm just checking on you."

"Okay. If you're in the neighborhood again, come by and see a fella."

My father was released before I had a chance to return. But the ordeal forced a reckoning: if he died, I'd be left with many unanswered questions. Although Hannah's birth had drawn us a bit closer—I loved the way he picked her up and trotted her around the garage whenever we stopped by—I still didn't know much about him or his side of the family. I realized that I needed to talk to him. But I couldn't do it as his daughter. I had to do it as a journalist. Although Kim and Debra discovered their daring as children, I'd found mine as a writer. My notepad doubled as my shield, my pen as my sword. To interview my father, I decided I would show up unannounced at the garage and spend as many Friday nights as I could talking to him. For the most part, the interviews would be organic. I would see where our conversations took us. But I did have three specific questions I had wanted him to answer for years: *What was your childhood like? On the night Kim died, what did you do after we left? Why did you choke my mother?* Interviewing 101 dictated that I begin with the softball question and finish with the one so combustible it could end everything, including all future interactions.

On a Friday night, two weeks after I visited Dad in the hospital, I drove to the city. I parked and walked into the taxi garage at about 10 p.m. Although Dad's shift started at 11 p.m., he always arrived an hour earlier. The red garage door was up and the menagerie of old mismatched chairs near the television was empty of the old mismatched behinds that used to occupy them. My father's blue sedan was in the mechanics area, sandwiched between two taxis with their innards spilling out. When I couldn't find him in either the dispatch office or the "boss's office," I sat down in one of the chairs to wait. A bulletin board hung over a set of green metal lockers. To my surprise, amid the banners announcing "Taxi alerts" and "Special notices from the police department" and "What's new about workers compensation and unemployment insurance" was a newspaper clipping of my latest column, published a few days earlier. I'd had lunch with Barack Obama, who was campaigning to become a US senator from Illinois. Among the questions I asked him was how he responded to critics who said he wasn't "Black enough." That explained the headline below my headshot: OBAMA UNFAZED BY FOES' DOUBTS ON RACE QUESTION. I was sure Ms. Clara had cut the column out of the newspaper and tacked it there. She told me she read everything I wrote. She used to remind Kim, every time she saw her, that she'd dispatched a cab for Mom the night Kim was born. She, however, never mentioned that she'd also sent a cab years later when Mom put Dad out.

Wearing his navy-blue smock, Dad walked into the garage, saw me, and stopped midstride. I could see all kinds of worry brimming inside him. The last time I came to him late at night, I was with his ex-wife and son-in-law delivering the news of his daughter's death. I empathized. After more than a decade, I still hated Sunday nights. Sometimes I turned the ringer off the phone, taking a page from Mom, who reminded family members, "Don't break up my rest to tell me somebody has died. If they're dead now, they'll still be dead in the morning."

Dad sat down next to me. "Everything okay?"

"Yes," I said, smiling. His body relaxed a bit as I reached into my book bag for my notebook. "How are you?"

"I'm fine. You should have told me you were coming. I've been here the whole time, in the back."

"I haven't been here very long."

"David and Hannah doing okay?"

"They're good."

"How about Granny and Doris?" He hesitated. "And your mama?"

"All good."

The way I held the notebook in my left hand, the edge rested on my baby finger and that made me glance at my father's hand. I flipped open my notebook.

"Where did you grow up?" I launched in, however inelegantly.

Maybe Dad had read my columns in which I'd referred to Mom or Granny or my in-laws and he had been waiting for his turn to tell his story. I don't know. But he never asked me why I was there or taking notes. And I, being his daughter, didn't ask him why he didn't want to know.

"I grew up"—he paused, maybe caught off guard—"in Hinds County, Mississippi, outside Vicksburg."

"On a farm, right?" I recalled bits of stories I'd heard over the years.

He nodded. "We had one hundred and sixty acres."

"It must have been unusual for a Black man to own that much land."

"It certainly was unusual. Your grandfather was no ordinary man."

As Dad spoke, he watched my pen move across the page as if I were performing a magic trick and he was waiting for the sleight of hand. After a few seconds, he stared beyond the garage door into a silty black sky, and a No. 3 King Drive bus hissed and groaned as it passed. Soon the present ceded ground to the past.

"My father was born in 1885 and bought the land 'on time,' with a bank loan during the Depression. Most people knew the Turners didn't like to work for nobody. Papa never sharecropped. He rented land. Do you understand what I mean?"

"No, I don't." I shook my head, eager to learn.

"Okay. In sharecropping, the landowner had to furnish the seeds and the housing and advance money for the sharecropper to live. Whatever he made from the crop, the owner kept fifty percent and the sharecropper got the rest minus the advance. At the end of the season, he was still broke. Sharecropping tied his hands, much like in slavery. But if you rented land, like Papa did before he got his own, you bought your own seed and provided your own housing. That's how he got started."

A boyish smile spread across Dad's face, showing a silver hook from bridgework I never knew he had. As I tried to remember the last time he smiled, I tried to recall the last time he taught me something. I'd learned how to ride a bike on my own. Debra and I had run alongside Kim, teaching her.

"Papa made enough money to buy a new Studebaker. In Mississippi, the white folks bought Fords, the Model T. They got so angry when they saw him driving around town, they told him that if he ever drove that car they would kill him. So he hired a Black man he knew to drive him."

"He did what?!" I proudly smiled.

"He bought another car and passed a white man on a two-lane, country road. That man found out where we lived, knocked on our door, and told my father, 'Nigger, if you ever pass me on the road again, I'll kill you.' Papa never saw the man again."

My father leaned forward, resting his hands on his knees.

"He wound up buying the one hundred and sixty acres and hiring sharecroppers. Papa wanted to treat them fairer than the white owners had. We owned three houses on the land and two of them went to the workers. They grew cotton and corn, peas and potatoes. We had peach, apple, and plum trees and an orchard of pecan trees. We would thrash the trees so the pecans could fall, or we'd wait for twister weather to toss them down to us. And we ate the good pecans until we got bellyaches. We set fire to the rotted ones and they would pop, pop, pop like the Fourth of July."

He started to fidget with his watch. It was a quarter to eleven. "Let me get on up and go to work," he said. "I'll walk you to your car."

"You don't have to."

"Yes, I do," he said. "You remember to call me when you get home."

When I made it home, I sat in the garage for a few minutes. My notebook lay open on the passenger seat and I picked it up. On the cover, I wrote in a rare legible print, "Friday Night Visits w/ My Father." Perhaps I was channeling author Mitch Albom's *Tuesdays with Morrie*, sans the life lessons, sage advice, affirmations, and otherwise warm and fuzzies.

The next Friday, I arrived at 10 p.m. and the garage door was down. Its once-shiny red paint was now chipped and the wood scarred. I entered the garage through the dispatch office and walked over to the television area to sit. Sometime during the past week, someone had hung a sign written in stenciled lettering:

DON'T INQUIRE WITHIN ABOUT DIRECTIONS
IF WE KNEW ANYTHING WE WOULDN'T BE HERE

A few minutes later, Dad's headlights illuminated the garage door's opaque windows and then the door lifted. Seeing me, Dad waved and rolled down his window.

"If I'd known you were coming, I would have been here earlier," he said, smiling. He parked and pulled his smock from the back seat. When he sat next to me, a knocked-up calico waddled over. She leered at me, meowing aggressively.

"No. No. No," he laughed, picking up the cat and placing her on his lap. "This is my oldest. She was here first."

"What's her name?"

"Meow," he said proudly, his devotion on full display as he adjusted her flea collar.

I felt silly envying the way the hem of his smock boxed her in, protecting her.

I flipped open my notebook. "Were you and your father close?" I asked. The question was unexpected.

"Papa would go on long trips, and of all my brothers and sisters, I'd be the only somebody waiting up for him. When I spotted his high beams cutting through the peach trees, I'd run to the garage. He always dug in his pocket to give me my candy."

I'd seen my father's angry face, his hurt face, his tired face, but this one was unfamiliar. He looked swaddled in the memory.

"I was eight or nine and Papa knew I liked to talk after the preachers."

"Talk after?"

"You know, imitate," he said. "Our church only had one service a month. Papa told me that I should memorize the sermons and then repeat them back to the ladies who couldn't make it to church. Where the minister cleared his throat, I cleared mine. Where he stomped his foot, I stomped mine. I'd go down to the pond where the women washed the white folks' clothes and my preaching made them feel better about working on the Sabbath. They took up a collection and gave me plenty of nickels."

Dad's spine straightened for the next part of the story.

"Then one Saturday evening in 1939, the year I turned twelve, I came home from the barbershop and my sister said, 'Buddy, Papa had an accident.' He was driving to Vicksburg on an old dirt road when a dump truck kicked up a cloud of dust. I don't know if my father ran a stop sign 'cause he couldn't see or if the truck ran the sign. But they collided. They took Papa to the Methodist hospital in Vicksburg. The car crushed his arms and legs. The accident was in the evening and he died at 4 a.m. the next morning. The funeral was that Tuesday. Papa was dressed up in his black suit and white shirt and black tie and carried in a simple pine box to the church. On the way to the cemetery, the hearse brought the body to the house because Daddy promised Mama that he'd always, always come back home. She made sure he kept his word."

Dad looked around the garage as if at least one of the old cabs could return him to that night and another could whisk him away.

I had a lump in my throat as my father spoke. He did so with an urgency of a man who had something to say to a daughter absorbing it all. When he grew silent, Meow looked up at him, her whiskers flaring like antennae. The entire time, she never left his lap, although she adjusted herself twice, snuggling her pregnant body against his midsection. As I wrote, I watched the way he tenderly stroked her head and scratched the scruff of her neck. He had a knack for strays, things that made no real demands. The way he touched her filled me with an unexpected sadness.

Once again, we were closing in on 11 p.m.

"When you come back, her kittens will be here," he said, walking me to my car.

By the next Friday, my father wasn't surprised to see me. He, however, did surprise me with a rendering, an old-time drawing of my grandfather. By some trick of DNA, Kim looked more like him than our father. She had his sly smile, strong chin, and thick eyebrows. I stared at my grandfather until Dad brought me back.

"Guess who had her kittens a couple of nights ago," he said, beckoning me to an alcove and pointing to a cardboard box, a quaint little refuge he'd created for the cat.

Inside the box, Meow lay on her side with four kittens nestled into her underbelly. Dad grunted as he stooped to pick up the brown kitten.

"I delivered a baby once when I was driving a cab, did you know that? I didn't eat nothing out of my hands for five days after."

The next Friday, when I sat down in a chair, he quickly tied up a conversation with a cabdriver and hurried over to me. I arrived with a box of photographs of Kim. He pored over each as though he were willing her to jump into his arms.

"The only picture I had of Kim, she looked like a wild rabbit," he said, laughing.

"On the night Kim died, what did you do after we left?"

"I couldn't stay home. I got dressed and came here. A few years before Kim died, she'd come here some nights and stay with me until the sun came up. The night of your wedding, she arrived here drunk and cursed me out for not coming."

He allowed a rueful smile.

I knew none of this. It was hard to fathom Kim cursing out our father and yet it wasn't. She was stalwart and her love for me made my heart ache.

I'd spend four months of Friday nights with my father. I was about to become too busy to continue our visits because I was part of a *Tribune* team covering the Democratic and Republican conventions for the 2004 presidential race. I knew I had one last night with Dad, and the time had come to ask him the hardest question of all.

On that night, Dad sat next to me, holding one of Meow's kittens.

"I've got to ask you something really important to me. And it's not an easy question." I looked him squarely in the eyes and my muscles tensed. "I need to know why you choked Mom that night."

He pursed his lips and stared out in front of him. I had seen him look this way when he was seated in the dispatcher's office, punching numbers on the adding machine while counting money. Now he was engaged in another type of calculation.

"Sometimes," he said slowly, "sometimes men just get really angry?" He was asking me, as though he wanted to know if he'd answered correctly.

"Why did you choke my mother that night? Had you ever done that before?"

"No," he said. "I—I was mad that night."

"While she was asleep?"

"A man should never hurt a woman." He clearly believed it was easier to concede.

"To this day, she sleeps with a glass of water beside her bed because she wakes up in the middle of the night choking."

Violence has a residue. The way it floods your pores and insinuates itself, causing a molecular mutation. Once again, I was that scared little girl who had opened her parents' bedroom door that night. Instead of crying into my pillow, I was now crying onto my notebook. Dad sat quietly, silenced by my tears or the question itself. Maybe sensing my father's distress, Meow leaped into his lap next to her kitten. Only this time, he didn't pet her the way he normally did. His hands remained at his side.

"I shouldn't have done that."

My father didn't use the words "I'm sorry." And I don't believe that's what I sought. What I wanted was akin to a truth-and-reconciliation moment, a healing. I needed him to acknowledge that he had hurt Mom and that he had changed her. I needed him to know that he had changed Kim and me, too, in ways that we would never fully comprehend. I was grateful that he didn't say what he did only happened once or that some men do far worse.

"Thank you for answering." I closed my notebook.

The next weekend I left for Boston for the Democratic National Convention. On the night Barack Obama introduced himself to the country, our newsroom emptied out to hear him talk about red states and blue states and the "audacity of hope." After the convention, Obama's autobiography, *Dreams from My Father*, went on to become a national bestseller.

I returned home from the Democrats' soiree, and then left the next month for New York with a team of *Tribune* journalists to cover the Republican National Convention. By the time Debra and I talked, she had a slew of questions. Was Obama as tall and handsome as he seemed on television? Did John Kerry, the Democratic presidential nominee, stand a chance? What did Hillary Clinton look like up close?

I'd told her about my Friday night visits with my father and we talked about my last night with him. Her father had grown up in the same neighborhood as Jiffy Cabs, a couple of blocks away. He was a boy when his family was among the first Blacks to integrate the block. For a while, a police car drove alongside him and his friends as they walked to and from school.

"If Dad had lived," Debra lamented, "I wouldn't have gotten into so much trouble."

"But you two butted heads all the time," I reminded her.

"I know," she said. "He would have made me listen. He would have saved me."

By November, when President George W. Bush was reelected, Debra dialed me, and I thought it was to talk about the election. But she told me she'd just received her mail and she was surprised to see that two letters she'd sent Mrs. Jones had been returned unopened. Mrs. Jones had always responded quickly.

A week before Thanksgiving, Debra was sitting in the day area of her dorm, reading the November 18, 2004, *Indianapolis Star*. She had read the story about the high number of Hoosiers being called to serve in the Iraq war; the opening of the Clinton library in Little Rock, Arkansas; and Bush nominating Condoleezza Rice to succeed Colin Powell as secretary of state.

Then Debra turned to the obituary pages, which she always read carefully because she had already lost friends and relatives since she'd been incarcerated. At the bottom of the page, there was no photo, just a few lines that said Margaret Myers Jones, seventy-four, Indianapolis, died November 15, 2004. It gave the name of the funeral home and said her services would be held in the Chapel of Peace.

"I cried when I got the news," Debra told me. "I hadn't cried that hard since my father died. I used to tell Mrs. Jones that when I got out, I would run errands for her. I just wanted to repay her kindness." I could hear Debra's voice breaking. "Inmates do their time differently when they're forgiven. I didn't deserve it, but from the very start, she gave me my life back. She didn't have to do that."

chapter thirty

"Down the Line"

. . .

After my tonsils were removed when I was eight, Aunt Doris sat with me for a week while Mom worked and Kim was at school. It was the only time I had Auntie all to myself, without my cousins or my sister. Every day she pulled a chair next to my bed and clicked on the television, toggling between game shows and soap operas. For lunch, she scooped ice cream in a bowl for me and one for her. Then she poured candy corn and peanuts into a cup, from which she dipped throughout the afternoon.

Over the years, Aunt Doris was my confidant, helping me navigate motherhood, my marriage, and even my relationship with my father. When I started spending Friday nights with him, I told her that I worried I was betraying Mom. Auntie said simply, "Child, your mother will roll her eyes, but she'll be fine." Then she offered one caution: "Just remember that your father adds yeast to his stories. Check behind him."

Aunt Doris was more than my aunt. She was my second mother. I felt that even more acutely when Mom called me to her apartment on a snowy winter day, just before Christmas, to tell me that her sister had been diagnosed with stage 4 lung cancer.

"Doctors give her less than a year," Mom said, wringing her hands, which she never did. "She's been around smokers, but she's never smoked a day in her life."

I left Mom and drove directly to Auntie's little blue frame house with the white trim. Uncle Henry was leaning on a snow shovel, looking as lost as I'd ever seen him. Snow still covered half the porch steps. I tapped my horn and got out of my car.

"Hey, Sugar Babe." Every other time he'd greeted me, he sounded like the happiest person in the world to see me. Now he just looked like it took everything he had to stand upright.

"Hey, Uncle." I opened the gate and he hugged me tightly. "I'm so sorry."

"We've been married forty-seven years," he said. "She was eighteen when she married me, and it was the first time she lived away from your mother and grandmother. I found us a dingy one-room basement apartment. It was all I could afford. We cooked on a hot plate. Forty-seven years. Not one has been easy. But she's my world."

"I know she is." I squeezed his arm and hugged him again. "Is she upstairs?"

He nodded. "See if she'll eat for you."

As soon as I entered the house, I could hear Aunt Doris's television blaring.

"Auntie," I yelled. "Your favorite niece is coming up. Are you decent?"

"I hope not," she yelled back, her voice lilting. "Hey, Sweet Sugar." She appeared at the top of the stairs wearing a brown jogging suit. I hugged her. It was the type of hug that you want to savor and sock away so you can borrow against it in the future.

"Your mother has a big mouth. Don't tell me she didn't tell you."

I looked up at the ceiling.

Her small bedroom overflowed with old magazines and clothes draped over too-big furniture. The heat stirred the smell of the eucalyptus oil she'd rubbed on her chest to quiet her cough. On the nightstand were the tea concoction composed of honey and melted butter that she'd been brewing to loosen phlegm and her signature bag of candy corn and peanuts. She began moving clothes off a chair for me.

"Auntie, I can do that."

"So can I. Now make yourself comfortable." She sat on her bed and propped herself against a stack of pillows. "I don't want everybody fussing all over me. Let me do while I can do."

On her bed, a *Jet* magazine lay next to a saucer holding one bar-
becued chicken wing, a tablespoon portion of string beans, and another of mashed potatoes. Nothing had been touched.

"Auntie," I said, pointing to the saucer. "Want to take a bite?"

"I will, later," she said, looking down at the food. "You know?
Men aren't worth one red cent. They pretend to be all big and strong.
But let a few clouds gather and they run for cover, under food." She
pushed the plate away. "I just don't want your uncle to start drinking
again. He's been doing so well all these years."

"But you do need to eat. Please?"

She ate a forkful of mashed potatoes, barely a forkful.

"Your mother insists on picking up Hen and me for my doctor's
appointments. She's always thought she was the boss. Did I ever tell
you that when we were little, I used to follow your mom to make
sure she was safe? I'd see her lying in the grass under clotheslines
with her hands folded behind her head. Or she'd be sitting outside
on a bench with this old lady, Mrs. Patterson."

"I remember Mom talking about her. The woman who'd been
a slave."

"That's her. Your mother was always going to the store for her
or she'd walk with her through the row houses and you'd see this old
stout woman rocking with her cane and this little sandy-haired child
holding her hand. They made the cutest couple."

Aunt Doris's only appetite now was for the past.

She talked about being fifteen years old in 1950 when our section of
Bronzeville was razed for Lake Meadows. On summer nights, when
the smell of death and decay from the stockyards wafted throughout
the community and swarms of flies followed suit, Aunt Doris stood
on the fire escape of a friend's apartment, peering at the construction
site north of 35th Street. Old doors from the soon-to-be demolished
buildings had been arranged side by side so they provided fencing
around portions of the demolition site. During the day, Mom, Aunt
Doris, and their friends would go to the site and peep through holes
in the doors where locks had been, glimpsing the future.

She saw me looking at the framed photos on her dresser of her
children, Kim, and me. One was from our Gospel Tour to New Or-
leans, where we stayed at the Hotel Monteleone. The swimming

pool was on the roof and we kids lived in the water. When we returned home, Mom said we were so dark Kim and I looked like little Africans.

"When you two were young your mom was always railing against your father. One time I interrupted her: 'He did two good things. We wouldn't have my nieces if not for him.' She looked at me and said, 'Damn it, Doris. There you go always looking on the bright side.'"

Aunt Doris and I howled, and we awakened the elephant in her bedroom. All the laughing brought on a wrenching coughing spell. I rushed over to give her a sip of cream soda and a gentle pat on her back. I asked her when she could take her cough syrup again. Over the next few weeks, her cough syrup was joined by a litany of other medicines and breathing apparatuses.

By the time we'd made it through the thick of winter, Auntie's brown jogging suit hung in folds on her shriveled body. Her glasses dwarfed her face. A pink bandana kept sliding off her bald head. Vanity always forced her hand up to her bandana, patting and adjusting.

From the moment Mom and Aunt Doris sat in Granny's living room and told their ninety-one-year-old mother that Aunt Doris had terminal cancer, Granny fell into total denial.

"Those doctors don't know shit from Shinola," Granny said, recalling the shoe polish. "My baby will be just fine. It's all in God's hands."

"Mama, she's not going to be fine," Mom said, glaring at her. "You've got to accept this. You understand?" Mom wasn't just angry that Granny refused to listen. Mom was perturbed that she had to say aloud words that made no sense to her either.

When spring arrived, Aunt Doris opened her bedroom windows. Experiencing a sudden burst of energy, and rocking a short Afro, she made a rare showing at church and sat next to Mom in the choir. At one point, as the music soared, Auntie got the Holy Ghost and ran out of the choir and all around the church.

Mom mumbled "Shit" to herself.

No longer a choir member, Granny sat on the Mothers Board and caught Mom's eye. She smiled and nodded a nod that said, *What did I tell you? She's going to be just fine.* Mom caught up with her sister and Auntie exploded into a coughing spell, forcing deacons to carry her to the back of the church. Nurses administered oxygen.

On a late April afternoon, Uncle Henry opened the door for me. The buttons on his blue shirt were misaligned. He looked painfully lost as he told me that the social worker was upstairs, and Aunt Doris had put him out of their bedroom.

"She told me to take my *4712* downstairs," he said, managing a smile. "She's up there signing papers." He looked down at hands that were calloused and chafing. "Doris used to have a beautiful handwriting. Now even that's tearing apart."

"I'll go up and see what's what, Uncle. Don't worry."

The social worker was a young white woman with spiky hair and a nose ring. She sat in a folding chair on the side of the bed near my aunt, typing on her laptop as Aunt Doris reviewed documents. Neither saw me. I stood there staring at my aunt's bare legs. Loose skin hung like stockings over purple veins resembling squiggly lines from a ball point. Gone were the smooth, shapely legs I used to stare at under the table.

"Doris," the social worker said. "I see you've signed the health-care Power of Attorney, but this is the Do Not Resuscitate order." She pulled out a green sheet of paper from a binder. "You said you wanted to sign it, too, but you forgot last time."

"Please call her Mrs. Reynolds," I said sharply. Aunt Doris looked up. The social worker angled around. "You're too young to address my aunt by her first name."

"Hey, Sweet Sugar." Aunt Doris cranked her body up and toddled toward me, enveloping me into her bony arms. "It's okay."

"No, it's not. It is not okay."

Even the social worker knew that I hadn't snapped because she took liberties with my aunt's first name. I'd snapped because of that bottomless binder she kept reaching into to hand my aunt papers. And because Auntie was using her *Jet* magazine to sign them on. And because of that day, months before, when Aunt Doris told me she was going to sign the DNR. But that was after the social worker had said, "Take your time and if you decide to sign, you can do so down the line."

We had arrived at *down the line*.

"I apologize," the social worker said to me. "I'm so very, very sorry."

When she left, Aunt Doris motioned for me to come sit next to her on her bed. She held my hand.

"Your mother has always been nosy. Did she ever tell you that when she was seven or eight—I can't remember—she liked to hide in the coat closet near the living room, listening to grown folks' business? One afternoon, she was in the closet and so tired that she accidentally fell asleep. When she woke up, it was pitch black and she had no clue where she was. So, your mother did what she knew best: she just started swinging. She beat the hell out of those coats and the hangers started falling down and slapping her in the face. She just fought harder. We heard all that commotion. By the time we got to her, she'd seen the light under the door and figured out where she was. Your great-granny Lessie opened the door and your mother stood there breathing hard, hair scattered all over her head. She told me, 'Doris, I thought I'd died, and I didn't want to die.' That girl was trying to beat the hell out of death."

Even though I wanted to laugh, I smiled because laughter is contagious, and I didn't want Auntie to get caught up in a coughing spell.

"Your mother takes me to chemo and gets mad at the nurses. She takes me to the gambling boat and dares anybody to smoke around me. She thinks all she has to do is come out swinging and she can save me. But she's wrong. You think as long as I don't sign papers, everything will be like you want it. But you're wrong."

I felt like a sprinkler, I was crying so hard. But Aunt Doris, ridiculed for years for being a crybaby, was as dry-eyed as I'd ever seen her.

"I've had a good run," she said. "You're going to have to let me go."

Aunt Doris moved into hospice in May. That first day, Mom and I were seated in her room, which was designed to look like a bedroom with a let-out sofa for family and floral wallpaper that matched the curtains and valance, and a plastic bouquet on the dresser. My cousins had been in and out, but at that moment it was just Mom and me. Aunt Doris had been sleeping, but she opened her eyes and she couldn't see.

"Mama?" she cried out. "Barb?"

"I'm right here, Sugar," Mom said.

"Touch me," Aunt Doris said, staring blankly. "Touch me."

Mom took both of her sister's hands in hers.

I was standing near the door about to run to get a nurse. Mom motioned with her head for me to come over to the bed.

She whispered, "I can't leave her, but I need you to go get Mama, right now."

I could hardly move.

"Don't just stand there with your mouth open. I need you to get her and drag her back here if you have to. I'll try to call her and let her know you're on your way."

I was staring at Aunt Doris's face, drawn and ashen.

"Go," Mom said. She couldn't yell it, but somehow that's the way it sounded.

I flew out of that room and down the hall. My slingbacks clacked across the white tiles and my face looked like I was running through a cascade of water. I was afraid I wouldn't get back in time. And I wasn't sure what I would do if my grandmother refused to come with me. I bolted across the parking lot to my car and I drove the six miles to Granny's apartment. Uncle Al had passed a few years before and Granny now lived in a courtyard building not far from Mom. She was waiting on the sidewalk when I pulled up. We didn't say much during the ride back to Aunt Doris. Granny looked out the window and not only did she understand that her daughter was sick, but she had arrived at the place that no mother can make sense of, no matter how many decades she'd been fortunate enough to have with her child. Ordinarily, Granny didn't so much lean on her cane as hold it up. But as we walked to Auntie's room, she relied on it. Mom was still holding Auntie's hand, frozen in place. I wondered if she'd moved at all while I was gone. Granny stood opposite of Mom, tenderly stroking Auntie's other hand and singing:

"I'm so thankful, thankful, thankful as I can be. God has been so good to me."

The way she cooed and sang, it sounded like a lullaby and I began sniffling. Mom and Granny glared at me. Auntie turned her head in my direction, and I don't know whether she could see me, but she started to moan as though she was sobbing. We soon realized she was actually laughing. Then Mom and Granny joined her. Their faces conveyed a clear message: *If you're ready to give up, leave. There is a process. There is a bridge. There will be a time for tears, but now isn't the time.*

The moment did come a week later, in the middle of the night, with Uncle Henry asleep on the hospice room sofa. Auntie passed away quietly in her sleep. My cousins had taped one of their parents' wedding photos over her bed. In the black-and-white image, Aunt Doris and Uncle Henry are cutting their multitiered wedding cake, getting ready to start their life together while Great-Granny Lessie and Granny look on smiling. Mom's smile is forced and she's looking side-eyed at her sister. I had seen that photograph for years and hadn't thought much of my mother's expression. But now I knew exactly what she was thinking:

I can't stand to see you leave me. Just go.

chapter thirty-one

Pomp and Circumstances

. . .

Inside the Rock's visiting center, Debra sat in a small room with her fingers laced together atop a table. An unarmed corrections officer stood nearby. Every time the guard moved and blocked her view of the security area, she leaned forward or to the side to see me pass through the metal detector. Our smiles met as I crossed over. A *Tribune* photographer accompanied me, and I waited for him to gather his tripod and gear. Then he turned on his video camera to capture me entering the room and embracing my friend.

Debra had been incarcerated for nine years. But she remained as healthy as ever, physically and mentally. Hair still in a bob and skin still flawless, she looked gorgeous. That day she wore iridescent teal-green eye shadow, accentuating the amber color of her eyes.

"I barely slept last night," she said. "I'm just really nervous."

"Don't be. I won't ask you anything you don't already know."

I motioned for her to sit at the head of the table and I took the seat on her right, outside the camera's frame. The photographer lay a microphone on the table between us and then snapped the video camera onto its tripod.

"Ready?" I asked Debra as I opened my notebook.

"I'm ready."

I turned to the photographer, who counted down from three and pointed to me. A tiny red light flashed, and I tossed aside my initial question. I imagined us in the shelter of her bedroom in Lawless, lying on her throw rug with the Tyrannosaurus rex I held, kissing her Brontosaurus, the two of us erupting in giggles.

"You loved dinosaurs," I said.

"Yeah," Debra nodded, her face still stoic.

"You were the only little girl who could name all of them—"

Her face ignited. "I still like dinosaurs," she said, emphasizing the word "still."

"You still like them?"

"Yes!" She smiled so hard her eyes became slits.

"What was the attraction?"

"Did you see that scene in *King Kong*?" She was referring to the 1960s movie *King Kong vs. Godzilla*.

Our laughter filled the room and the officer suppressed his smile.

"You're about to complete your bachelor's degree," I said. "And I'm writing a story that will accompany this video. What does your upcoming graduation mean to you?"

"Well," she said, once again serious. "I never thought I was smart—"

"For the record," I said, "you're graduating summa cum laude."

"I know I'm smart now. But I wish someone had told me when I was younger. Maybe I wouldn't have given my teachers so much grief. I don't know. Most of the long-timers here go to school. Some go because it trims a few years off your sentence. But for a lot of us, it's the first time we've really accomplished something."

"What do you want people to know about your conviction?"

"From day one, I've never denied that I was guilty of something. I'm not a murderer, the *charge* is murder. I would rather have a reckless homicide charge. When people hear the word 'murder,' you think of the *Psycho* movie." She mimed stabbing from the movie's shower scene. "Being in here, when I read the horrible, horrible crimes and intentional acts that have been committed, I'm like, 'God, they're convicted of murder and I'm convicted of murder.'"

"You've appealed your case and the Indiana Supreme Court upheld the trial court's decision. Then you applied for post-conviction relief and then stopped the application process. Why did you do that?"

"I needed to do my time, for society, for the family, for me, for

God. I made a mistake, a horrible mistake, and it caused a lot of pain. It trips me out to know that I'm responsible for something like that. At one time I wanted to be a nurse to help people."

"Do you think a lot about Raymond Jones, your victim? Is it like grief, where, over time, it may become more bearable?"

"I don't know if I'd say bearable. It becomes more, I want to say, more real. It becomes more a part of me. I threw my whole life away and somebody else's. Raymond wasn't a bad person. He was an addict like me. Maybe about a year ago, it hit me that I'd apologized to Raymond's mother, to God, to Raymond's family. I said, 'Debra, you've never apologized to Raymond.' I was in my dorm and I found myself by my locker just crying and telling him, 'I'm so sorry, I'm so sorry.'"

Debra and I talked for about an hour, taking stock of her crime and how her years in prison had recontoured her life. The Kroger food store ads in the newspaper reminded her how much she missed shopping, cheese that actually melted, and the drive-through of her favorite Taco Bell. She worried about whether she'd be able to find a job once she was released. Who would hire an ex-felon in her fifties? She longed for dreams with settings beyond the prison walls. She had reconciled that she would never give birth, and more than anything, she feared her mother might die while she was locked up. She broke down when she talked about her drug use and how she couldn't hold a job and had tried to take her life.

For my final question, I asked her what she wanted to do upon her release.

"Talk to young girls," she said. "These girls out here, between ten and thirteen, are so vulnerable. I was thirteen when I had my first joint. My father was strict. He told us not to do any drugs. But I didn't listen. I was wild. I tried crack for the first time the day after we buried him. I thought it was just any old high. I didn't know that I would submit to it and give my life to it."

"You didn't listen to your father. Why will young girls listen to you?"

"I have to try. I can say, 'Look at what happened to me.' Not what might happen. I can ask them, 'Is the ride you're about to take worth your life?'"

———

For much of the drive home, I thought about Debra wanting to reach out to "tweens"—porous and vulnerable preadolescents. I had a tween. Hannah was twelve, and while I'd always worried about her health, my focus now was on peer pressure and drugs and sex. Of course, most parents steeled themselves for puberty's invasion. But in the back of my mind and careening forward were Debra, Kim, and me as tweens. Kim was ten when she started cutting class. Debra smoked weed for the first time at thirteen. And I was thirteen that summer when the man on the lakefront assaulted me. To this day, I shudder to think about what might have happened had Debra not been with me.

I was obsessed with history not repeating itself with my tween. On the night Debra was arrested, Darlene had asked her sister, "When did we lose you?" I had asked myself that about Kim. I was determined to never have to ask my child.

As I pulled into my driveway, I could see light seeping around the blinds in Hannah's bedroom. The lamp in David's office was on, too. He had finished law school a couple of years before and passed the bar. He was working full-time designing legal software for a company but also trying to start a law practice on the side. We both worked constantly and rarely spent time together.

Inside, I walked upstairs and tapped on Hannah's door.

"Hey, Mom," she said, removing her headphones. "You have a good trip?"

I walked over and sat on her bed. She still looked just like David but with hair. I rubbed her back.

"I need you to know that you can always tell me anything."

"I know. You've told me a million times."

"I'm saying it again. If you don't want to talk to Dad or me, you can confide in Grandma or your aunts." Her surrogate "aunts" were three of my closest girlfriends. Holding her face in my hands, I stared into her eyes with a sincerity she readily recognized. "I need you to not go to prison and to never die."

That sounded morose, but she'd heard about Debra and Kim for years and understood the references.

"Okay," she said. "Not part of my plan."

A few days later, I stood in the parking lot in Lawless Gardens with the *Tribune* photographer who taped my interview with Debra at the Rock. He wanted footage of the old neighborhood to pair with the video from the prison. While he set up his gear, I looked around the complex. Although I'd stood outside the fence seven years before when I worked on the Joseph's Coat story, I hadn't gone inside. I was surprised to see that the landscaping no longer looked well-maintained and was strewn with garbage. The merry-go-rounds, swing sets, and sandboxes in Lawless's playgrounds had been dismantled and sod laid down over the areas.

Later, one of Mom's Lawless friends would tell her that teens were getting high in the playgrounds, which explained why they were removed. She'd add that as the Ida B. Wells housing project was being vacated, some of its residents were using government housing vouchers to move across the street, behind the fence. The newcomers were being blamed for polluting the once-pristine environment. That was one of the fears former housing project residents had around the city—that residents paying market rate would blame them for any and everything.

When the photographer began recording, he gave me the cue and I pointed to Debra's and my old eleventh- and twelfth-floor bedroom windows and then to the sidewalk in front of me.

"There were many times when we would kind of run up and down this little sidewalk going from place to place," I said into the lens. "This is where the roots are. It wasn't quite solidly middle class, but it also wasn't the housing project that was just to the east."

The interview ended and my colleague left, but I spent a few minutes looking up at our eleventh- and twelfth-floor bedroom windows and wondering how many times Debra and I had looked out at the same time and never knew it.

O n my return trip to Rockville that spring, I entered the recreation building for Debra's commencement ceremony. Folding chairs had been arranged for nearly 180 visitors. Balloons and crepe streamers adorned the blue-gray cinder-block walls. At the front of the room was a makeshift stage with a podium and a basket of rolled-up graduation certificates. The ceremony was about to start when I arrived. I quickly found Mrs. Trice and Darlene and sat with them.

When the sixty graduates marched in, dressed in their black caps and gowns, they began filling in the empty rows at the front of the room. Debra saw us and waved.

Of all the people who spoke that day, the inmate who delivered the keynote address stood out. Poised and eloquent, she was fifty-six years old with auburn hair and what her fellow inmates called "girl next door" looks. She was doing time for voluntary manslaughter. She walked up to the microphone and owned the stage:

> As most of us can attest to, life can at times literally bring us to our knees. It is during this time we realize that if we stay down, we will remain at this point forever. I believe that this is God's way of making us slow down for a minute to ask for his guidance in helping us to reevaluate and reorganize our priorities in life. Being human makes us vulnerable to making mistakes along the way. It is our personal show of determination and sincere willingness to learn from these mistakes that define who we are in terms of inner strength and moral character. There is no promise in life that guarantees us complete happiness. . . . We may often wonder about or question the direction that our lives have taken. But we must keep in mind that whatever was is in the past and whatever is is what's important. Today is here and we have only this moment, a moment that we have earned, a moment in which we can be truly proud.

I joined in the standing ovation.

During the ceremony, I kept looking at Debra and her peers. Women who had been broken and plagued by low self-esteem were being lauded for their hard work and perseverance. When it was time, Debra crossed the stage, accepting her bachelor of arts degree in business administration from the representative from Oakland City University. Darlene cried the whole time. I thought about Debra's road there and how within the cinder-block walls and iron gates she had transformed herself far beyond what it took to satisfy the requirements for a degree. I thought about my own college graduation and the sense of accomplishment and pride I'd felt walking across the stage.

When the ceremony ended, the graduates filed into the prison yard, flinging their caps in the air. They hugged their family members and one another. Inmates looking out from the windows of the housing units, as well as those hanging out in the yard, burst into applause and whistles and yelled their congratulations. Graduation was the only time the corrections officers didn't write inmates up for the noise.

"I'm about twenty years late." Debra frowned as she walked up to me. "I wish Mrs. Jones could have seen me and I wish I could have done this on the outside."

We both knew she could not.

My column on her graduation ran that November. Beyond the background of reminding readers about Debra's and my childhood together and the events surrounding Raymond Jones's death, I wanted the ending to focus on her transformation:

> *I used to believe that the hardest thing you could do is watch, even from afar, as a friend destroyed herself. But it's equally hard watching that friend rebuild, especially if the process is occurring behind bars.*
>
> *This is Debra's story. But it's mine as well. We all make mistakes. We all make good and bad choices. Life can change in an instant and sometimes we avoid peril not because of any series of things we've done perfectly but by a grace far bigger than our own steps and missteps.*
>
> *After years of searching, Debra believes she's finally rediscovering herself. I believe she is as well. . . .*
>
> *Now, after all these years of us traveling down two completely different roads, it appears our paths once again are converging, and it doesn't matter that we couldn't occupy two more distinct worlds.*

It became one of my most popular columns ever and readers contacted me from all over the country and world via letters and emails. Many of the comments were positive, with teachers hoping to use

Debra's story as a cautionary tale for their students. Some readers lamented the waste of talent. "All these brilliant minds, locked up," wrote a man from Memphis. "It makes you wonder how much better our world would be if these ladies would have made the most of the opportunities on the outside."

Readers also focused on forgiveness: "Fantastic article," wrote one. "I never thought I could feel anything for anyone who committed murder, but this story changed that. If the mother of the victim could forgive, who are we to ask why and not forgive. I pray Debra makes it all the way out."

When the letters no longer fit in my mailbox cubby, an editorial assistant transferred them to a plastic bin the size of a small trunk. He set it next to my desk and I opened a few envelopes a day. Maybe a week after the story ran, I had a stack on my lap, getting ready to slice open the first letter when I locked in on the name above the return address. It was from Terri Jones, Raymond's widow. I had left voicemail messages for the Jones family to get a comment for the column, but no one responded. I threw the other envelopes back into the bin and opened Terri's.

"I don't care what she's done in prison or how many degrees she's gotten," Terri wrote. "I don't care that she's the person you grew up with. The person described in your story is not the person I saw in the courtroom. She's a murderer, an evil woman who left a man to die in the street. How dare you uplift her? Because of her, I don't have a husband and my children don't have their father. Raymond never got the chance to change his life."

I immediately dialed the Jones family hoping to get Terri's telephone number. No one answered. But what would I have said to Terri had I reached her? I spent the day turning the letter over and over in my head. Terri was right about Raymond not having the chance to change his life. He didn't get a chance to graduate from his addiction or have his family celebrate his transformation. He wouldn't have a redemption story that recounted his before and after.

Over the years, I'd tried to understand how people changed their lives before the clock ran out. Kim had not been able to do so. Debra had only figured it out behind bars. That question of how a person managed to start over was at the heart of the stories I pursued, the people I most enjoyed talking to, and the way I parented. I didn't want Hannah to get swept up in some addiction from which she'd have to fight her way back.

Earlier in the day, I'd called David to tell him about Terri's letter. As I climbed into bed that night, flopping down onto the pillow, he could tell that the letter's full weight still bore down on me.

"We want to believe that people change eventually," he said.

"I used to tell Kim that she could change her life, as long as she had breath." It was what one of the men said at the Alcoholics Anonymous meeting we attended.

"I know," he said. "But what if Kim never changed? What if she had only got worse?"

In bed, our feet used to always touch, one finding the other. But they didn't anymore, and I couldn't tell if I was mad about that or what he'd just said.

"How could you say that? Of course that was a possibility, but I always believed that even if Kim had to hit bottom, she'd eventually change direction."

"Sometimes people don't change for the better," he said. "We say to ourselves, there's a chance they will get better. But there's a chance they won't. That's the alternate story nobody wants to see."

chapter thirty-two

Girls School Road

. . .

A few months after Debra's graduation column ran, Barack Obama, now a Democratic presidential candidate, won the Iowa caucuses, astounding the country. With Iowa being such a white state, I asked my editor if I could create an online forum about race. I called it "Exploring Race," and I worked with the *Tribune*'s graphic designers to create a forum where readers could feel free to ask questions about race they wouldn't ordinarily ask, fearing they might be deemed a racist. Some of the most popular and most sincere questions had nothing to do with such touchstones as affirmative action or interracial neighborhoods but . . . hair. One man said he was a white guy with a Black girlfriend and asked, "Why doesn't she let me touch her hair?" I also wanted participants to contribute essays about race. A white woman penned one about having a "Black"-sounding name and how people were surprised to see her when her name preceded her on a job application or even a Starbucks cup. A South Asian woman lamented not being able to tell her mother that she wasn't looking for a suitable boy but for a suitable girl. A Japanese American woman outlined the downside of being part of "the model minority."

I enjoyed the online forum and columns on race, but I also missed the type of writing that I loved: telling the stories of people who changed their lives. My editor agreed to a new series of columns called "Short Stories."

In the March 11, 2011, *Tribune*, I wrote about Brenda Myers-Powell, a former prostitute who had become a member of the Cook County Sheriff's Office Human Trafficking Response Team. When it came to changing one's life, she was an exemplar and a testament to how difficult a task change was, but how remarkable it could be if mastered.

I had first met Brenda a decade before. I'd received a call from a reader pitching a story about an organization that helped women transition from a life on the streets. I visited Brenda in the new apartment she'd gotten through the program. That first meeting, she was meek and self-conscious. We were sitting on her sofa and she told me that her earliest memories of being raped went back to when she was four years old.

"Then, when I was nine years old, I remember identifying with the women on the street corner because they wore shiny clothes and I wanted to be and feel shiny. They looked like the Supremes. I was living with my grandmother and I asked her what they were doing. She told me they were taking their panties off and men were giving them money. I could identify with that scenario, too, because men had been taking my panties off. And I thought, 'Wow, I'll probably do that one day.' It seemed normal and inevitable."

The inevitable arrived a few days before Brenda's fifteenth birthday. She had two daughters, one who had just turned a year old and an infant whom she'd just taken for her six-week checkup. They were living with Brenda's grandmother in her one-bedroom West Side apartment and they needed money for food and rent. On the evening of Good Friday, 1973, Brenda put on her two-piece lime-green dress with the puffy sleeves. It cost $3.99 from a store called Three Sisters and she'd worn it to Sunday school. She slipped on a pair of her grandmother's cinnamon-colored stockings and then into her $2.99 black shoes that made a crunching sound. She stood on the corner in front of the Mark Twain Hotel on West Division Street on Chicago's Near North Side. Her orange lipstick somehow made her look even more like a girl but that didn't matter.

"I remember getting in a car and the man teaching me how to give him oral sex," she'd said. "We had a debate about the price. I'd read *Hustler* magazine and I thought all prostitutes got one hundred dollars. But he said, 'I don't want to buy you, I just want to rent you.' He gave me forty and then an extra twenty. I asked the other guys for a hundred and some gave it to me. I remember one Italian guy with cologne and a gold chain. He gave me one hundred and fifty dollars."

That night, she made enough money to pay the rent, buy groceries, and buy her children Easter clothes. She even bought her baby a fluffy bunny rabbit.

After that Good Friday, Brenda's life in prostitution would drag on for twenty-four years and include a stint in California and an addiction to crack. She'd dig her way out on April 1, 1997, just days away from her fortieth birthday, after a customer didn't want to pay her and shoved her out of his car. Her dress caught in the door and he dragged her for six blocks. She lay in a hospital bed for a week with injuries to the left side of her body and most of her face. She almost lost her left eye.

In 2011, when I met Brenda a second time, she was still a member of the human trafficking response team, but she'd cofounded the Dreamcatcher Foundation, a nonprofit that works to prevent young girls from entering the sex trade and help those already entrenched to burrow their way out. She'd coauthored research projects for DePaul University, including the study "From Victims to Victimizers: Interviews with 25 Ex-Pimps in Chicago," with law professor and senior research fellow Jody Raphael. That March, I attended a symposium on human trafficking and Brenda was on a panel designed to help social workers understand the sex trade. I eagerly wrote a follow-up column about her.

Debra read the column and asked me to bring Brenda to the Indiana Women's Prison, where Debra had transferred as part of an effort to ease overcrowding in Indiana prisons. She was one of the leaders in the PLUS program, a purposeful-living initiative that helped women reenter the outside world cleansed of their demons. Debra lived in a dorm with about sixty other women who were in the program and on a similar path. She was part of a team responsible for bringing in motivational speakers.

Located on Girls School Road, the prison was a collage of buildings that once housed juveniles, girls under age fifteen whose conduct the state deemed incorrigible. The prison chaplain greeted Brenda and me on the day we arrived and escorted us through security. She took us to a building that used to be a high school, through hallways lined with lockers and to a classroom that doubled as a chapel.

A small stage was dressed in purple bunting and held a cross made of stained glass and a couple of chairs with a table between them. I left the room for a second and saw the inmates standing in line waiting to enter. The majority of the women were white and appeared to be in their early to mid-twenties and could easily pass for high school or college students. When I heard a familiar laugh, I looked toward the back of the line. Lifting up on tiptoes, Debra was trying to peer over the crowd. Seeing me, she smiled and waved her extravagant, SOS-like wave. Her hair was still in that neat bob, but time had begun to gently etch small creases around her mouth. Still, Debra was as buoyant as ever. She looked at the guard for approval to step out of line and when the woman nodded, my friend hurried toward me, flinging her arms around my neck.

"Debra!" I sang. I hugged her tightly.

"I'm so glad you're here," she said. "I really am."

I led her inside the room to Brenda and introduced them. They shook hands and Debra cupped her hand around Brenda's. "Thank you so much for making the trip," she said. "I've heard so much about you."

"And I've heard a lot about you, too," Brenda said.

"I've got to do a few last-minute things," Debra said. "But we can talk more later."

When it was time for the program to start, she stood near the front and quieted everyone. Brenda was on the stage, but I tried to take a seat in the audience.

"No, Dawn," Debra said, "I want you up there, too. Please."

I followed instructions.

"Can everybody hear me okay?" Brenda said, standing. Debra had placed a handheld microphone on the table between us, but Brenda preferred not to use it.

Pacing the length of the stage, she said, "How many of you have ever done something you regret?"

We all raised our hands.

As a primer, she talked about her life in prostitution. She stressed that she understood how difficult it is for someone to change her life.

"No little girl or little boy wakes up one morning and says, 'I think I'll be a prostitute when I grow up. I think I'll waste my life away in back alleys or in the back seats of cars or in nasty motel rooms.'"

As Brenda spoke, my attention shifted around the room to the women. Once again, I'd gotten permission to bring a notepad and I started to jot down what I saw and heard. Some of the women leaned forward in rapt attention. Some leaned away, still skeptical and not yet ready to buy in. One woman with hauntingly blue eyes watched Brenda intently as she walked back and forth across the stage, surveying her shoes, her long feathery lashes, and the way her hair lay flat, pulled into a taut bun.

When Brenda finished speaking, the women applauded and Debra invited some of the inmates to the stage to share their stories. Ashley, a white woman, had long black hair and spoke in a mild southern dialect. She said she thought she had to enter prison and be tough. For five years, she did nothing. No programs, no therapy.

"Eight months ago, I transferred here, got my GED, and became a part of the PLUS program for the time cut. I came for the wrong reason. But, as we say, it doesn't matter why you come. It matters that you get what you need."

Brittany, a white woman with glasses and short mousy-brown hair, was next. I was smiling until she began by admitting that for a long time she hated herself and wanted to die.

Her hands trembled as she told us that she was ten when her stepfather molested her. He touched her privates and made her touch his. She moved out at thirteen and went to live with her father. Brittany described him as the type of man who met you at the door with a loaded gun. She was bisexual and he didn't approve of her girlfriends. Her father moved to Indiana and she spent her high school senior year there. Two weeks before she graduated in 1992, she became pregnant and had to get married. The marriage was far from happy. After the baby was born, she had postpartum depression so bad that the child was taken into foster care. She gave birth again and her postpartum depression worsened. That child also went into foster care and her parental rights were later terminated. By then her marriage was over. She met a friend and got pregnant again.

"My son was born six weeks early," she said. "This time, I had a support system of women I'd told about my history of postpartum depression. When he was three months old, I became paranoid. The day I took my son's life, I was in a psychologist's office earlier that morning and he was telling me what a good mother I was. I can't tell you when exactly I lost my temper with my son. I remember he was crying, and I shook him. He died three days later. The hospital called the jail for me to give them permission for my baby to be an organ donor. I've been incarcerated eleven and a half years. I've forgiven the people who have hurt me. But I can't forgive myself."

By the end of her story, I'd stopped writing. The women applauded and I realized they had told their stories before. I couldn't fathom another way a person learns to open up about such shame and heartbreak without having been offered some degree of grace.

Debra walked up to the stage and held Brittany's hand.

"I want to thank everyone for coming—as if y'all had a choice," she laughed. "Most of all, I want to thank Miss Brenda and my best friend."

Debra walked over to me as I stood. She hooked her arm around mine.

"I used to hate women who had been convicted of murdering or hurting their children. Most of them denied the charges. But Brittany was the only woman I met who said, 'I killed my child.' I saw how sincere she was about changing her life and I figured, 'Who am I to keep her pinned to her demons?'"

The women began to get back in line to return to their dorm. When the chaplain passed us, Debra asked if Brenda and I could see the living quarters.

"Of course," the chaplain said.

As we left the building, the chaplain walked ahead, and I caught up with her.

"The stories were powerful," I said.

"We try to drill down to what happened to each woman," she said. "Rather than say, 'What's wrong with you?' we try to frame it as 'What happened to you?'"

"That's huge," I said. "It lets them know they are not inherently bad even though they're here because they did something bad."

She nodded. "And, it says, 'Now, let's try to figure out who you really are. Let's surround you with people who'll listen to you and support you.' We all need people. The majority of the women in prison have been physically or sexually abused, many before puberty. If that had been my history, I would have used drugs, too."

We walked across the quadrangle to the one-story dorm pod that housed members of the PLUS program. Inside, a group of women surrounded Brenda in a common area. Debra took my hand.

"Let me show you around," she said, leading me to her dorm room, thirteen by nine feet with three beds, including a set of bunk beds. "I only have one bunkie right now and she's a chatterbox."

She patted the spread. "This is me." Her bed was next to the window and she had a small television set and a radio. My mind colored in her pink-and-white Lawless bedroom and the little girl who'd proudly shown me that she could climb to her sister's top bunk and jump.

Debra dragged a box from a corner.

"It's my keepsakes box," she said.

Inside were letters she'd received from pen pals, relatives, and friends; books from when she was in school; and newspapers that had begun to yellow. She unfurled the articles that I'd written about her and the ones I'd sent her from my coverage of Hurricane Katrina, the 2004 and 2008 presidential elections, and from Obama's inauguration. I'd told her that I'd stood directly under the podium where he was sworn in on one of the coldest days of my life.

I sat on the bottom bunk of the empty bed and she sat next to me, side by side, shoulders touching. It was the first time since she'd been in prison that we were able to do that.

"I need to be careful because I still have eight whole years and Mama's getting older," Debra said. "She's been in and out of the hospital. Darlene and I are going to take care of her when I get out. We don't ever want her in a nursing home unless she needs medical care that we can't possibly provide."

Debra got up and pointed to an old photo of Hannah taped to the wall. It was the one I sent to her after I learned she was in jail.

"Why don't I have a more recent picture?"

"I'll get you one," I said. "She'll be seventeen. She's a good kid. Her grades are less than stellar, but she's a good kid."

"Her mother is an author and journalist and her father is an estate planning lawyer," Debra said. "Cut the girl some slack. How is David?"

I hesitated. "We're in this weird place. But we've been trying counseling. Our therapist is a marathon runner and he said our problem was akin to an ingrown toenail. It hurts a bit when you run but you can get through it. David and I left the office and laughed all the way home. We just need to fix it and we will."

Brenda peeped in to tell me it was time to leave. I stood and Debra looked at my hair—curly and pulled back into a ponytail. She tugged on it. "Why don't you straighten your hair?"

"I do sometimes, but it's too much work."

Then, as if we were young again and the world still stretched out perfectly and neatly without disappointments and failures and grief, as if we were twelve or thirteen and she was innocently planning a slumber party, she smiled broadly and said, "When I get out, you know what I'm going to do? I'm going to flat iron your hair for you."

chapter thirty-three

Fast-Forward Not Available

- - -

After Kim died, when Mom told me she couldn't dream about her daughter, I loaned Mom the videocassette of my wedding. The photos she had all around her apartment and on her nightstand just weren't enough. She wanted to see Kim in perpetual motion, eternally young. In the video, Kim is walking down the center aisle of the church. Her gait is methodical like she's balancing on a tightrope. Her pink, three-quarter-length gown matches the blush on her cheeks and her bouquet of plastic roses is slightly shaking. She's walking toward the camera and smiling brilliantly. During the rehearsal, the videographer had told us not to look directly at the camera and when she does, she catches herself. Behind her, you see the church's wood-paneled walls and its lone window. The walls are sweating, as are the people she passes. At this point in the video Mom always says everybody looked like they had fever from consumption. But they are fanning and watching Kim as though the heat doesn't really matter. Kim passes the front row and the camera focuses on Mom, Granny, and Aunt Doris before it follows my sister to the altar. The music from the part-time pianist still grates. Over the years, it has done what we once thought impossible—gotten worse.

When Aunt Doris died, Mom watched the video to see her,

and after Granny died at the end of 2011, having recently turned ninety-eight, Mom watched it to see her mother. With the exception of Granny's last two bedridden years, she'd been spry and congenial in her old age, spending her afternoons watching bad reality television and sucking on Werther's Original candies, handing them out to Hannah, whom she called "Little Lady," and to the handsome home health-care nurse, with whom she flirted. And to me. I still have one wrapped in its gold foil, unopened, undisturbed. During the last year of her life, her memory was in tatters. Although she no longer remembered my name or Mom's, she somehow remembered David's without fail. Mom cared for her until the end. And when Granny died on a November morning under a familiar blue sky, one as pale blue as any bird or ornament in her collection, Mom looked as lonely as I'd ever seen her. We held Granny's funeral at the First House of Prayer Church.

I hadn't seen the wedding video in years, but I remembered David's face as I walked down that center aisle. He was smiling but straining, his body quaking, trying not to laugh at the inept pianist. I couldn't look at him because if we'd caught each other's eye, we would have cracked up at how earnest the pianist's face was despite how poorly he played. In that moment, we were happy, the happy that radiates and changes the atmosphere of a room. The happy that feels bottomless and covers faults. The happy that makes you believe you will be able to withstand everything.

Fast-forward not available.

I was thinking about the video on a Saturday morning when Mom buzzed me into her apartment building. She lived on the third floor and typically I climbed the steps two at a time. But that morning, I walked up so slowly she said, "What's the matter with you?" She leaned over the banister. "Why are you ass-dragging?"

"I'm good," I said, smiling up at her.

She hugged me when I reached the top. We walked back to the kitchen where a television with a built-in VHS player sat on a counter next to a stack of videotapes Mom made of my various television appearances. Among the tapes was my wedding video.

"What's going on that you have to see me first thing on a Saturday morning?" she asked, leaning against the counter. When I didn't say anything, she added, "You know I don't like anybody who chews on her words too long."

"As I said, everyone is healthy and fine, but I need you to sit down."

She slowly sat on a counter stool.

"I've asked David for a divorce. It's so hard to explain why, but I'm also so sorry it's come to this."

My mother's brows knitted. More than confused, she looked hurt and disappointed. A month before she'd bragged to her church friends that her daughter and son-in-law were celebrating twenty-four years of marriage.

"We told Hannah last night. It blindsided her, too. She wrote on her Facebook page: 'My life has just been devastated.' My friends texted me, asking what was wrong. I didn't want to tell them before I told you."

"I'd say devastated is right," Mom said. "Every marriage has its ups and downs."

"I know. I think David described what happened to us best by saying we started out riding in the same car and then we began taking two separate cars. Gradually, we were heading in opposite directions and didn't mind it."

My mother swiveled absentmindedly on the stool, at a loss for words.

I looked out the kitchen window. "You enter marriage with a list of things you tell yourself you would never put up with. But what happens when that thing that destroyed your marriage wasn't on your list? He didn't cheat or do drugs. He didn't hit me. He didn't squander money. And neither did I."

A scowl descended over Mom's face. "Don't do anything rash, okay? Just give it some time."

"It's been eleven years. I can tell you when it all started. It was when I put Hannah in that private school. She was only there for second grade. Afterward, she went back to a public school. But he's never forgiven me. It was like he saw me as a traitor, someone who no longer shared his values or dreams."

"You thought you were doing what was best for your daughter."

"Exactly. But after he saw me as a traitor, that was further validated when I stopped eating meat or if I asked him to read something and didn't take his suggestions. It's hard to live with someone who doesn't like you. We both changed, but not together."

"Where is he now?"

"He's still in the house. He just sleeps in his office."

When I left, Mom looked like I'd delivered news that someone had died. I felt horrible, but I also felt resolute and relieved.

I told my friends and family members about my decision, and when Debra called me, I told her, too. She was sorry to hear it but understood.

"Damn," she said. "You won't be a Trice anymore."

"Nope, no more."

A few months later, a friend encouraged me to apply for a Nieman, a prestigious journalism fellowship at Harvard University. For years, several *Tribune* colleagues who had won the fellowship had urged me to apply, but I never thought I was good enough to be chosen. I loved to tell the stories of ordinary people. They were the types of emotionally engaging columns that certainly were impactful, inspiring readers to respond with donations, or to ask: "What can I do?" But I doubted that my work rose to the level of winning a Nieman.

I also never pursued it because the time never seemed right to take off a whole year from work and uproot my family. But that year, tumult was already in play and it felt like the right time. I went through the application process, became a finalist, and flew to Cambridge the following May for interviews. At the time, Ann Marie Lipinski, a Pulitzer Prize winner and the former editor of the *Tribune*, had been the curator of the Nieman Foundation for Journalism for three years. She started early that morning, calling the winners, twelve international fellows and twelve from the States.

I tried not to stare at the phone. The fellowship would be an opportunity for me to reboot and renew on both personal and professional fronts. I wanted it more than I'd wanted anything in a long time. At 7 a.m. Chicago time, the phone rang.

"I'm pleased to offer you a space in our 2014–2015 class," Ann Marie said.

I thanked her profusely.

I'd told David how much I'd wanted the fellowship and he ran in the bedroom and hugged me, despite the fact that we no longer shared the room.

Hannah asked to take the semester off from her college to come with me. I agreed. David's and my split had upended her life, too, and it seemed the least I could do. As a Nieman affiliate, she also would be able to audit classes.

I wrote a "Farewell for now" column, announcing the fellowship, and Hannah and I arrived on campus a couple of days before orientation. My rental apartment, a vintage two-bedroom, was a half block from the Charles River and four blocks from Harvard Yard. We unpacked and spent the second day walking around the campus, finding the Walter Lippmann House, the headquarters of the Nieman Foundation, and sampling from the quaint ice cream shops and delis.

I bought a bike and rode with a group of Niemans from Cambridge to Walden Pond and back. I rode to Black Lives Matter protests and discussions about the Michael Brown shooting in Ferguson. I rode to my seminars at Lippmann House and to my classes, including one taught by the famed attorney Charles Ogletree, examining race and the criminal justice system through the lens of the HBO series *The Wire*. I rode along the Charles River and wrote in coffeehouses and read tons of books.

I returned to Chicago for Christmas break and cooked a feast for the extended family. It was Hannah's birthday and we always celebrated, and I didn't want that year to be any different. Everyone knew that David and I were divorcing, but they were surprised by how cordial we were, how I laughed at his jokes, how we worked together serving the food.

"Can't you mend things?" Mom asked pleadingly. "You clearly still love each other."

"We do. We just don't like each other enough to live together. When everyone leaves, he will go to his room and I will go to mine."

On New Year's Eve, I boarded a plane and spent ten days all by my lonesome in Barcelona. Hannah stayed behind to return to college. And when my plane touched down at Boston's Logan Airport, I taxied to my apartment and spent the spring semester in the

East Coast's record snowfall, working on screenplays and novels and absorbing every glorious moment of the experience. It was my first time in more than twenty years living alone and I reveled in the solitude, the time to think and wonder and create.

Among my classes that semester was one on revitalizing American cities taught by Ogletree. It was held in the law school's Kirkland & Ellis Hall, named after a large Chicago law firm. My childhood friend Thomas worked there for years as a senior corporate paralegal in investment funds. Every time I entered the class, I thought about how instrumental he'd been to my education. Thomas and I would go a couple of years without talking and reconnect as though no time had passed. We had dialed each other during the important milestones of our lives, but I hadn't yet told him about the impending divorce or the fellowship.

On a rainy Sunday afternoon, I called him, and we talked for more than five hours. Before we hung up, I told him that I might not have been on campus if not for him and that my life might have been so different. That sounded hyperbolic, but it felt true.

"Get out of here," he said.

"No, seriously. I got into the program at the University of Chicago because of you. And if it hadn't been for me competing with you, who knows where I might have landed."

Thomas's laugh was still somewhat squeaky, like when his voice was changing.

"The reason I signed up for the program had nothing to do with academics," he confessed. "I found out that its students didn't have to take gym at the high school. I was a gay boy who did not want to be in anybody's locker room."

"So, my life is based on you not wanting to swim and get your hair wet?"

"Exactly!"

How lucky am I?

When the school year ended I returned home, and a few weeks later David moved out. Our divorce was finalized that fall. I kept delaying my return to the newspaper, but when I did go back,

I stayed for about three months and determined it was no longer the right fit. My last day was just before Thanksgiving.

I also wanted to return to the city. I prepared to sell the house by hiring workers to paint and fix things. In clearing out clutter, I began with my home office, rummaging through old bins.

One held items from travels that I was saving for Debra when I learned she was deathly afraid of flying: a matchbox from a Paris café; a scarf from London; a charm bracelet from Madrid. I would later add items from Amsterdam, Accra, Shanghai, Nice, and, among other places, Sydney, Australia. In Sydney, I'd talk about the unlikely presidency of Donald Trump, along with race, class, and growing up in Bronzeville on a national radio show.

In another bin, I found my eighth-grade autograph book, Doolittle, Class of 1979. I flipped through it, and on Kim's page she wrote three inscriptions:

"Aries are pests, but you're the best, good luck in everything, Kim."

"Roses are Red Violets are Blue, I love you much, I hope you love me, too."

"Lucky, lucky am I. I picked the best, now when I rest, and no matter how long I live, to me you will always be the best, Kim." She was ten years old when she wrote that. She'd been gone twenty-two years, almost as long as she was alive.

I had left a page for Debra with her name on it, but she never wrote on it. I don't remember writing in her book either. That was the year we rarely saw each other.

I found the four reporter's notebooks that held my father's stories. Tucked in one was a copy of a deed for the 160 acres that my grandfather owned. Having heeded Aunt Doris's advice, I'd checked most of what Dad told me. When I asked my cousin Samuel Turner Jr., a retired second judicial circuit court judge and family historian, about the property, he mailed me the document. It was signed by the chancery clerk on March 30, 1928, and read, in part:

In consideration of the sum of Four Thousand ($4,000.00) Dollars . . . I convey and warrant to the said Clem Turner the following described land situated in the Second District

of Hinds County State of Mississippi . . . 160 acres more
or less. . . . It is further agreed and understood that the
said Clem Turner is to have all rents and revenue from said
lands and pay all taxes against said lands.

My father and his siblings sold off much of the property in the
1970s. Sam, who lives in Memphis and is an ordained minister, remembered it as some of the most verdant land Mississippi had to
offer, with pecan and peach trees anointed by God.

After those Friday nights with my father, I'd seen him a few
times a year. We talked on the phone about his health, and he'd re-
galed me with a few more stories of his past. In the fall of 2010, I
stopped by Dad's place because I happened to be in his neighborhood reporting on a column. He was living with my half-sister, her
husband, and their two daughters. He'd stopped coloring his hair
and was grayer. His heart issues had caught up with him and he was
thinner. He told me that he often watched me on television, and he
read my column. He smiled but didn't say much more than that.
When it was time for me to leave, he walked me to my Toyota. I
hugged him for the first time in my memory and I kissed him on
his cheek. He'd told me to call him when I got home. A month later,
Dad passed away in his sleep.

Below the notebooks, I unearthed a shoebox of letters I'd mailed
to Kim while I was in college. I read through them, identifying a
refrain: "You can change your life."

There were letters and photographs from Debra, including one
that came after her graduation. It showed Debra in her cap and
gown standing with her mother. The inscription on the back of the
picture read: "To Dawn, Friends 4 life! Deb." As she had for years,
ever since elementary school, she signed her name and added a heart.

At the beginning of 2016, Debra called to tell me she, too, was
packing up and leaving. She'd been at the Indiana Women's
Prison on Girls School Road for seven years and was transferring
to the Madison Correctional Facility, a minimum-security prison
in Madison, Indiana, where she'd spend her remaining three years.

Located near the banks of the Ohio River, the facility is a step-down prison and the most concrete sign so far that her sentence was coming to an end. The prison was nearly two hours southeast of Indianapolis and Debra knew that her mother's failing health would prevent any more visits.

Every time Debra and I talked, she mentioned how hard Darlene was working to care for Mrs. Trice. Debra wished she could be by her mother's side. One time when I visited Debra, I asked Mrs. Trice if I could stop by to see her and she grew quiet. I knew she didn't want me to see her ill, so I changed the subject. Debra's greatest fear had always been that her mother might die while Debra was in prison. She had already felt the loss of her grandmother, Mrs. Jones, and a couple of high school friends. But Debra also knew that her mother was in pain and when Debra called me to wish me a happy Easter, she said, "I don't want her to suffer anymore."

I had officially put the house on the market that May when Debra called to tell me Mrs. Trice had passed away. Debra was hurt but ready.

"I'm just sorry she won't see me on the outside."

"She'll see you," I said. "And she was so proud of you."

Debra wasn't crying, so it didn't seem appropriate for me to. But I could hear my voice breaking.

"My family is going to video the services," she said. "And Mama and I did a video visit a while ago. I still have that."

"We've been lucky to have such good mothers, Debra. Your mother loved you dearly."

"I know," she said, her voice petering out. "I really have been lucky."

chapter thirty-four

Two Good Families

• • •

04/26/18

Debra,

Hello, my name is Whitney Jones and I'm the daughter of Raymond Jones. I'm writing you this letter today because me and my mom are at a place in our lives where we are ready to sit down and hear your side of the story. I know your release date is rapidly approaching, so me and my mom feel that this will be the best time to visit you. It hasn't been easy for any of us since my Daddy has been gone, but I think once we get the answers that we've been looking for we will finally get the closure we need and can start the process of forgiving. If you would be interested in meeting us as well, please let me know and me and my mom can start making arrangements!

God Bless,
Whitney Jones

5/17/18

Hello Whitney,

Let me start by saying that honey you need no introduction—I knew exactly who you were the minute I saw your name on the *envelope. You and your brother Jaylon have been on my mind and in my heart ever since this nightmare began. Before I even read your letter, I was crying, shaky and nervous. You see, deep in my heart, I always knew this day would come. I have prayed for this day and have looked forward to being able to talk with you and Terri. I have so much to say and at the same time, I don't know what to say. You have no idea what your letter means to me. I am humbled beyond words and I spent the next day crying on and off and sharing your letter with my closest friends. I have spent decades soul-searching and trying to figure out how the paths in my life led me to that day.*

We have a lot to talk about. Right now, I am waiting to get an appointment with the warden. I do not want us to talk in the visiting center during regular visits. I am requesting a special visit where we can talk more comfortably. So please be patient with me while I set this up—I know you don't know but the wheels turn very slow in prison. I will let you know what needs to be done so don't for one minute think I have forgotten. Talking to you and your Mom is the most important and most serious thing I have ever had to do in my entire life.

Will be in touch soon,
Deb

Debra scheduled the reconciliation meeting and asked me to join her. The night before, I could hardly sleep. As I lay in my hotel bed, my mind raced across the stories I'd covered over the years about forgiveness. In September 2015, I traveled to Mother Emanuel African Methodist Episcopal Church in Charleston, South Carolina, a few months after white supremacist Dylann Roof massacred nine church members. They had invited him to join in on their Wednesday night Bible study. Despite the prevailing narrative that Emanuel's parishioners had forgiven Roof, several told me they hadn't and might not ever. Long before that story, I'd written others about Chicago parents who'd lost their children to gun violence. They often tried to wrest meaning from the tragedy by starting foundations or delving into other types of advocacy work so their child's death wouldn't be in vain. But I'd never been in a situation like this one: the person convicted of murder was my childhood friend. I kept wondering: *What do you say to the woman who took your loved one's life and, by doing so, forever changed yours?* As for Debra, *What do you say to the wife and child of the man whose life you took?*

The Madison Correctional Facility is a series of stand-alone and connected terra-cotta-colored brick buildings that sits at the end of the tree-lined Bus Stop Drive. I was surprised to see that it's part of a campus that includes the Lide White Memorial Boys & Girls Club and the Indiana Veterans Memorial Cemetery. How strange to have both so close to a prison. I parked and walked up to an outpost that sits off the road. Chain-link fencing with figure-eight-shaped loops of razor wire enveloped the property. As soon as I opened the door, I saw a woman seated on a bench beyond the metal detector. She was dressed in a T-shirt, black skinny jeans, and low-top All Stars. Her hands were folded in her lap.

"Whitney?" I said it low, worried that saying it louder would startle her.

She smiled nervously. "Yes. Hi, are you Dawn?"

"I am."

Now twenty-nine years old, she looked like someone waiting for a train but hating that she had to get on it.

"Are you alone?" I asked.

"No, my mother's in the bathroom." She pointed to the door across from her.

I was wearing earrings and a bracelet that a female corrections officer told me I had to take to the car. I did, and when I walked back, Debra stood a few yards away but on the other side of the fence. I waved with both hands and she waved back. For the first time since I'd been visiting her, I felt no butterflies, no lump in my throat. In a few minutes, she was about to be face-to-face with two people who had suffered because of her and neither one of us saw this as a nostalgic or celebratory moment. We had no idea what to expect. What I remembered about Terri Jones was the letter she'd written me a decade ago, furious about the column on Debra's graduation.

When I returned to the security area, Terri had come out of the restroom and was sitting next to her daughter. She wore a beige outfit with gold ballerina flats. The most striking thing about her was her eyes, large and doleful. She, like her daughter, was very pretty. The two watched me pass through the metal detector. It pinged, and I had to take off my shoes and walk through again.

"Now I have to pat you down," the guard said. "Face the window."

Distracted and not really listening, I turned toward her instead.

"If you don't face that window," said another female corrections officer, "that pat down is going to feel like a big ol' uncomfortable hug."

I smiled and followed directions. After passing through the metal detector, I introduced myself to Terri as I gathered my things. She was a bit more reserved than Whitney and harder to read.

An officer led us through a metal door and then a gate to the building where the meeting was to take place. We entered the visitation area, a room with large windows and filled with round tables and chairs. No one was in the room except for Debra and a middle-aged woman with dark blonde hair. The woman, holding a bundle of papers and a cloth bag, introduced herself as one of the prison counselors and said she would be supervising the visit.

My friend looked as scared as I'd ever seen her. I imagined this was the way she looked the night she turned herself in. Or maybe when she was in the courtroom during the trial or during the sentencing. Debra's entire being fixed on Terri and Whitney and her face showed a concentration, a contrition I'd never seen. She stood with her arms to her sides.

"Hello?" It sounded more like a question. "Thank you for coming."

"Thank you," Terri said.

Debra did not know what to do with her arms. She looked like she wanted to embrace them, but her arms only lifted halfway. She looked like she was going to extend her hand for a handshake, and she drew it back.

Whitney and Terri stood in front of me and I couldn't see their faces. But Debra's told me that they were offering a degree of kindness and I could see Debra's chest swell, as though she'd taken her first breath in a while.

The counselor said the room where we were scheduled to meet wasn't ready yet. And the moment felt interrupted, as though precious momentum had been lost.

"Ms. Trice," the counselor said, "you and your guests can get something from the vending area while you wait."

"I have quarters," I said, reaching into my pocket. Debra had asked me to bring them. "It's on me."

"No, thank you," Terri said. Whitney smiled.

Debra and I walked over to the vending area.

"I'm so scared, Dawn," she whispered.

"Just breathe. You will be fine."

No officers were around, so I handed her quarters.

"I don't know what to say." She retrieved a Mountain Dew Code Red from the machine.

"You will know when the time comes."

"We're ready now," the counselor said.

She led us to a room called the Family Preservation Center, where inmates visit with their children. Posters of Winnie-the-Pooh, Big Bird, and Mickey and Minnie Mouse hung on the wall near books and toys occupying a bookcase. Debra eased down in a chair adjacent to a red sofa. Terri sat on the part of the sofa closest to Debra, and Whitney followed. I sat on the end, next to Whitney.

The counselor piled her papers on top of a desk a few feet away. It was so quiet in the room that when she pulled out the chair, we turned toward the scraping sound. The counselor reminded me of a teacher getting ready to oversee detention hall.

"I'd like to start by saying I am humbled," Debra said. "I've been waiting on this moment for a long time. I was praying that this day would come and when I received Whitney's letter . . ." Debra began to cry, so she unfurled the bathroom tissue stuffed in the pocket of her khakis. "The day I received the letter, it was late at night after count. I'd gone down to the mailroom. Whitney, I saw your name and I just had to be still."

Debra curled the tissue around her finger and dabbed at her eyes.

"I took the letter back to the dorm room. I shared it with six other women. They said, 'Trice, what's wrong?' I could hardly open it. I want you both to know how sorry I am for the pain I inflicted on your family. I want you to know that it wasn't something I set out to do. I come from a good family. I am not a bad person. What I did to you and your family was a horrible thing. Raymond came from a good family. Terri, I remember in court when you said you had two young children that you had to now raise by yourself and while I knew all along what I did was wrong, that's when it hit me. I've always loved children and to think that I took away these kids' father. I'm so very sorry."

The counselor looked up from her paperwork. She had been writing, but now her attention was on us. She'd later tell Debra that she thought she was merely sitting in on a special visit among family. Sometimes the prison made accommodations for family members who couldn't come during regular visiting hours. But when she understood that this was a reconciliation meeting between Debra and her victim's family, she stopped working.

As Debra spoke, Terri sat with her back straight and her ankles crossed, and hands folded in her lap. She nodded and listened. Whitney began to cry, and Debra tore off a section of the tissue paper and handed it to her. They laughed as pieces stuck to their wet fingertips.

"I'm sorry Jaylon couldn't make it," Debra said.

"He's entering his senior year at the University of Central Missouri," Terri said of her twenty-three-year-old son. "He's studying sports medicine. He had just left for school and couldn't attend."

"I understand," Debra said.

"Whitney told me the date of the meeting," Terri said. "And I was scheduled to be out of town."

"I'm such a 'fraidy-cat," Whitney said. "I've always been so fearful of everything, but I told Mom that I would come alone."

"And I told you," Terri said to her daughter, "I was never going to let you come by yourself."

Debra leaned forward. "You can ask me anything, okay?" she said. "Either of you. Anything."

"I've always wanted to know about the night my father died," Whitney said. "It's been a missing piece in my life. But this past Easter, me, my mom, and grandmother went to church and then to dinner at Red Lobster and I told Mom that I wanted to reach out to you. I remember over the years that you wanted to contact us. All I'd ever heard from that night is what someone else had told us. They told us why you shot my father, but I never heard your side. The only person left to talk to was you. I needed the closure. I wanted to know who you were and where you came from. I knew I was doing well in my life. I'd had a child. And I said to myself, 'Let's work on this weight I still have about my dad.' And it took until now for me to feel comfortable to handle the truth."

Debra sat up, as though she needed her back straight for what she said next.

"Raymond was a good man," she said. "I never would have brought him to my mother's house if he wasn't. We had become friends and were both so tired of our addictions."

The first part of the story was familiar. She talked about that exceptionally hot day, July 20, 1998, that pushed her and Raymond into her mother's air-conditioned house so that they could smoke crack. She told them that her mother's rings came up missing and that Debra believed Raymond had them. She was drunk when she went to get them back. She took a shotgun to protect herself against feral dogs. While talking to Raymond, it somehow fired.

The way Debra looked while speaking was earnest and sincere but also composed. Although she cried, her voice never quivered. And she never failed to maintain eye contact with either Whitney or Terri. Debra stopped every now and then, leaning forward to hand Whitney more tissue from her pocket. It was still difficult to read Terri's face—even when Debra said she remembered Raymond falling to the ground, and she kept talking to him as if he were standing, and she wanted to believe he was just fine.

Debra told them that she remembered driving off. Sometime during the middle of the night, it had begun to rain and that extra-hot day that forced Debra and Raymond inside had finally cooled off. Debra called Mrs. Trice, waking her up to tell her that she thought she'd shot someone, but she wasn't sure.

"My mother said, 'What have you done? Who have you shot?'"

The next morning, Debra went home, and Mrs. Trice handed her an *Indianapolis Star Tribune* article. It said Raymond Jones had died of a shotgun blast to the chest and police were searching for a woman driving a tan Mazda 626 whose license plate had a handicap decal.

"My mother said, 'Debra, did you kill that man?' I didn't answer her. And to this day I will never forget what she said to me next." Debra wadded the tissue. "She said, 'Debra, I could have bought new rings. No amount of jewelry was worth a man's life.'

"I left the house," Debra said. "I had to turn myself in, but I didn't know how. I found out it's hard to turn yourself in for murder. I stayed away for eight days."

By the time Debra finished speaking, Terri had uncrossed her ankles and was leaning forward, resting her clasped hands on her knees.

"I remember getting the phone call," Terri said.

Now our attention was on her. "It was about one o'clock in the morning and I remember how hard it was raining. One of Raymond's relatives told me that Raymond had been shot and that we needed to get to the hospital. I got up and started getting the children ready. We'd just celebrated Whitney's ninth birthday. Jaylon was three. I was told that I shouldn't worry about driving and that someone would pick us up. I told myself, 'He's been shot. He may need surgery, but he will be fine.' We went to two hospitals and he was at the second. The waiting room was filled with Raymond's family. I remember taking Whitney and Jaylon to sit with them so I could go back to the room. I remember walking toward where they had Raymond and I saw a chaplain and nurse walking toward me. When I saw that chaplain, I knew he was gone. I'm a nurse myself. I know when the chaplain shows up, it's not good."

I didn't say anything, but I felt like I'd just recognized a fellow traveler in a crowd. Terri made me think of the chaplain who greeted us on the night Kim died.

"The nurse said, 'Are you Terri Jones?' I said, 'Yes.' She said, 'Please come with us.' I entered the room and Raymond's mother was over to the left, doubled over in a chair, crying. That's when they told me unfortunately they were unable to revive him. It was just unbelievable. They had him on a stretcher and he was covered up to the neck with a sheet. And he had a tube in his mouth. I just cried. A couple of detectives, one Black and the other white, were in the room and they began interrogating me. I'm looking at the blood on Raymond. They're asking me if I knew who could have done this.

They knew he'd worked in St. Louis. Maybe the family told them. They wanted to know whether anyone there could have come here and done it. I just kept saying, 'No.'

"I left that room thinking about Whitney and how in the world was I going to tell this little girl that her dad is gone. I'm trying to dry my eyes. My son was three and didn't understand. But Whitney understood. Raymond called her his 'Poosha' and she called him 'DaDa.' He took her everywhere. Hair combed or not. They went to museums, art houses, and the park. Telling her was one of the hardest things I've ever had to do. At the funeral, Whitney stood near her father's coffin and she wouldn't move. I remember people saying, 'Somebody go get that child.' And my family was looking over at me and I would look at her and she just stood there for the longest time by his side. So I said to myself she needs to be there. This is the last time she's going to see him. Maybe I asked her, 'Whitney, do you want to sit down?' and maybe she said no. But I thought, *I'm going to let her stand right there for the entire wake*. Jaylon wanted to kiss Raymond. So I picked him up and let him kiss his father's forehead."

Whitney touched her mother's wrist. "I felt paralyzed. I didn't want to move. At the hospital, I didn't get a chance to see him. But at his wake, I wanted to stand there forever. Later, I used to go outside and look up to the sky whenever I wanted to talk to him. I needed a sign that he was okay. But the sign never came and for years I wondered why I couldn't at least dream about him."

Whitney turned to Debra. "I work in customer service and as I started thinking about writing to you, I had a client named Raymond Jones and I would keep hearing from Raymond Jones and I started to think maybe that's my father saying it's okay to contact you. It's time. I was fourteen when my mother gave me a plastic bag of my father's personal effects. It had come from the funeral home and held a necklace and the American flag that was draped over his coffin because he served in the air force. In the middle of it all was his autopsy report. I don't think it was supposed to be in there. But it detailed all the drugs in his system. That's when I knew it was just a matter of time before he died. So, I want you to know that I forgave you a long time ago. I also want to thank you. I'd heard the story about him stealing from you, Debra, but I didn't know the details.

Him being in your mother's house and the jewelry—both were new to me."

Terri said that, in the beginning, she never believed the jewelry story.

"I kept saying all these years that it was a lie," she said. "But I was thinking of the Raymond I knew and not the Raymond he'd become."

During the nearly two hours we were together, I, like the counselor, had tried to not be intrusive in any way. But Terri turned to me.

"You're the one who wrote the article about Debra graduating college," she said.

"I am."

"When I read it, I was still angry. I know now that you were writing about the friend you grew up with. I wrote you an awful letter. I have to apologize for that."

"Oh, no, you don't. You were entitled to feel every emotion you felt. And I've received far worse from people who have far less of a reason to write me."

Terri nodded. "I remember feeling, who cares that she graduated from college in prison? Raymond didn't get a chance to do that. He wouldn't see his children grow up to be the beautiful people they are. Both are college graduates. It wasn't easy being a single parent. I cried at every track meet, at band concerts. Whitney ran track. Her brother played football. To have them both be good kids and go down the right path was a blessing. I had a lot of help from my parents and it was God's grace. In 2001, I got involved in correctional nursing. I went to work at the Marion County Jail as a nurse. I met people who had gotten caught up. I met people who had done things that they never meant to do. I think that started to soften me because before that I thought Raymond's mother, Mrs. Jones, was a traitor because she was corresponding with you. I said, 'Why are you talking to that woman?' She said, 'You're going to have to forgive her, Terri.' God bless Mrs. Jones. For her, forgiveness was instant. But I was furious. Mrs. Jones was one of the sweetest women I knew. I told her, 'I don't forgive her. I won't forgive her. Nope. Nope. Nope. No way.'

"On the drive here today, I thought about Mrs. Jones the whole time because she said this day would come. She was laying the groundwork because I couldn't hear it back then. I couldn't hear it for years. But after working at the jail and meeting people, I got to know them beyond their crime. It started to change my heart. It took some time, Debra. I had said that I wasn't going to come here angry. I wouldn't come until I could say 'I forgive you' and mean it. And I mean it now. I forgive you."

Debra hung her head and her shoulders shook as she wiped her eyes.

"I want to thank you for seeing us," Whitney said. "You didn't have to."

Debra smiled. "I want to thank you for coming and I don't want this to end, but I've got to use the bathroom so bad."

The entire time, she had been sipping nervously from her Mountain Dew Code Red.

She looked at the counselor. "Can't I just leave for five minutes?"

"I'm afraid that if you leave, it's over, Ms. Trice."

"I'm sorry," Debra said to Terri and Whitney. "I really don't want this to be over. I shouldn't have drunk that pop."

She leaned forward and took Terri's hands in hers. I jumped a bit because it seemed like such a risky thing to do. I wasn't certain how Terri would respond to Debra touching her. But Terri didn't pull away.

Then Debra added a part to the story from 1998 that she never told me.

"I live in my head," she said. "I always try to figure things out and for years I tried to narrow down the moment when my life and Raymond's life changed. That very hot day when we were heading to my mother's house, we got to my block and a guy I knew pulled up beside us in his car. He wanted me to jump in and go get high with him. I put my hand on the door handle, but he told me Raymond couldn't come with us. I told him I wasn't going to leave my friend. I let go of the handle. To this day, and for the rest of my life, I will regret not getting in that car.

"If Jesus told me that I could bring one person back from heaven—as much as I loved my parents, as much as I miss my mother—I promise you, I would choose Raymond."

chapter thirty-five

The End Date

. . .

Terri and Whitney's visit, their forgiveness, liberated Debra in ways she never expected. Although her crime would haunt her for the rest of her life, she started to imagine entering the world beyond the razor-wire fence. It was an indulgence she hadn't allowed herself since years ago, when she tried to appeal her case. She began to count down and divide time into days and months rather than swaths of years and decades. She let herself think about her release date, just over a year away. The Indiana prison system gives inmates one day for every day served, and from the onset, Debra knew she was staring down twenty-five years. But her bachelor's degree and involvement in various programs knocked off another four years.

Inmates reaching the end of their sentence often acquired "short-timers" syndrome and Debra was not immune. Mostly everything about living communally now irritated her like never before. When we talked, she complained about the women who left dirty dishes in the kitchen sink or hair in the shower stalls or monopolized the television. She hated her "lumpy-ass mattress," and because Madison was one of the older facilities, she couldn't stand the dull floor tiles.

As part of Madison's work-release program, Debra got help finding employment. On a mid-September Sunday afternoon, she and twelve other inmates boarded a van to prepare for job interviews. Before that day, the only time she had left prison grounds was to transfer from one facility to another. But that day, the women were taken to a cosmetology school to get their hair, makeup, and nails done, and then to JCPenney's to purchase civilian clothes and shoes at discounted prices.

Debra called me after the outing. "Girl, I just tried on my first pair of skinny jeans."

I was in my kitchen chopping onions, carrots, and celery for a minestrone soup. Balancing the phone between my ear and shoulder, I couldn't help but smile.

"I'm not used to skinny jeans," she said. "I've worn the same baggy-ass clothes for twenty-one years and my body has changed. The styles have changed."

"It's hard for anyone to feel comfortable in those things," I chuckled. "You just have to find the right fit."

"My ass used to look great in jeans. Now I have that sit-down ass, the kind that comes from years of not moving."

"Whatever you do, avoid three-way mirrors. They're the devil!"

"I've got to get to a gym. But I still can't wait to have real pork bacon. And a meal with everything on the same plate. And fried food. I'll give it all up later, but when I get out, I'm eating every fried animal I can find."

"What outfit did you get for your interview?"

"I found a black jacket that was so cute with a pair of black pants. But I was so upset because the jacket was a size medium and it was too snug. I just got a blouse."

"Perfect," I said. I sprinkled fresh thyme into my pot. "You'll make this work."

"My feet are hard to fit so I got a pair of patent leather slides with heels. I haven't worn heels in twenty-one years."

"Slides are good! With your pants—boom!"

"I know. When we returned to the prison, we put on a fashion show with our new outfits. It was such a confidence builder."

Debra gave me the date of the job fair, and on the morning the women boarded the van for their interviews, I began my day at my desk working on a screenplay and pretending I wasn't worried about what this moment meant to her. Since she'd been in prison, one of her greatest fears was how she would support herself once she was released. Debra has always been smart and personable. But I thought about how she was doing as I rode my bike along the lakefront and then returned home to work some more.

Later that evening, when my cell phone rang, it was on the kitchen counter. I saw it was the prison and snatched it up. "Tell me every detail!"

Debra laughed. "They took us to Ivy Tech Community College and the interviews were held in this conference room. The woman who interviewed me worked for a factory that makes auto parts. She told me that I was such the conversationalist. I thought, *Let me be quiet. They're supposed to be interviewing me.* I told her I've never even been inside a factory before. I sent her a thank-you letter, letting her know that she made me feel like I was a part of the team."

Debra got the job, which paid $13 per hour, and was determined to learn everything she could about becoming a machine operator, including working a forklift.

Over the years, Debra had tried to prepare herself for life on the outside by keeping abreast of every tidbit of news. She understood how Google and Amazon and GPS have transformed the world and that nearly everything was on demand. She had gone from sending me letters, when she first entered prison, to sending emails. That Thanksgiving she texted me on a new cell phone that her aunt Linda, her mother's youngest sister, bought her. Linda had promised her sister that she would help look after her nieces.

Debra could only call me during certain hours of the day, but it still felt good opening our conversations without a recording. The day she got full access to the Internet, she called me, laughing. "Dawn, I've been typing in names and I typed in yours and then our third-grade teacher's. Girl, the Rebecca Love I got is a porn star!"

Her job, her phone, her curiosity all led me to believe that her transition would be fairly seamless. Until she told me about an outing to the grocery store.

The prison allowed the transitioning inmates to shop at Walmart. One day, Debra missed the van with the other women and had to ride alone in another one. When she got out of the van, she stood on the sidewalk in front of the store. Then something happened as she watched the prison van circle out of the parking lot.

She began to feel unsteady as she walked to the store's main entrance. She labored to breathe, and her chest tightened. She realized she was having a panic attack. Stopping abruptly, she began scanning the bushes around the store, looking for sharpshooters and wondering if their red dots were trained on her forehead. Deep down, she knew no one was there. But it was the first time in years that she'd been without a guard nearby monitoring her every move and telling her what to do next. She looked at the parking lot and main thoroughfare and realized she hadn't had to worry about cars and crossing streets in decades.

When Debra told me about it, my greatest fear was that she had become *institutionalized*. It was a concept I wasn't familiar with until the movie *The Shawshank Redemption*. It referred to the mental state of former inmates who couldn't make it on the outside.

During Debra's time in the Indiana prison system, she'd known two women who had two distinctly different outcomes after leaving prison. Paula Cooper was sixteen in 1986, when she made international headlines for being this country's youngest death row inmate. Paula left prison in 2013 and struggled mightily to navigate the outside world. I didn't know her but I remember feeling heartbroken when she committed suicide two years later. The other woman was Michelle Jones, who at one time was Debra's roommate. She excelled as a published scholar of American history while in prison. She left in August 2017, after serving twenty years. I had the privilege of meeting Michelle in New York a few months later when she invited me to a screening of Anna Deavere Smith's film *Notes from the Field* on America's school-to-prison pipeline. Michelle had become a doctoral candidate at New York University and has since created the nonprofit Constructing Our Future. It buys dilapidated Indianapolis homes in ravaged neighborhoods and provides safe housing to women who are formerly incarcerated. The nonprofit also offers jobs by having these women rehab the structures. Michelle continues to thrive.

Debra worked through that Walmart outing and plowed forward, fighting for her future and counting down. The prison allowed her to create a Facebook page, and she introduced herself as a "Humble Recipient of True Forgiveness and Second Chances." She reconnected with friends she had known at Pershing, Doolittle, and Northwest High School and with former inmates. She posted a video explaining that she was in her final months of a prison sentence for murder. "Friending" Terri and Whitney, Debra introduced them in a post as being her victim's widow and daughter. She thanked them for their forgiveness. Debra "liked" Whitney's super-cute photos of her daughter and Terri's posts about her travels, including an upcoming trip to Honolulu for work.

On Father's Day, a month before Debra was scheduled to leave prison, Whitney posted a photo of Raymond holding her as a newborn. In it, she is on his lap facing him, and the two are staring into each other's eyes. Raymond, dimple showing, is half smiling and transfixed. Whitney's post read: "Happy Heavenly Father's Day, DaDa! This is one of my absolute favorite pictures of us!! It's been a long twenty-one years without you but I'm still standing strong and you will ALWAYS have a special place in my heart. . . . I promise to continue to make you proud!! Love you forever."

Debra saw the post and called me, sobbing.

"I want to respond. But I don't know what I should write. I did this to them."

"They've forgiven you, Debra. You can't change the past."

"I know," she moaned.

"It's like what Mrs. Jones told Terri. 'One day you're going to have to forgive her,' and that 'her' is you."

"I know."

"Years ago, you told me that there's an art to serving a long sentence. You said that if your mind wandered too far in the past or the future, you got upset. You said the worst thing a long-timer could do was just sit around. You keep going or you sink right in place. Then you said, 'I won't sink, Dawn. I can't.' You feel me?"

"I feel you."

chapter thirty-six

"Crack the Gate!"

. . .

Every time I wrote about Debra in the *Tribune*, readers and colleagues would say how lucky she was to have me as her friend. I found that utterly offensive. I would always say, "No, we're both lucky." I understand that going to prison can be a relationship deal breaker. But I knew Debra long before her addiction and her crime. People reading her story just saw her as being broken. They didn't take into account that we all are broken. We are nicked and chipped, bruised and battered. Like my grandmother's glass figurines, we position ourselves to hide our defects. We learn how to move forward.

I couldn't wait to see my friend on the outside.

I was sitting up in the bed in an Indianapolis hotel room on July 28, 2019, when my cell phone rang. I answered, smiling wide.

"This is a call from an inmate in the Madison Correctional Facility. . . . Press zero to accept this call."

When Debra came on the line, I said, "After tonight, we will never, ever have to hear that fucking recording again."

We screamed like schoolgirls.

"I can't believe I'm leaving this place!" Debra squealed. "How much is left?" She was referring to the money on my prepaid phone account with the prison, which was over one hundred dollars at the beginning of the week.

"We're just under five dollars now," I said.

"I'm going to keep calling until it's all used up!"

"Listen," I said. I felt around the bed for my notepad. "About going to Walmart after we pick you up. Darlene, Linda, and I aren't too keen on hanging around a small Indiana town after midnight. Linda wants you to give me a list of what you want, and she'll pick up most of it before we head your way."

"But I don't think Madison is like that, Dawn."

"We don't want to find out, sweetie. Give me your list."

She had me hold on for a few seconds and she came back to the phone.

"Olay Regenerist face cream," Debra said. "It's in a red jar and fights wrinkles."

We were in our fifties, but I couldn't help but think about the two girls who slathered Noxzema on their faces and stood before that bedroom mirror with their training bras raised, staring at their budding breasts—poised on the other side of time.

"It costs about twenty-five dollars."

"Got it. What else?"

"I need a litter box, litter, and a scoop. I just got this rescue cat. Her name is Shelby and she's coming with me."

"Does Frank know about the cat?"

Frank was a close friend of Debra's and had invited her to stay with him until she found her own place. Because she would be on parole for the next two years and had to remain in Indiana, the prison still held sway over her life and had to approve her housing arrangement.

"Not yet, but he'll love little Shelby," she cooed.

"I hope so," I laughed. "Or you both may be out on your asses."

"We had a lot of cats down here, Dawn. Mama wouldn't let us have a dog." She paused, her mother's absence momentarily snagging on the memory. "I had a tarantula and a scorpion. I was about to get a baby boa constrictor, but I thought you had to feed them live rodents. I found out later they sell the things vacuum packed!"

"I've always preferred vacuum-packed rodents to live ones," I laughed.

Debra rounded out her list with kitty treats, eggs, spicy breakfast sausage, wheat bread, milk, almonds, and cashews.

I had rented a van and at 8:30 p.m. I picked up Darlene and Linda. The prison allowed inmates to leave after midnight on their release date. Although Debra didn't mind waiting until the next morning, I didn't want her to spend an extra second there.

I pulled into the loading area of the prison and drove to the back gate alongside a fence topped with razor wire. Air thick with humidity and smelling of wet grass met us as we exited the van.

"There's my sister," Darlene said, pulling out her cell phone.

Inside the building, Debra was arranging a stack of boxes and plastic bins. She wore a white T-shirt, white gym shoes, and a pair of skinny blue jeans with a hoodie tied around her waist. When she stood in the doorway, the outdoor lights shone on her hair, dyed deep blue. Seeing us, she ran outside to the gate.

"Hey, y'all!" She waved with both hands and then looked down at her watch. "It's almost time."

Darlene began to stream live on Facebook as Debra moved her boxes and bins outside the building, stacking them near the gate.

A male guard stood nearby, watching the clock and pacing.

"My watch says 11:59," Debra said, hoisting Shelby's lavender traveling case on top of a large box. The cat's meows drew another cat roaming the yard.

"It's 23:58," the guard said, smiling. "You know I can't let you out until midnight."

"Oh, I know." Debra ran back into the building and returned with her last item, a rolled-up white canvas.

The guard handed her a manila envelope with her release papers, diploma, certificates, state identification card, and parole instructions. Then he looked at the clock one last time and yelled to his right, "You can go ahead and crack the gate so she can start hauling out."

"Crack the gate!" Debra repeated as it opened. She ran out with one of the boxes and placed it and the canvas in the back of the van. She hugged each of us and we began taking turns streaming live on her Facebook page and filling the van with her belongings. At one point, Debra beckoned me toward her and unfurled the canvas. It was a drawing of a little girl standing outside her house, praying up to the night sky.

"When Whitney came to the prison, you remember the story she told us about being a girl and searching the sky for Raymond?" Debra asked.

"I do," I said. "I love it!"

"This is rough. I paid someone to draw it. I just hope they can use it as part of the foundation Whitney is starting in her father's name."

Debra rolled up the canvas. The guard helped her move the rest of her belongings outside the gate so that he could lock up.

"Look, he's closing the gate for the last time," Debra said. "Hear that click?" She cupped her hand over her ear. "I'll never have to go through that gate again."

We erupted in cheers. Debra faced her sister's phone, thanking her coworkers and bidding farewell to friends, inmates she left behind. At least one was serving a life sentence.

"I'm free," she said with a shrug. We cheered and clapped again. "Wait a minute, hold up. I said I was going to do this. Let me see if I can get back up."

She knelt and kissed the ground.

We finished loading the van and Debra grabbed my arm. "You know, Dawn, my original best friend, I'm so glad my mother told me to go play with the girl downstairs."

"I'm so glad I was that girl," I said, giving her a big hug. "I sincerely am."

She climbed into the back seat next to Darlene. I got into the driver's seat and turned around. A shadow fell on Debra's profile as I watched her struggle to buckle herself in. She gazed up nervously, and I could see her eyes—her joy, her fear, but most of all, her determination. Linda, Darlene, and I waited for a few seconds and then we heard the second momentous click of the night. And once again, we cheered.

"You're all set?" I asked Debra.

She nodded and smiled.

"Then let's go home."

chapter thirty-seven

"Lordy, Lordy, Lordy"

■ ■ ■

The flat-screen in Mom's kitchen blared the morning news. I heard it as soon as Mom opened the door for me. I took off my winter coat. "I want you to see this," I said, carrying my laptop as we walked through the apartment to the kitchen. I placed it on the table. My childhood friend Bruce Wilson, who grew up in the Ida B. Wells Homes, had tagged me on a Facebook post displaying hundreds of vintage photographs of people and places in Bronzeville, spanning the early 1900s through the early 2000s. It was a treasure trove and I wanted to show Mom the photos, hoping they might spark a memory, coax a story.

As I scrolled, Mom leaned forward, her left leg bouncing. Some of the photos showed our section of Bronzeville before the Ida B. Wells Homes, Lake Meadows, and Lawless were built. There were aerial shots in color and black-and-white. Photos of the side streets and stores with billboards promoting Black Kow Soda and Sweet Georgia Brown Hair Dressing Pomade. In a 1947 photo of a delivery room at Provident Hospital, a newborn lay on a table surrounded by Black doctors. Provident was the country's first Black-owned hospital. A black-and-white photo taken circa 1942 at the Supreme Life Insurance Company showed a group of Black women in starched blouses with high collars sitting behind desks, tapping on typewriters and adding machines, poring over actuarial tables.

"Supreme Life," Mom said.

"It's that little vagina coin purse that I remember."

Smirking, she sucked her teeth, looking so much like Granny and Aunt Doris. She recognized it, too, and told me that some days she stood in front of the mirror and said, "Good morning, Mom, good morning, Sis!"

In every photo of little girls, jumping double Dutch or playing Ring Around the Rosie, I looked for my mother. The sandy-haired girl with the winsome smile. One photo showed seven cheerleaders with perfect press-and-curls and the letter "P" emblazoned on their sweaters. They attended Wendell Phillips High School, Mom's alma mater. She had always reminded me that the late soul singer Sam Cooke was an alum. But this time she didn't. Her eyes lit up.

"Do you know these girls?" I asked her.

"Do I know them?" She eagerly began to tick off their names and then sadly pointed to the one girl who died young.

We continued to stare at the screen until Mom grabbed my hand, forcing me to stop. In front of us was a black-and-white photo of an old woman with white cottony hair and smooth brown skin seated next to a boy who was standing. Mom's back straightened.

"Mrs. Patterson!" Mom beamed as though the woman had just miraculously materialized before us.

"You're kidding me!"

"That's Ella Patterson!" My mother was normally nonchalant, hard to excite. She was in her early eighties, but in that moment, she was five years old again.

"The woman who had been a slave?"

"Yes, the woman I went to the store for. The one who gave me the shiny pennies that looked like they'd been dipped in copper. I asked Mrs. Patterson why her eldest daughter was so white-looking. Mrs. Patterson said the ol' masters used to take girls in the barn and do whatever they wanted. When people say they sat at someone's knee, I did just that and she told me stories of slavery."

In the photograph, Mrs. Patterson has a congenial smile and her chin is slightly elevated. She wears round wire-rimmed eyeglasses and a floral dress and is seated, holding the hook handle of a wooden cane.

I've always enjoyed the story of Mrs. Patterson, but as I got older, the idea of Mom knowing a woman who had been a slave seemed far-fetched. As I sat there, I searched a newspaper database on my laptop and before long found two front-page *Chicago Tribune* articles. The first story ran in 1941, when Mom was five, and featured the Ida B. Wells Homes's oldest resident. The headline:

FORMER SLAVE AT 101 RECALLS PLANTATION LIFE
Most Vivid Memory Is Sale at Auction

The story went on to say that she remembered standing on the auction block with her siblings and their new master giving the girls red sticks of candy.

I showed my mother the screen. "It says her first name is Kate."

"Child, please. That's Mrs. Ella Patterson. I don't know what she had to tell those white folks who interviewed her."

The photo on the front page of the newspaper was the same as the one we'd just seen. The young boy standing next to her was said to be her great-grandson.

Mom fixated on Mrs. Patterson's face. "She was my best friend."

I knew exactly what my mother was feeling—that swell of memory and rekindled emotion that accompany recalling a person you met when you were brand-new and beginning. That person who entered your life at a critical moment and, no matter how long she was gone or how she left, would always be with you.

Mom still drove, but I was the one behind the wheel a couple of months later when she, Hannah, and I were leaving downtown and I detoured through the old neighborhood. Mom hadn't been there in years.

Condos were selling for nearly half a million dollars. White people were moving in. A friend who owns a lot of real estate told me that King Drive was being billed as the Drive. What's happening in the old haunt is happening in Harlem, now sometimes called Central Park North. I wondered how long before Bronzeville's history will be erased despite the nearly one hundred bronze plaques embedded in the sidewalks and medians, commemorating some of the neighborhood's most-esteemed former residents.

We drove south on King Drive and stopped at the now-shuttered Griffin Funeral Home. In the years following Candy Love's funeral, the Black owner hung the Confederate flag outside the building so that it waved alongside the American flag, the African American flag, and one for prisoners of war. He said he did it because the funeral home sat on land where Confederate soldiers had died. He wanted to honor them.

"Utter nonsense," Mom said now, peering at the area where the flag once flew. "Why do we always have to be the ones who forgive?"

I circled around to Lake Meadows. It has remained one of the area's jewels. It was no accident that the development wasn't named after a prominent person as the Theodore K. Lawless Gardens Apartments, the Clarence Darrow Homes, and the Ida B. Wells Homes had been. Lake Meadows's name—and those of the nearby developments Prairie Shores, South Commons, and Long Grove Village—was derived to pay homage to the idea of peace and tranquility. That was fine. The other names were hollow gestures because the city didn't live up to the principles of the people whose names were on the buildings. As always, I stopped at Debra's and my ledge. It was fenced off years ago so that nobody could climb up there and sit. We weren't the only children who saw its worth.

I left there and crossed 35th Street to Lawless Gardens, passing the little blond-brick outpost and parking outside the fence. My mother sat in the passenger seat, staring at the vast expanse of grass and concrete that once held the Ida B. Wells housing project. Its last building was razed in 2011. For the most part, the city's plan to transform public housing had been completed about a decade before. In the words of James Baldwin, urban renewal had once again only meant Negro removal. How successful the plan has been depends on the rubric used. One of the plan's goals was to move residents into mixed-income communities, but a 2017 study by the award-winning journalist Natalie Moore at Chicago's WBEZ radio station and Northwestern University showed that only eight percent of residents had achieved that.

Mom had read news stories about the demolition but hadn't seen it.

"Lordy, Lordy, Lordy," she said, looking as though she was unsure whether this was the land she roamed as a child and teenager.

Having come of age in Bronzeville, Mom had seen urban renewal several times over. She'd known this geography back when the area teemed with tenement housing, cold water flats, and kitchenettes. She had moved her family into Lawless around the time the Ida B. Wells Homes had begun its slide. The city's housing authority had stopped screening applicants as it once had, and not long afterward it would get rid of its on-site janitorial staff. It simply stopped demanding of itself and its residents the things required to maintain a healthy and humane development. Later still, residents would have to contend with dysfunctional policing practices and crooked cops. The acclaimed investigative reporter Jamie Kalven, a dear friend, would write extensively about a team of corrupt Chicago officers who operated for years in the Ida B. Wells housing project and others. Then the world would look at what ails Chicago, particularly its violence, and pretend to wonder how it happened and how to fix it.

Decades had passed, and with the deaths of Granny, Aunt Doris, and Kim, Mom had experienced the type of loss that felt bottomless. But looking out on the barren land, too, left her bereaved. How unsettling, disorienting for her to see that her childhood buildings had been erased and very little had risen in their place.

Buildings are like mountains. They don't disappear without a fight. And when they are intentionally taken down, you almost have to bear witness to the demolition. You need to see the process, the wrecking ball's work: the gaping holes and the rubble with its stacks of bruised bricks; the mortar that has returned to dust. You must view the remains.

But now there was nothing left.

"When I was about eight years old," Mom said, turning to Hannah in the back seat, "I used to wait for the milkman to drop off bottles of milk at neighbors' doors and I would go from stoop to stoop slurping off the cream that had settled on top of the milk. I'd drink until I got full." She looked back out the window. "Lordy, Lordy, Lordy."

We got out of the car and walked a bit. The property used to display signs showing architectural renderings of the new "mixed-income" development called Oakwood Shores. But the signs had been removed, and in the distance only a scattering of low-rise buildings stood just to the east.

"I'm so turned around," Mom said wistfully. "Lordy, Lordy, Lordy."

"Grandma," Hannah said, holding Mom's hand. "You've said that over and over."

Mom nodded. "I know, baby. I guess time brings about change."

chapter thirty-eight

Three Girls from Bronzeville

. . .

Ihave this fantasy: It's a Sunday morning and Debra, Kim, and I are having brunch in a restaurant in one of Bronzeville's new cafés. Debra helms the pediatric nurses unit downtown at Northwestern Memorial. It's the reason she moved back to Chicago. Kim runs a nonprofit for teenage mothers. She has a master's degree in social work from the University of Chicago. Because it's my fantasy, she tells the young women she works with what I told her: "You can change your life. It's never too late." The three of us lean into one another at the table, laughter tossing our heads back the way it once did with Mom, Granny, and Aunt Doris. They are the original three girls from Bronzeville. Only Debra, Kim, and I take measure of how ridiculously happy and fulfilled we are. As we dine, we talk about the past. Lawless. Our old apartments. That stairwell. Miss Polaroid. Doolittle. Our tin of discarded items we believed could be made whole and new again. We figure out who will host the next holiday meal. We debate who gets to choose our next movie. We set a date for our next brunch. We jump in our cars and head in three different directions.

The fantasy brings me comfort, joy, even though, of course, it is no more than a rueful indulgence.

Sometimes I think about the girls Kim, Debra, and I once were, and it astounds me the paths we took. I used to believe that it was their daring that led to their undoing and that ours was a story about choices—three girls who made vastly different ones. But it's really a story about second chances. Who gets them, who doesn't, who makes the most of them.

I've thought about how much my sister's death and my best friend's imprisonment changed me and how they continue to shape my writing and the stories I tell. In that way, our separate roads have merged into one and we are forever connected.

We will always find each other.

acknowledgments

The process of excavating the past for this memoir often required me to dig with one end of the shovel and beat myself about the head with the other. Early on, I wondered: *Can I do this?* While I eventually determined I could, I knew I could never do it alone.

I will be forever indebted to my Simon & Schuster editor, Christine Pride, my North Star. I am thankful for her editorial prowess, but also for helping me to understand when I needed to be a journalist searching for the truth and when I needed to just be a big sister, best friend, or daughter feeling all the feels. How she was able to wade through and help me make sense of some incredibly raw drafts, I will never know. But I extend my sincerest gratitude.

A huge thank-you to Simon & Schuster's tireless editorial and production teams, including copyediting, marketing, publicity, and sales. The stars aligned for me in finding the perfect publisher for this project.

I am deeply thankful to literary agents Steve Ross, who believed in this book from its inception, and David Doerrer, for his steady hand in navigating it through the production process.

Many thanks to readers who took on various iterations of the book and made crucial suggestions as well as offered a shoulder to lean on. Among them are: Patrick Anderson, James Baer, Lee Bey, Rita Coburn, Elaine Copeland, Rob Copeland Jr., Joyce Gay, Dahleen Glanton, Deborah Grant, Linda Jenkins, Jamie Kalven, Beth Kujawski, Gracie Lawson-Borders, Linda Loewenthal, Marcia Lythcott, Michelle Mann, Jeanne Miller, Paul Miller, Kareem Rogers, Steve Rogers, Richard Steele, Darlene Trice, and David Trice.

My year as a fellow at the Nieman Foundation for Journalism was transformative. Thank you to Ann Marie Lipinski, the curator and fearless leader, and to my entire Nieman class. I offer a special thanks to my narrative nonfiction seminar mates: Abeer Allam, Melissa Bailey, Gabe Bullard, Farnaz Fassihi, Irina Gordienko, Miguel Paz, Laurie Penny, Alicia Stewart, Linda Golden, Yessi Crosita, and Carmen Gómez Menor; and to our instructor, the talented author Steve Almond.

Thank you to David Axelrod and his University of Chicago Institute of Politics, where I spent my fellowship leading a seminar on the policy impacts of racial images in the media. I met brilliant students who believe in our democracy and our political system, and are eager to work to improve them.

I relied heavily on research from a number of places, but a special thanks goes to the Chicago Public Library's Vivian G. Harsh Research Collection, the Chicago History Museum, and the *Chicago Tribune* archives, as well as to officials at Indianapolis's Marion County Jail; the Indiana Women's Prison; the Rockville Correctional Facility; the Madison Correctional Facility; the Court of Appeals of Indiana; the Indiana Supreme Court; the Indianapolis Metropolitan Police Department's Administration Division; the Indiana Department of Correction; and the Indiana Historical Society.

Thank you to my James R. Doolittle Jr. Elementary teacher Janet Sheard for sharing her stories and photographs, and to my Doolittle classmates who recounted memories of key events. I'm particularly grateful to my dear friend and classmate Bruce Wilson, who was always willing to read chapters and direct me to people who could help.

A special thank-you to Debra. It is difficult for anyone to change her life, but two years after her release from prison, Debra continues to thrive. I thank her for allowing me to witness her journey, which began so many years ago, and for her love and friendship. I'm also deeply grateful to Terri Jones, Whitney Jones, and Jaylon Jones for the generosity of their time and for the grace that they extended to my friend.

Lastly, to my daughter, Hannah, who is my heartbeat, and to Kim, Mom, Auntie, and Granny—four incomparable women who wrapped me in a cocoon of love that I still feel to this day. I adore you!

about the author

Dawn Turner is an award-winning journalist and novelist. A former columnist for the *Chicago Tribune*, she spent a decade and a half writing about race and people whose stories are often overlooked and dismissed. Her commentary has appeared in the *Washington Post* and on *PBS NewsHour*, CBS News' *Sunday Morning*, NPR, and elsewhere. She has held fellowships at Harvard University, the Maynard Institute for Journalism Education, and the University of Chicago. In 2018, she established the Dawn M. Turner and Kim D. Turner Endowed Scholarship in Media at her alma mater, the University of Illinois at Urbana-Champaign.